Reading and
Word Study

PE
1128
C7.8

Reading and Word Study

For Students of English as a Second Language

HIGH INTERMEDIATE LEVEL

by

Kenneth Croft

The American University Language Center
Washington, D. C.

PRENTICE-HALL, INC. • *Englewood Cliffs, N. J.*

Library of Congress Catalog Card No. 60–10176

Printed in the United States of America

75674-C

Fourth printing............June, 1963

ACKNOWLEDGMENTS

The editor acknowledges the following sources of the original stories which have been adapted for this book, and expresses his appreciation for permission to use copyrighted material.

THE STORY OF RIP VAN WINKLE. Adaptation of "Rip Van Winkle," from *The Sketch Book* by Washington Irving (New York: G. P. Putnam, 1849).

THE OPEN BOAT. Adaptation of the story "The Open Boat" by Stephen Crane, from *Scribner's* (June, 1897). Copyright 1897 by Charles Scribner's Sons.

A WHITE HERON. Adaptation of the story "A White Heron," from *A White Heron and Other Stories* by Sarah Orne Jewett (New York: Houghton, Mifflin and Company, 1887). Copyright 1886 by Sarah Orne Jewett.

TAPPAN'S BURRO. Adaptation of the story "Tappan's Burro," from *Tappan's Burro and Other Stories* by Zane Grey (New York: Grosset & Dunlap, n. d.). Copyright 1923 by Zane Grey; used and adapted by permission of Zane Grey Inc.

A NEW ENGLAND SPINSTER. 3500-word adaptation of "A New England Nun," from *A New England Nun and Other Stories* by Mary E. Wilkins Freeman. Copyright 1891, 1920 by Harper & Brothers. Used by permission of Harper & Brothers.

THE MURDER OF MR. HIGGINBOTHAM. Adaptation of the story "Mr. Higginbotham's Catastrophe," from *Twice Told Tales* by Nathaniel Hawthorne (Boston: American Stationers Co., 1837).

THE EGG. Adaptation of the story "The Egg," from *The Triumph of the Egg* by Sherwood Anderson. Copyright © 1920 by Eleanor Anderson. Reprinted by permission of Harold Ober Associates Incorporated.

THE MAYSVILLE "POET". Adapted from "The Maysville Minstrel" in *Round Up* by Ring Lardner, copyright 1929, Charles Scribner's Sons; renewed copyright © 1957, Ellis A. Lardner. Used and adapted by permission of Charles Scribner's Sons.

A PIECE OF RED CALICO. Adaptation of the story "A Piece of Red Calico," from *The Lady, or the Tiger? and Other Stories* by Frank R. Stockton (New York: Charles Scribner's Sons, 1884). Copyright 1884 by Charles Scribner's Sons.

THE HEADLESS HORSEMAN. Adaptation of "The Legend of Sleepy Hollow," from *The Sketch Book* by Washington Irving (New York: G. P. Putnam, 1849).

Preface

This text, devoted to reading and word study, was prepared for students of English as a second language at a high intermediate level. It consists of two parts: (I) twenty-four reading selections—American short stories which have been adapted for foreign students—with comprehension exercises; and (II) twenty-four chapters concerned with the study of English words—word classification, word formation, and recognition of word classes—also with exercises and drills.

According to the author's plan, the text was designed for a semester course of three hours per week, with forty-eight class lessons, one for each class hour of the semester. The rate of speed with which a given class will be able to proceed with this text, of course, depends on the students' previous English training. Very advanced groups may complete the book in fewer than forty-eight class sessions. Most classes, however, should proceed at the average of a lesson for each class session, or even at a slower rate. All the lessons do not have to be completed in one semester; it may be desirable in some cases to use the book for two semesters.

It was planned that the reading selections would be assigned in order, each one to be followed by the study of the corresponding chapter in Part II; that is, the first reading selection followed by Chapter 1, Part II; the second selection by Chapter 2, Part II; etc. From experience in class-testing the material, however, I know that some teachers will be interested only in Part I—Reading for Comprehension—for certain classes and only in Part II—Word Study—for certain other classes. Generally, the two parts of the text are most effective when used jointly. This is especially true since the reading selection is frequently the starting-place for the corresponding word-study chapter, in that words have been drawn from the reading selection for discussion in the word-study part of the book.

If the study of this text is systematic and thorough, the student will increase his vocabulary to about 4,000 words. This is the principal aim of the book. In addition, the student will become familiar with the stories of a number of well-known American writers, many American idioms, and many sentence patterns commonly used by American writers. The stories themselves have been rewritten within the 2,000-item vocabulary list (*A General Service List of Words*) edited by Michael West. Where other vocabulary appears in the stories, footnote explanations and, in some instances, pictured illustrations are given. The words used for systematic study and drill in the second part of the book were drawn from the stories and the West vocabulary list—words of high-frequency occurrence in written English. We start with a vocabulary level of approximately 2,000 words and proceed by introducing new vocabulary and new forms built from already familiar word elements until we reach a level of approximately 4,000 words.

It has been stated above that this text is for students at a high intermediate level in their study of English. By "high intermediate level" I mean that the student should have a vocabulary of at least 2,000 words and at least fair facility in reading. A good test of this proficiency is whether or not the student can read this preface and understand virtually all of it. If the student cannot read it with understanding he is not yet ready to use the text.

Most of the stories which have been included are works of American literature. Through adaptation I have shortened the stories somewhat and divided them into convenient parts for class use. I have also controlled the vocabulary so that the student would not be faced with a large number of unfamiliar words at one time; on the average twelve "new" words appear in each reading selection. Adaptation has not changed the original stories much, although an author's style is inevitably affected to some extent by this amount of editing. Even so, I believe the student will find the stories interesting and will gain some familiarity with the writings of the authors represented here.

My approach to English word study will probably differ from any which is already familiar to the student. The original plan was to present only certain basic information about the derivation of English words. A number of texts for students of English as a second language treat word inflection in considerable detail, but few of them provide even a summary treatment of derivation.

When the preparation of this material started, however, the need became apparent for an objective method of separating the major word classes. The syntactic analysis made available in Dr. Charles C. Fries' *The Structure of English* (1952) proved especially useful in this connection, as well as the extensions and applications of Fries' approach presented in Dr. Paul Roberts' *Patterns of English* (1956) and Dr. W. Nelson Francis' *The Structure of American English* (1958). I acknowledge my indebtedness to these authors, and particularly to Dr. Paul Roberts, whose book provided not only guidelines but actual methods which I have followed. Although I have drawn many ideas and in some cases procedures from the books mentioned, any errors of analysis, classification, or interpretation found in this book are entirely my own.

I gratefully acknowledge the assistance of Dr. Harry Freeman, Dr. Walter P. Bowman, and Dr. Marie Gadsden of The American University, who used this book experimentally in their classes during the 1958–59 school year and offered valuable suggestions and criticism. Equal thanks are due to Dr. A. L. Davis, former director of The American University Language Center, who checked early drafts of this material for inaccuracies and provided me with many good suggestions for improving the presentation; to Mr. Ralph Beckham, also of The American University Language Center, who assisted in the development of the word-study drills which appear in the second part of the book; and to Dr. Edith Fries Croft, who adapted a large part of the story "The Headless Horseman" and whose critical evaluation of the reading selections has been enormously helpful. I also express my appreciation to all the teachers at The American University Language Center and elsewhere who have tested this material in their classes and offered useful comments and advice. Last, but by no means least, I acknowledge my indebtedness to Dr. Harold V. King of the University of Michigan, Dr. Walter P. Allen of the University of Miami, and Dr. Westbrook Barritt of Washington and Lee University, who read the manuscript of this work before it was printed and whose critical comments have enabled me to produce in the end a much better book than would otherwise have been possible.

KENNETH CROFT

Contents

Part I: Reading for Comprehension

Part II: Word Study

CONTENTS

CONTENTS

Reading for Comprehension

Subjects

The Out-of-Doors
The Forest
The Mountains
The Desert
The Sea
The Farm
The Village
The Town

SELECTION 1

THE STORY OF
RIP VAN WINKLE

Washington Irving

PART 1

Rip Van Winkle lived in a little village at the foot of the
Catskill Mountains. This was in the old days when the country
was still a province of Great Britain.[1] It was an old village built
by Dutch colonists during the government of Peter Stuyvesant.
Some of the houses of the original settlers were still standing—
houses built of yellow bricks brought from Holland.

---

1 **province of Great Britain,** land belonging to Great Britain

Rip was a friendly man. He was a kind neighbor and an obedient hen-pecked husband.[2] Since he was a favorite among all the good wives of the village, they took his part in all family arguments and blamed the family difficulties on Mrs. Van Winkle. The children of the village liked him too. He taught them games, made them playthings, and amused them with stories. No dog in the neighborhood ever barked[3] at him.

Rip's great fault was his extreme dislike of all kinds of profitable work. This does not mean that he was lazy, for he would sit on a wet rock all day holding a heavy fishing rod, even without catching a single fish; or he would carry his gun for hours through the forest and swamp,[4] up and down hills, in order to shoot a few squirrels[5] or wild pigeons. He never refused to help a neighbor with the most difficult kind of work, such as building stone fences. The women of the village employed him too for little bits of work their husbands would not do for them. Rip was ready to attend to anybody's business but his own; he found it impossible to do his family duty and keep his farm in order.

squirrel

He said it was useless to work on his farm; it was the most worthless piece of land in the whole country; everything about it was wrong, or would go wrong in spite of him. His fences were continually falling to pieces; his cow continually wandered away; weeds were sure to grow quicker in his fields than anywhere else; and rain always came the moment he had some outdoor work to do. So his farm went from bad to worse; it was in the worst condition of all the farms in the neighborhood.

His children wore old, torn clothes and received little care.

---

[2] **hen-pecked husband,** a husband ruled by his wife
[3] **bark,** make a loud, sharp noise
[4] **swamp,** soft, wet land
[5] **squirrel,** a small bushy-tailed animal that lives in trees (see picture)

Thus his son Rip inherited [6] the idle habits along with the old clothes of his father.

Rip Van Winkle, however, was one of those happy souls who take life easy. They eat white bread or brown, whichever they can get with the least thought or trouble. If left to himself, Rip would have been a contented man. But his wife continually complained of his idleness, his carelessness, and the ruin he was bringing on the family. Morning, noon, and night, her tongue was going. It was Rip's habit to say nothing and go outside the house—the only side which, in truth, belongs to a hen-pecked husband.

Rip's only domestic companion [7] was his dog Wolf, who was as hen-pecked as his master. Mrs. Van Winkle regarded them as companions in idleness and looked upon Wolf as the cause of his master's lack of attention to his family duty. He was a courageous dog, unafraid of any wild animal in the forest. But one needs more than courage against the terrors [8] of a woman's tongue. The moment Wolf entered the house, his tail dropped to the ground or curled between his legs; he watched carefully, and any suspicion that Mrs. Van Winkle might throw something caused him to run quickly to the door.

Times grew worse for Rip Van Winkle as years of married life continued. When driven from home, he frequently met with other idle persons of the village. They had formed a kind of club and held meetings on a bench [9] in front of a small inn. Here they used to sit in the shade through a long, lazy summer's day, talking over village gossip,[10] or telling endless sleepy stories about nothing. However, when, by chance, an old newspaper fell into their hands, some lively dis-

bench

---

6 **inherit**, receive money, property, etc., as the descendant of a person
7 **domestic companion**, companion at home
8 **terror**, something causing great fear
9 **bench**, a long seat (see picture)
10 **gossip**, talk which concerns the affairs of other people

cussions took place. They listened very attentively to the contents of the newspaper, read by Derrick Van Bummel, the village schoolmaster. And they discussed in detail public events several months after they had taken place.

The opinions of this group were completely controlled by Nicholas Vedder, an old gentleman who owned the inn. He sat at the door of the inn from morning till night, just moving enough to avoid the sun and keep in the shade of a large tree. The neighbors could tell the hour by his movements almost as accurately [11] as by a clock. It is true he rarely spoke but smoked his pipe continually. His companions understood him perfectly and knew how to gather his opinions. When he was displeased by something read or said, angry puffs [12] of smoke came forth from his pipe. But when pleased, he blew smoke slowly and quietly, sometimes taking the pipe from his mouth and letting the smoke curl about his nose.

The unlucky Rip was finally driven away from this restful group by his scolding wife; she even accused the worthy Nicholas Vedder of encouraging her husband in habits of idleness.

Poor Rip was at last reduced almost to despair. To escape work on the farm and his wife's loud voice, he would take his gun in hand and walk away into the forest. He would sometimes sit at the foot of a tree and share a little food he had brought with Wolf. "Poor Wolf," he would say, "you lead a dog's life. But don't worry; you'll have one friend at least as long as I live." Wolf would look into his master's face, and his eyes showed both pity and love for the unhappy Rip.

One day Rip had unconsciously climbed to one of the highest parts of the Catskill mountains. He was hunting squirrels—his favorite sport—and had broken the silence many times with the shots from his gun. Becoming tired, he threw himself, late in the afternoon, on the ground near a cliff. Through an opening in the trees he could see the lower country for many miles—many

---

[11] **accurately**, exactly; correctly
[12] **puffs of smoke**, small clouds of smoke

miles of rich woodland. He saw the great Hudson River in the distance, far, far below him, and on it the reflection of a purple cloud or the sail of a small boat.

On the other side he looked down into a deep valley, wild and lonely, the bottom scarcely lighted by the rays of the setting sun. For some time Rip lay looking at this scene; evening was gradually advancing; the mountains began to throw long blue shadows over the valleys. He realized that it would be dark before he could reach the village and he thought of Mrs. Van Winkle's anger when he did arrive.

About to descend, he heard a voice from a distance calling, "Rip Van Winkle! Rip Van Winkle!" He looked around but could see nothing but a crow [13] flying across the mountain. He thought perhaps his ears had deceived him and turned again to descend when he heard the same cry ring through the still evening air: "Rip Van Winkle! Rip Van Winkle!"—at the same time Wolf gave a low growl,[14] looking fearfully down into the valley. Rip looked anxiously in the same direction and saw a strange figure climbing slowly up the mountain and bending under the weight of something he carried on his back. He was surprised to see any human in this lonely place but, supposing it to be someone of the neighborhood in need of help, he hurried down.

Soon he was again surprised by the strangeness of the person's appearance. It was a short, old fellow, with thick bushy hair and a gray beard. His clothes were Dutch fashion—but the fashion of many years before. He was carrying a heavy keg [15] that seemed full of liquor,[16] and he made signs for Rip to help him with the load. Though rather distrustful of the stranger, Rip agreed, and the two of them climbed with their load up the mountain path. As they moved slowly upward, Rip now and then heard long rolling noises, like distant thunder, that seemed to

---

13 crow, a large black bird with a harsh cry
14 growl, a low threatening sound
15 keg, a small barrel
16 liquor, a strong drink containing alcohol

come from between two great rocks directly ahead of them. He paused for an instant, but supposing the noise to be due to one of those thundershowers which often take place in mountain heights, he went on. Passing between the two great rocks they reached a hollow, surrounded by mountain sides almost straight up. During the whole time Rip and his companion carried their heavy load in silence, although the former wondered why they were taking a keg of liquor up this wild mountain. The strangeness about the unknown, however, kept him silent.

On entering the hollow, new objects of wonder came before his eyes. On a level spot in the center there was a group of odd-

looking characters playing a game of ninepins.[17] They were dressed in the same manner as his guide, in Dutch clothes of an earlier time. Their faces were strange too; one had a large beard, broad face, and small eyes; the face of another seemed to consist entirely of nose. They all had beards of various shapes and colors. There was one who seemed to be the chief. He

ninepins

was a fat gentleman with a weather-beaten [18] face. The whole group reminded Rip of figures in an old Flemish painting [19] in the home of Dominic Van Shrack, the village minister, who had brought it over from Holland at the time of the settlement.

What seemed particularly strange to Rip was that, though these folks [20] were amusing themselves, their faces showed serious expressions, and there was a mysterious silence everywhere—the saddest party of pleasure he had ever witnessed. Nothing interrupted the stillness of the scene but the noise of the balls, which, when they were rolled, sounded along the mountains like thunder.

---

[17] **ninepins,** a game in which a ball is rolled at nine wooden bottle-shaped "pins" (see picture)
[18] **weather-beaten,** made rough by the weather
[19] **painting,** a picture drawn and colored by a brush
[20] **folks,** people

As Rip and his companion came near them, they stopped playing and stood looking at him with such strange expressions on their faces that his knees began to shake. His companion emptied the keg into a large vessel and made signs for him to wait on the group. He obeyed with fear and trembling. They drank the liquor in silence and then returned to their game. By degrees Rip's fear disappeared. He even tasted the liquor and found it had an excellent flavor. He was naturally a thirsty soul and soon took another taste. One drink suggested another, and after several visits to the liquor vessel, his senses became dull and he fell into a deep sleep.

On waking, he found himself back where he had first seen the old man with the keg of liquor. He rubbed his eyes—it was a bright sunny morning. The birds were jumping about in the bushes, and an eagle [21] was flying over-head. "Surely," Rip thought, "I have not slept here all night." He suddenly remembered what had happened before he fell asleep—the strange man with the keg of liquor—the game of ninepins—the party—the vessel of liquor—"Oh! that vessel of liquor!" Rip thought—"What excuse shall I make to my wife?"

eagle

In place of his clean, well-oiled gun, he found an old rusty gun beside him. He now suspected that the group of mountain characters had tricked him—while he was under the influence of liquor, perhaps they had robbed him of his gun. Wolf, too, had disappeared. He whistled for him and shouted his name, but no dog came in sight.

He decided to revisit the scene of the last evening's party, and if he met any of the group, he was going to demand his dog and gun. As he rose to walk, he found he was stiff in the joints and unable to walk as well as usual. "These mountain beds are bad

---

[21] **eagle,** a large bird that attacks and eats other birds and small animals (see picture)

for me," Rip thought. With some difficulty he started down into the valley. He found the place where he and his companion had started their climb the evening before. But he was astonished to find a mountain stream where the path had been. Somehow he made his way up to the two great rocks which he and his companion had passed between; but he found no hollow—the rocks formed a high wall over which sheets of water fell into a broad deep basin below. Here poor Rip stopped to think. He again called and whistled for his dog. What was to be done? The morning was passing away, and Rip felt hungry from the lack of breakfast. He regretted giving up his dog and gun; he was afraid to face his wife; but he certainly did not want to die from hunger among the mountains. He shook his head, placed the rusty gun on his shoulder, and turned his steps toward home.

EXERCISES

A. Put a check mark (✓) in front of the item (a, b, or c) which best completes each unfinished sentence.

1. Rip Van Winkle's farm—
   .... a. was in good condition.
   .... b. was in better condition than most farms in the neighborhood.
   .... c. was in the worst condition of all the farms in the neighborhood.

2. Rip met with other idle persons of the village—
   .... a. in the mountains.
   .... b. in front of an inn.
   .... c. in the village schoolhouse.

3. The women of the village—
   .... a. threw stones at Rip.
   .... b. employed Rip.
   .... c. disliked Rip.

4. Rip's favorite sport was—
   .... a. hunting rabbits.
   .... b. hunting crows.
   .... c. hunting squirrels.

5. While in the mountains one day—

.... a. Rip met a stranger with a broken leg.

.... b. Rip met a stranger with a keg of liquor.

.... c. Rip met a stranger with a dog.

6. The stranger wanted—

.... a. Rip to go away.

.... b. Rip to help him.

.... c. Rip to smoke his pipe.

7. When Rip and the stranger entered a hollow they found—

.... a. other strange characters.

.... b. Mrs. Van Winkle.

.... c. Derrick Van Bummel and Nicholas Vedder.

8. Rip served liquor to the group of strangers and—

.... a. gave some to Wolf.

.... b. drank some himself.

.... c. poured the remainder into the river.

9. In the morning when Rip woke up, he found—

.... a. a clean well-oiled gun beside him.

.... b. a keg of liquor beside him.

.... c. an old rusty gun beside him.

10. Since Rip felt hungry, he decided to—

.... a. build a fire and cook breakfast.

.... b. return to the village.

.... c. look for food in the mountains.

B. Write T for *True* in front of each sentence below which is true according to the story. Write F for *False* in front of the sentence if it is not true.

.... 1. Rip Van Winkle did not like to work on his farm.

.... 2. Mrs. Van Winkle never complained.

.... 3. The idle group Rip met with sat in the shade of a tree.

.... 4. Rip always refused to help his neighbors.

.... 5. The name of Rip's only domestic companion was Wolf.

.... 6. While in the mountains one day Rip became tired and lay down on the ground.

.... 7. The man who called Rip was dressed in old-fashioned Dutch clothes.

.... 8. After Rip made several visits to the liquor vessel, he fell asleep.

.... 9. When Rip woke up he tried to find his dog and gun.

.... 10. After a thorough search, Rip finally found the mountain characters.

C. Put a check mark (√) in front of the meaning (a, b, or c) which best fits the numbered word or phrase.

1. **squirrel:**
.... a. a kind of bird
.... b. a kind of animal
.... c. a kind of fish

2. **accurately:**
.... a. timely
.... b. exactly
.... c. understandably

3. **liquor:**
.... a. something to drink
.... b. something to eat
.... c. something to wear

4. **keg:**
.... a. a small bench
.... b. a small table
.... c. a small barrel

5. **folks:**
.... a. eagles
.... b. clothes
.... c. people

6. **weather-beaten:**
.... a. smooth
.... b. rough
.... c. sad

7. **growl:**
.... a. noise made by a dog
.... b. noise made by a bird
.... c. noise made by a cow

8. **gossip:**
.... a. talk about the distant thunder
.... b. talk about the affairs of other people
.... c. talk about the mysterious silence

9. **swamp:**
.... a. soft, wet land
.... b. mountainous woodland
.... c. large, flat rocks

10. **inherit:**
.... a. receive something
.... b. lose something
.... c. give something

This lesson is to be followed by Chapter 1 of Part II, p. 227: "Nouns and Verbs: Differences in Patterning."

THE STORY OF
RIP VAN WINKLE

PART 2

On entering the village Rip met a number of people but recognized none of them. This surprised him, for he thought he knew everyone who lived there. Their clothes, too, were of a different fashion from what he was accustomed to see. They all looked at him with equal signs of surprise—each time they looked, they felt their chins.[1] This caused Rip to do the same, and he was astonished to discover that his beard had grown a foot long!

As he went on into the village, a group of children ran alongside him, pointing at his gray beard. Not being someone they recognized, the dogs too barked at him as he passed. The village had changed; it was larger, and the population had increased. There were rows of houses which he had never seen before, and the familiar houses had disappeared. Strange names were on the doors—strange faces at the windows—everything was strange. Surely this was his native village, which he had only left the day before. There stood the Catskill Mountains—there ran the Hudson River at a distance—there was every hill and valley exactly as it had always been. Rip was puzzled. "That liquor last night," he thought, "has completely confused my thinking."

[1] **chin,** the part of the face below the mouth

With some difficulty he found the way to his own house; every step of the way he expected to hear the loud voice of Mrs. Van Winkle. He found the house in decay—the roof had fallen in, and the windows were all broken. A dog that looked like Wolf was wandering about. Rip called him by name, but the dog barked, showed his teeth, and passed on. "Even my own dog has forgotten me," poor Rip thought.

He went into the house, which Mrs. Van Winkle always kept in neat order. It was completely empty. He called loudly for his wife and children; the lonely rooms rang for a moment with his voice, then all was silence again.

He hurried to the village inn, but it was gone too. A large wooden building stood in its place, with some of the windows broken and mended with old hats and shirts, and over the door a sign was painted, "The Union Hotel." Instead of the big tree that used to shelter the quiet little inn, there was now a tall pole,[2] with a flag at the top composed of stars and stripes. All this was strange and mysterious.

flagpole

There was, as usual, a crowd of people around, but none that Rip remembered. Everything about the people seemed changed. The village appeared noisy and active instead of quiet and sleepy. He looked for the wise Nicholas Vedder with his broad face, double chin, and long pipe, producing clouds of tobacco smoke instead of idle speeches; or Van Bummel, the schoolmaster, reading aloud the contents of an ancient newspaper. In place of these, a thin fellow with his pockets full of handbills[3] was speaking to a group about the rights of citizens—elections—members of Congress[4]—liberty—Bunker's Hill—heroes[5] of seventy-six—and other words which were meaningless to Van Winkle.

---

[2] (flag)pole, a long, round piece of wood (or metal) with a flag at the top (see picture)

[3] handbill, a printed notice or advertisement given out by hand

[4] Congress, a group of elected government officials in the United States who make the laws for the country

[5] hero, a very brave person

Rip's appearance, with his long, gray beard, his rusty gun, his old clothes, and an army of children following him, soon attracted the attention of the politicians. They crowded around him, looking with curiosity. The thin fellow with the hand-bills drew him partly aside and asked, "On which side did you vote?" The question meant nothing to Rip and he answered nothing. Another short but busy little fellow pulled him by the arm and inquired, "Are you a Federal or a Democrat?" [6] Rip could not understand this question either. An important-looking old gentleman came through the crowd and demanded to know why he had brought a gun to the election. "Please, gentlemen," Rip answered, "I am a poor quiet man, a native of this village and a loyal subject of the King."

A general shout burst from the on-lookers—loyal to the King? —a spy, no doubt!—take him away from here! With some difficulty the important-looking man was able to restore order,[7] and he demanded to know why Rip had come there. The poor man said he meant no harm—that he had only come in search of some of his neighbors who used to spend time around the inn.

"Well—who are they?—name them."

Rip thought for a moment and inquired, "Where's Nicholas Vedder?"

There was a silence for a little while; then an old man replied in a thin voice, "Nicholas Vedder! Why, he died eighteen years ago!"

"Where's Brom Dutcher?"

"Oh, he went off to the army at the beginning of the war; some say he was killed at Stony Point—others say he was drowned in a storm at the foot of Anthony's Nose. I don't know—he never came back."

"Where's Van Bummel, the schoolmaster?"

"He went off to war, too, and now he's in Congress."

Rip's heart became sad on hearing of these changes in his home and friends, and finding himself thus alone in the world.

---

[6] **Federal, Democrat,** a member of the Federalist or Democratic party—the two
political parties in the United States at the time of this story
[7] **restore order,** bring back order

Every answer puzzled him, too, because it suggested the passing of long periods of time and brought up matters he could not understand: war—Congress—Stony Point—he had no courage to ask about other friends, but cried out in despair, "Does anyone here know Rip Van Winkle?"

"Oh, Rip Van Winkle!" two or three answered. "Oh, yes! That's Rip Van Winkle over there, leaning against the tree."

Rip looked and saw a man that looked as he did the day he went up the mountain. The poor fellow was now completely confused. He wondered whether he was himself or another man. Then someone asked what his name was.

"God only knows," he replied; "I'm not myself—I'm somebody else—that's me over there—no—that's somebody else in my shoes—I was myself last night, but I fell asleep on the mountain, and they've changed my gun, and everything's changed, and I'm changed, and I don't know what my name is, or who I am!"

The on-lookers now began to look at each other and tap their fingers against their foreheads.[8] There was a whisper, also, about taking his gun, and keeping the old fellow from doing harm to himself or others. At this moment a fresh, attractive young woman pressed through the crowd to see the man with a gray beard. She had a fat little child in her arms, who began to cry. "Hush,[9] Rip," she said; "the old man won't hurt you." The name of the child, the appearance of the mother, the tone of her voice, all seemed familiar to him. "What is your name, my good woman?" he asked.

"Judith Gardenier."

"And your father's name?"

"Ah, poor man. Rip Van Winkle was his name, but it's been twenty years since he went away from home with his gun, and nobody has seen him since. His dog came home without him. Nobody knows what happened to him. I was a little girl then."

---

[8] **forehead,** the part of the face above the eyes
[9] **hush,** be quiet

Rip had only one more question to ask: "Where's your mother?"

"Oh, she died a short time ago."

There was a drop of comfort, at least, in this bit of information. The old man caught his daughter and her child in his arms. "I am your father!" he said. "Young Rip Van Winkle once— old Rip Van Winkle now! Doesn't anybody know poor Rip Van Winkle?"

All stood silent, until an old woman came through the crowd and studied his face for a moment. "Sure enough!" she replied, "it is Rip Van Winkle! Welcome home again, old neighbor. Where have you been these twenty long years?"

Rip told his story—briefly, of course—for the whole twenty years had been only one night for him. The neighbors listened and shook their heads. Probably nobody believed the story.

It was decided, however, to accept the opinion of old Peter Vanderdonk, who was seen slowly advancing up the road. He was a descendant of the historian [10] by that name, who wrote one of the earliest accounts of the province. Peter was the most ancient inhabitant [11] of the village and was familiar with all the wonderful events and beliefs of the neighborhood. He recognized Rip at once and accepted his story as the truth. He told of strange beings who lived in the Catskill mountains, a fact recorded by his ancestor, [12] the historian. It is said that the great Hendrick Hudson, the first discoverer of the river and country, with the men from his ship the Half-Moon, visited the mountains every twenty years; this way they guarded the river and the city called by his name. Peter said his father had once seen these characters in their old Dutch clothes playing ninepins in a hollow of the mountains, and he himself had heard, one summer afternoon, the sound of their balls, like distant thunder.

To make a long story short, the group broke up and returned to the more important concerns of the election. Rip's daughter

---

[10] historian, one who studies and writes history
[11] inhabitant of the village, one who lives in the village
[12] ancestor, a person from whom one is descended

took him home to live with her. She had a comfortable, well-furnished house, and a strong, cheerful farmer for a husband, whom Rip remembered as a child. As to Rip's son, who was exactly like himself, seen leaning against the tree, he was employed to work on the farm; but like his father, he was ready to attend to anything else but his own business.

Rip now resumed [13] his old habits; he soon found many of his former friends and made many new friends among the younger people of the village.

Having nothing to do at home, and having reached that happy age when a man can be idle without being scolded, he took his place on the bench at the door of the inn and was considered one of the wise old men of the village and an authority [14] on old times "before the war." It was some time before he learned enough about village affairs to take part in local gossip or could understand the strange events that had taken place during his absence.

There had been a war of independence; the country was no longer a part of old England; instead of being a subject of the King, he was now a free citizen of the United States. Rip, in fact, was no politician; the changes of states and empires interested him very little; but there was one kind of government he violently disliked—female government in the household. Happily that was at an end; he no longer had a wife and could go in and out as he pleased.

He used to tell his story to every stranger that arrived at the hotel. He was observed, at first, to add and omit certain details every time he told it; this was due perhaps to the fact that he had so recently waked up. It at last settled down to the story I have just told, and every man, woman, and child in the neighborhood knew it by heart. Some always pretended to doubt its reality and insisted that Rip was out of his head.[15] Almost all the old Dutch inhabitants believed it. Even to this day, when

---

[13] **resume**, go back to; take up again
[14] **authority**, one who has considerable knowledge of a subject
[15] **out of his head**, mad

they hear a thunderstorm in the Catskills on a summer after-noon, they say Hendrick Hudson and his men are playing a game of ninepins; and all the hen-pecked husbands of the neigh-borhood, when life is difficult at home, wish that they might have a quieting drink from Rip Van Winkle's vessel of liquor.

EXERCISES

A. Put a check mark (√) in front of the item (a, b, or c) which best completes each unfinished sentence.

1. When Rip entered the village—
.... a. he recognized everyone he saw.
.... b. he saw nobody he knew.
.... c. he found the village unchanged.

2. The roof of Rip's house—
.... a. was new.
.... b. had a flag on it.
.... c. had fallen in.

3. The thin fellow, talking about the rights of citizens, elections, members of Congress, etc., was—
.... a. a politician.
.... b. Nicholas Vedder.
.... c. Rip's son.

4. When asked about voting in the election—
.... a. Rip did not understand the questions.
.... b. Rip said he voted for the best man.
.... c. Rip went back to the mountains.

5. Rip discovered that he had left the village—
.... a. the day before.
.... b. twenty years before.
.... c. two weeks before.

6. The first person who recognized Rip Van Winkle was—
.... a. Peter Vanderdonk.
.... b. Brom Dutcher.
.... c. an old woman.

7. Rip went to live—
.... a. at the hotel.

.... b. with his daughter.

.... c. with the politicians.

8. One thing Rip violently disliked was—

.... a. local gossip in the village.

.... b. female government in the household.

.... c. a ship called the Half-Moon.

9. The people in the village considered Rip—

.... a. an authority on old times "before the war."

.... b. an authority on farming.

.... c. an authority on the game of ninepins.

10. Rip's son—

.... a. was employed on a farm.

.... b. was employed at the inn.

.... c. was employed by the King.

B. Write T for *True* in front of each sentence below which is true according to the story. Write F for *False* in front of the sentence if it is not true.

.... 1. After entering the village Rip discovered that his beard had grown a foot long.

.... 2. On the day Rip arrived in the village there was an election.

.... 3. Rip found Mrs. Van Winkle at the inn.

.... 4. Rip voted in the election on the side of the Democrats.

.... 5. Judith Gardenier was Rip Van Winkle's daughter.

.... 6. Everybody believed the story Rip told about the mountain characters and the vessel of liquor.

.... 7. Peter Vanderdonk said he had seen the strange characters playing ninepins in the mountains.

.... 8. During Rip's absence there had been a war of independence.

.... 9. Rip found out that his wife had died a short time before he returned to the village.

.... 10. After the war of independence, Rip was still a subject of the King.

C. Put a check mark (√) in front of the meaning (a, b, or c) which best fits the numbered word or phrase.

1. **historian:**   .... a. one who makes history

                        .... b. one who writes history

                        .... c. one who buys history books

2. **hush:** .... a. make a low noise
.... b. cause fear
.... c. be quiet

3. **chin:** .... a. part of the face
.... b. part of the foot
.... c. part of the chest

4. **Congress:** .... a. a list of accepted opinions
.... b. an ancient book
.... c. a group of law-makers

5. **Federal:** .... a. member of the King's guards
.... b. member of Hendrick Hudson's group
.... c. member of a political party

6. **authority:** .... a. person who knows a lot about a subject
.... b. person who knows a little about a subject
.... c. person who knows nothing about a subject

7. **out of his head:** .... a. worried
.... b. unhappy
.... c. mad

8. **restore order:** .... a. lose control
.... b. bring back order
.... c. put out of order

9. **ancestor:** .... a. person interested in many things
.... b. person from whom one is descended
.... c. person in need of assistance

10. **handbill:** .... a. something causing pain
.... b. talk about local affairs
.... c. printed notice or advertisement

This lesson is to be followed by Chapter 2 of Part II, p. 232: "Words Which Pattern as Both Nouns and Verbs."

SELECTION 3

THE OPEN BOAT

Stephen Crane

PART 1

None of them knew the color of the sky. Their eyes were on the waves that came toward them. These waves had a reddish-blue color, except for the tops which were white, and all the men knew the colors of the sea. The horizon seemed to rise and fall, and all around them there was nothing to see but the edges of the waves, which looked like the points of sharp rocks.

Many people have bathtubs larger than the boat they were attempting to steer on the open sea. The waves were tall and powerful, and each one made traveling in the small boat a real problem.

The cook sat in the bottom and looked with both eyes at the side of the boat—about six inches high—which separated him from the ocean. His sleeves[1] were rolled up, and the two sides of his unbuttoned shirt hung loose as he bent to bail out[2] the boat. Often he said, "We certainly had a narrow escape!" As he said it, he looked eastward over the rough sea.

The oiler, steering with one of the two oars in the boat, sometimes raised himself suddenly when water rushed in over the stern.[3] It was a thin little oar, and it often seemed ready to break.

The correspondent,[4] trying to row with the other oar, watched the waves and wondered why he was there.

The injured[5] captain, lying in the bow,[6] was thinking sadly that sometimes, for no good reason, the business fails, the army loses, the ship goes down. The master of a vessel is like a part of the vessel; if the vessel is destroyed, the master feels destroyed, for a while at least. Finally the captain spoke. Although it was steady, his voice sounded extremely unhappy.

"Turn the boat a little more south, Billie," he said.

"A little more south, sir," repeated the oiler in the stern to show that he had heard the order.

A seat in this boat was not unlike a seat on a wild horse, and a horse, by the way, is not much smaller. The boat went left and right and up and down; bow up, stern down; then bow down, stern up. As each wave came, the boat rose like a horse jumping a high fence. One disadvantage of riding on the sea is that after you pass over one wave successfully there is another

[1] **sleeve,** the part of a shirt (or coat, or dress) that covers the arm
[2] **bail (out),** throw water out of a boat with a bucket or other container
[3] **stern,** the back part of a boat or ship
[4] **correspondent,** a person who sends news and other writings to a newspaper to be printed
[5] **injured,** hurt; wounded
[6] **bow,** the front part of a boat or ship

wave behind it just as important and just as ready to fill your boat with water. In a ten-foot dinghy [7] one sees and feels the tremendous force of the waves and realizes the damage they can cause. Waves striking the sides of a large ship, on the other hand, do not seem nearly so dangerous. As each wall of water came, the men in the boat could see nothing else; they probably thought that each wave was bigger and more powerful than the last one.

In the pale light the faces of the men were probably gray. Their eyes turned eastward as the sun came up slowly into the sky; they knew it was day even without seeing the sun, for the sea changed from reddish-blue to green, and the foam [8] was like snow. What happened in the sky at daybreak was unknown to them; they only knew what happened to the color of the waves that rolled toward them.

In disconnected sentences the cook and the correspondent argued about the difference between a life-saving station and a house of refuge. [9] The cook had said: "There's a house of refuge a little north of the lighthouse at Mosquito Inlet, and as soon as they see us they'll come in their boat and take us to shore."

"As soon as who sees us?" asked the correspondent.

"The crew," [10] answered the cook.

"Houses of refuge don't have crews," said the correspondent. "Houses of refuge are places where clothes and food are stored for shipwrecked people. They don't have crews."

"Yes, they do," said the cook.

"No, they don't," said the correspondent.

"Well, we're still rather far from Mosquito Inlet," said the oiler in the stern.

"Well," said the cook, "perhaps it's a life-saving station near the lighthouse, and not a house of refuge."

---

[7] **dinghy**, a small rowing-boat carried on a ship
[8] **foam**, small balls of air in liquid (bubbles) producing a white color
[9] **refuge**, shelter; protection (from danger)
[10] **crew**, a group of persons working together

"We're not there yet," said the oiler.

The wind blew hard against their faces and pushed their hair this way and that way.

"It's a good thing the wind is blowing toward the shore," said the cook.

"That's right," said the correspondent.

The busy oiler also agreed.

Then the captain in the bow laughed a little. "Do you think we can save ourselves, boys?" he asked.

The other three were silent. They were hopeful, but at the same time they were doubtful. To express certainty in their situation seemed childish and stupid.

"Oh, well," said the captain, "we'll get ashore all right."

But the tone of his voice was not comforting, and the oiler added, "Yes, we'll get ashore if the wind doesn't change." And the cook, still bailing, added, "Yes, if the waves don't overturn the boat or fill it with water."

Sea gulls [11] flew around them. Sometimes they sat down on the sea near bunches of brown seaweed that rolled over the waves. The birds sat comfortably in groups; the men in the boat envied them, for the roughness of the sea did not disturb them at all. Often they came close to the boat and looked at the men with their tiny [12] black eyes. The men shouted at them, telling them to go away. One came, and decided to sit down on the captain's head. The bird flew alongside the boat and did not circle, but made short jumps in the air like a chicken. Its black eyes were fixed on the captain's head. "Ugly old bird," said the oiler. The cook and the correspondent swore at the creature. The captain wanted to hit it with a heavy rope that lay in the boat, but he was afraid that the sudden move-

sea gull

---

[11] (sea) gull, a large, graceful seabird (see picture)
[12] tiny, very small

ment might overturn the boat; and so, with his open hand, the captain gently and carefully waved the gull away.

The oiler and the correspondent rowed. At first they sat together on the same seat, and each rowed with one oar. Then the oiler took both oars; then the correspondent took both oars; then the oiler; then the correspondent. While one rowed, the other lay down in the stern. Then they changed places. It was in reality easier to steal eggs from a hen [13] than to change seats in a dinghy. Every movement in the boat was made with extraordinary care. As the two slid past each other, the others kept watchful eyes on the coming waves, and sometimes the captain would shout: "Look out, now; careful!"

The brown bunches of seaweed that appeared from time to time were like islands, little bits of earth. From all appearances they were traveling in no single direction. They seemed to remain more or less in the same place. By watching the seaweed, however, the men could determine that the boat was slowly making progress toward land.

The captain, raising his head cautiously in the bow, said he could see the lighthouse at Mosquito Inlet. Presently the cook remarked that he could see it. The correspondent was rowing then, and for some reason he too wished to look at the lighthouse; but his back was toward the shore, and he had to keep his eyes on the waves. So for some time he had no opportunity to turn his head. But at last there came a wave more gentle than the others, and while the boat was on top of it he quickly passed his eyes over the western horizon.

"See it?" asked the captain.

"No," answered the correspondent slowly; "I didn't see anything."

"Look again," said the captain. He pointed. "It's exactly in that direction."

At the top of another wave the correspondent did as he was told, and this time he caught sight of a small, still thing about

----
[13] hen, a female chicken

as big as the point of a pin. It took sharp eyes to find a lighthouse so tiny.

"Think we'll reach the shore all right, Captain?" someone asked.

"If the wind continues and the boat doesn't get full of water, we can't do otherwise."

The little boat, lifted and pushed by the waves, made some progress, but it was slow. Occasionally a great quantity of water poured into the boat from an extra-large wave, and the captain shouted for the cook to bail faster.

It would be difficult to describe these men as a group. They had little in common. There was a captain, an oiler, a cook, and a correspondent—and they were all friends, bound together in an effort to save themselves from drowning. The hurt captain, lying against the water jar [14] in the bow, spoke always in a low tone and calmly; but he never commanded a more swiftly [15] obedient crew than the three in the dinghy. There was something more than a mere recognition of what was best for the safety of all. Besides the feeling of loyalty to the commander of the boat, there was friendship and companionship which

jar

the correspondent felt was the best experience of his life. But no one said this was so. No one mentioned it.

"I wish we had a sail," remarked the captain. "Let's put my overcoat on the end of an oar, and you two boys can rest a while." So the cook and the correspondent held the oar and spread out the overcoat; the oiler steered with the other oar; and the little boat made good time with her new "sail." Sometimes the oiler had to stand up to steer properly, which was dangerous, but otherwise sailing was a success.

Meanwhile the lighthouse was growing larger. Now it had some color and looked like a gray shadow against the blue

[14] jar, a container made of glass (see picture)
[15] swiftly, quickly; rapidly

sky. The man with the oar turned his head often to see this
little gray shadow. At last the men in the boat could see land.
As the lighthouse was like an upright shadow on the sky, this
land was like a long black shadow on the sea. "We're probably
near New Smyrna," said the cook, who had been along this
shore often in various ships. "By the way, Captain, I believe
they abandoned [16] that life-saving station there about a year
ago."

"Did they?" said the captain.

The wind slowly died away. The cook and the correspondent
now had to hold the oar with the "sail" higher than before.
But the waves continued to hit the sides of the boat and make
it go up and down again. Since the wind was no longer pushing
the boat, the waves seemed to attack more fiercely. The oiler
and the correspondent took the oars again.

Shipwrecks usually come without warning. If men could
train for them and be in good condition when they happen,
there would be less drowning at sea. None of the men in the
dinghy had slept for two days and two nights, and in the
excitement of leaving the sinking ship they had forgotten to
eat anything.

For these reasons and others, neither the oiler nor the correspondent was fond of rowing at this time. The correspondent
wondered how it was possible that some people enjoyed rowing a boat. It was no joy for him; it was real punishment,
and nothing could persuade him to believe that rowing was
anything but misery to a person's arms and back.

"Take it easy now, boys," said the captain. "Don't exhaust
yourselves. If we have to swim ashore, you'll need all your
strength."

EXERCISES

A. Put a check mark (√) in front of the item (a, b, or c) which
best completes each unfinished sentence.

---

[16] abandon, leave unattended; desert

1. The four men in this story were traveling—
.... a. on a horse.
.... b. in a bathtub.
.... c. in a boat.

2. They found traveling difficult because—
.... a. the waves had a reddish-blue color.
.... b. the waves were tall and powerful.
.... c. they had no oars.

3. The person in charge of the dinghy was—
.... a. the captain.
.... b. the correspondent.
.... c. the cook.

4. The men were trying to reach the shore after—
.... a. swimming in the ocean all night.
.... b. a shipwreck.
.... c. visiting a life-saving station.

5. Sometimes they were bothered by—
.... a. sea gulls.
.... b. the hot sun.
.... c. other boats.

6. Two of the men rowed:—
.... a. the captain and the cook.
.... b. the cook and the oiler.
.... c. the oiler and the correspondent.

7. They could determine that the boat was moving toward land by—
.... a. watching the waves.
.... b. watching the seaweed.
.... c. watching the sun.

8. The men made a "sail" with—
.... a. an overcoat
.... b. a towel.
.... c. a shirt.

9. None of the men in the dinghy had slept for—
.... a. ten days and ten nights.
.... b. three days and three nights.
.... c. two days and two nights.

10. Before leaving the sinking ship—

.... a. they had eaten some bread and meat.

.... b. they had eaten nothing.

.... c. they had eaten breakfast.

B. Write T for *True* in front of each sentence below which is true according to the story. Write F for *False* in front of the sentence if it is not true.

.... 1. One of the men in the boat was a cook.

.... 2. The correspondent could not row because he was injured.

.... 3. As the sun came up the sea changed color.

.... 4. According to the correspondent, houses of refuge do not have crews.

.... 5. A sea gull tried to sit down on the oiler's head.

.... 6. It is easy to change seats in a dinghy.

.... 7. There was a lighthouse at Mosquito Inlet.

.... 8. The correspondent enjoyed rowing.

.... 9. The cook's job was to bail out the water.

.... 10. Shipwrecks usually come without warning.

C. Put a check mark (√) in front of the meaning (a, b, or c) which best fits the numbered word.

1. **sleeve:**   .... a. a part of a ship

                      .... b. a part of a shirt

                      .... c. a part of the body

2. **bail:**   .... a. throw water out of a boat

                      .... b. jump from a boat

                      .... c. put water into a boat

3. **bow:**   .... a. the back part of a boat or ship

                      .... b. the front part of a boat or ship

                      .... c. the sail of a boat or ship

4. **dinghy:**   .... a. a kind of bird

                      .... b. a kind of jar

                      .... c. a kind of boat

5. **tiny:**   .... a. very quick

                      .... b. very small

                      .... c. very large

6. **correspondent:** .... a. a person who writes for a newspaper

                      .... b. a person who commands a ship

                      .... c. a person who lives in a lighthouse

7. **injured:**
.... a. wet; soaked
.... b. hurt; wounded
.... c. dead; lifeless

8. **swiftly:**
.... a. slowly; unhurriedly
.... b. thoroughly; completely
.... c. rapidly; quickly

9. **crew:**
.... a. a group of people
.... b. a group of ships
.... c. a group of oars

10. **refuge:**
.... a. shelter
.... b. waste
.... c. container

This lesson is to be followed by Chapter 3 of Part II, p. 236: "Noun and Verb Suffixes."

THE OPEN
BOAT

The shore now had the appearance of a line of black and a line of white—trees and sand. Finally the captain said that he could see a house on the shore. "That's the house of refuge, I'm sure," said the cook. "They'll see us soon and come to help us."

The distant lighthouse was clearly in view. "The keeper of that lighthouse can surely see us now," said the captain. "He'll tell the life-saving people that we're out here."

"I imagine that no one on shore knows about the shipwreck, and I doubt that any of the other boats from the ship have reached land yet," said the oiler. "Otherwise the life-saving people would be searching for us in their boats."

Slowly and beautifully the land appeared before them. The wind came again. It had changed from the northeast to the southeast. Finally a new sound fell on the ears of the men in the boat. It was like thunder—the waves striking the shore. "We'll never be able to reach the lighthouse now," said the captain. "Turn the boat a little more north, Billie."

"A little more north, sir," said the oiler.

They all expected to be ashore within an hour. The correspondent thought that his clothes were completely wet, but when he happened to feel in the top pocket of his coat, he found eight cigars.[1] Four of them were soaked,[2] but the other four were perfectly dry. After a search, somebody produced three dry matches. They now rode in their little boat, certain of their rescue in the near future, and smoked the big cigars. Everybody took a drink of water.

"Cook," remarked the captain, "there are no signs of life at that house on the shore."

"No," replied the cook. "I'm surprised that they don't see us!"

The roar of the waves striking the shore sounded louder than ever. Being closer to the shore the waves were also bigger than ever. As the men sat in the boat, they expected to find the boat full of water at any moment.

"I wonder why they don't see us," one said. Then another said the same thing; then another.

It is fair to say here that there was not a life-saving station within twenty miles in either direction; but the men did not know this, and we shall not record the words they used in talking about the eyesight of the nation's life-savers.

Their confidence of an immediate rescue completely faded.

"Well," said the captain. "I suppose we'll have to try to reach land without any help. If we stay here too long, we'll not have the strength to swim after the boat fills up with water."

And so the oiler, who was at the oars, turned the boat toward the shore. There was some thinking at this time.

"If we don't all get ashore," said the captain, "you fellows can tell my relatives what happened to me."

Then they briefly exchanged some addresses. As for the men's thoughts, there was a great deal of anger in them. They probably thought, "If I'm going to drown now, why was I allowed to come this far and see sand and trees and not be able to save myself? Why didn't I drown at the shipwreck,

---

[1] **cigar,** a roll of tobacco leaves for smoking
[2] **soaked,** thoroughly wet

or at least before all the hard work in order to come this far. But no; I can't drown now—not after all that hard work."

The oiler found the boat more and more difficult to manage. It almost overturned several times.

"Boys," said the oiler, "in this kind of water we can't last more than three minutes, and we're too far from the shore to swim. Shall I take the boat back to sea again, Captain?"

"Yes. Go ahead!" said the captain.

This oiler, by a series of quick twists and fast and steady oarsmanship,[3] turned the boat around and took her safely to sea again.

There was silence as the boat moved along, rising and falling, to deeper water. Then somebody spoke: "Well, anyhow, I think some of the people on shore have seen us by now."

The gulls were now turning sideways as they flew into the wind. There was a windstorm southeast of them; they knew this by the color of the sky; some clouds were dirty-gray and some a brick-red, like smoke from a burning building.

"What do you think of those life-saving people? After all this time, there's no sign of them."

"It's strange they haven't seen us."

"Maybe they think we're out here for a good time. Maybe they think we're fishing. Maybe they think we're just stupid—being out here in an open boat."

It was a long afternoon. The wind and waves forced them northward. Far ahead there were little dots which seemed to be a city on the shore.

"St. Augustine?" somebody asked.

The captain shook his head. "No. We're too near Mosquito Inlet."

And the oiler rowed, and then the correspondent rowed; then the oiler rowed again. It was very tiring. The human back can become the center of more aches and pains than any other part of the body; at least it seemed so to them.

---

[3] **oarsmanship**, skill in rowing

"Did you ever like to row, Billie?" asked the correspondent.

"No," said the oiler; "never!"

When one exchanged the rowing-seat for a place in the bottom of the boat, he looked as if he didn't have enough strength to move a finger. Cold sea water covered the bottom of the boat, and he lay in it. His head, resting on an arm, was sometimes drenched [4] by more water coming into the boat. But these matters did not annoy him. If the boat had turned over he would have fallen into the ocean thinking it was a nice soft bed.

"Look! There's a man on the shore!"

"Where?"

"There! See him?"

"Yes. Sure. He's walking along."

"He's waving at us!"

"I believe he is."

"Ah, now we'll be all right. Now a boat will come for us."

"He's going on. He's running. He's going to the house there."

The distant beach [5] seemed lower than the sea, and it was difficult to determine exactly what the little black figure was doing. The captain saw a floating stick, and they rowed to it. Tying a bath towel to the stick, the captain began to wave it. The oarsman did not dare turn his head, so he could only find out what was happening by asking questions.

"What's he doing now?"

"He's standing still again. He's looking, I think. There he goes again—toward the house. Now he's stopped again."

"Is he waving at us?"

"No, not now."

"Look! There comes another man!"

"He's running."

"I think he's riding a bicycle. Now he's met the other man. They're both waving at us. Look!"

---

[4] **drenched**, covered with water

[5] **beach**, that part of the seashore nearest the water, usually covered with sand and small stones

"There's something big moving on the beach."

"What is that thing?"

"It looks like a boat."

"Certainly. It's a boat."

"No; it's on wheels."

"Yes. It's probably a lifeboat. They put lifeboats on wagons [6] to move them around on the shore."

"That's a lifeboat, sure."

"No. I think it's an omnibus." [7]

"I tell you it's a lifeboat."

"It is not! It's an omnibus. I can see it clearly. See? One of those big omnibuses that hotels have."

wagon

"You're right. It's an omnibus. What do you suppose they're doing with an omnibus?"

"There's a fellow waving a little black flag. He's standing on the steps of the omnibus. Two other fellows are with him. They're talking. Look at that fellow with the flag!"

"That isn't a flag. That's his coat. Certainly. That's his coat."

"Yes. He's waving his coat."

"There's no life-saving station on the shore there. That's a hotel omnibus that brought some guests down to the shore to see us drown."

"What is that fellow with the coat trying to tell us?"

"I think he's trying to tell us to go north. Maybe there's a life-saving station in that direction."

"No. He thinks we're fishing. He's just waving to say hello."

"Well, I wish I could understand what his signal means. Surely the signal means something. He's just standing there waving his coat around like a wheel."

"Some more people are joining him."

---

[6] **wagon,** a four-wheeled vehicle for carrying people or things, often pulled by horses (see picture)

[7] **omnibus,** a vehicle with seats inside and sometimes outside used by hotels to take passengers to and from the railroad station

"Look! He's still waving his coat. What's the matter with that fellow? Doesn't he ever get tired? Why doesn't he get some men and come out here? A big boat—one of those fishing boats —could come out here all right."

"Now that they've seen us, we'll have some help soon for sure."

A faint yellow color came into the sky, and the shadows on the sea slowly deepened. The wind became colder, and the men began to shiver.[8]

"Golly,[9] it's cold," one of them said. "I hope we won't have to stay out here all night."

"Don't worry. They've seen us, so it won't be long before a boat comes for us."

The shore grew darker. Finally the man waving the coat was swallowed in the darkness, as well as the omnibus and the group of people.

"I'd like to catch that fellow who waved the coat. I feel like hitting him in the eye."

"Why? What did he do?"

"Oh, nothing, but he seemed so cheerful."

In the meantime the oiler rowed, and then the correspondent rowed, and then the oiler rowed again. The form of the light-house had disappeared from the southern horizon; finally a star appeared just above the level of the sea. All around them the light of day was fading into darkness. They knew they were still close to land, for they could hear the waves striking the shore.

It was certainly a quiet evening. All except the oarsman lay restlessly in the boat's bottom. As for him (the oarsman), his eyes were just able to observe the tall black waves that rolled toward the boat.

The cook's head was raised slightly and he looked without interest at the water under his nose. He was thinking of other things. At last he spoke: "Billie," he said with a sleepy voice, "what kind of cake do you like best?"

---

8 **shiver**, shake or tremble with cold
9 **golly**, a word used to express discomfort, surprise, unhappiness, etc.

"Cake!" replied the oiler and the correspondent. "Don't talk about things like that!"

sandwich

"Well," said the cook, "I was just thinking about sandwiches,[10] and—"

A night on the sea in an open boat is a long night. The moon in the south produced a reflection on the water. On the northern horizon a new light appeared, a small bluish light on the edge of the water.

They were so close together in the tiny dinghy, that the rower was able to keep his feet partly warm by putting them under his companions. The legs of those in the stern extended far under the rowing seat until they touched the feet of the captain in the bow. Sometimes, in spite of the efforts of the tired oarsman, icy water spilled into the boat and soaked them again. They would twist their bodies for a moment and groan[11] and then return to an uncomfortable sleep.

The plan of the oiler and the correspondent was for one to row until he lost the ability and then wake the other from his seawater bed in the bottom of the boat.

The oiler rowed until his head fell forward and sleepiness blinded him; and he rowed even after that. Then he touched the man in the bottom of the boat, and called his name. "Will you relieve me for a little while?" he asked.

"Sure, Billie," said the correspondent, waking and dragging himself to a sitting position. They exchanged places carefully, and the oiler, lying down in the sea water at the cook's side, seemed to go to sleep instantly.

EXERCISES

A. Put a check mark (√) in front of the item (a, b, or c) which best completes each unfinished sentence.

---

[10] **sandwich,** two pieces of bread with meat, egg, cheese, or tomato, etc. between them (see picture)
[11] **groan,** make a deep sound, usually to express pain

1. The sound like thunder was—
.... a. the waves striking the boat.
.... b. the waves striking the shore.
.... c. the waves striking the lighthouse.

2. In his coat pocket the correspondent found—
.... a. a jar of water.
.... b. a sandwich.
.... c. some cigars.

3. As land appeared before them and they saw a house on the
   shore, the men expected—
.... a. to spend several days in the boat.
.... b. immediate rescue.
.... c. to drown.

4. When no help came, they thought of trying to reach the
   shore without any help,—
.... a. so they rowed to the shore and landed the boat.
.... b. but they decided this was too dangerous.
.... c. so they jumped into the water and swam ashore.

5. The men wondered—
.... a. why no one on land had seen them.
.... b. why the gulls flew sideways.
.... c. why they had no water to drink.

6. The bottom of the boat was—
.... a. dry.
.... b. covered with mud.
.... c. covered with sea water.

7. A man on the shore saw the men in the boat and began to—
.... a. swim toward them.
.... b. wave at them.
.... c. sing to them.

8. The men in the boat saw people on the shore and also—
.... a. a lifeboat.
.... b. a flag.
.... c. an omnibus.

9. During the evening they all lay in the bottom of the boat
   except—
.... a. the rower.

.... b. the captain.

.... c. the cook.

10. The cook began to think of—

.... a. sea gulls.

.... b. food.

.... c. cigars.

B. Write T for *True* in front of each sentence below which is true according to the story. Write F for *False* in front of the sentence if it is not true.

.... 1. The cigars the correspondent found were all soaked.

.... 2. Although the men could see a lighthouse on the shore, there was no life-saving station within 20 miles.

.... 3. The oiler was not a good oarsman.

.... 4. Rowing made the correspondent and the oiler very tired.

.... 5. The oiler found that he could lie down in the boat and row at the same time.

.... 6. The men in the boat decided to catch some fish for food.

.... 7. A man on the shore waved his coat at them.

.... 8. As evening came, the wind became colder.

.... 9. A fishing boat came to rescue them.

.... 10. The men in the dinghy were comfortable.

C. Put a check mark (√) in front of the meaning (a, b, or c) which best fits the numbered word.

1. **soaked:**   .... a. wet

.... b. comfortable

.... c. lifted

2. **shiver:**   .... a. rescue

.... b. shake

.... c. ache

3. **sandwich:**   .... a. something to wear

.... b. something to eat

.... c. something to drink

4. **oarsmanship:**   .... a. skill in throwing oars

.... b. skill in rowing

.... c. skill in swimming

5. **cigar:**   .... a. something to eat

.... b. something to smoke

.... c. something to row

6. drenched:
.... a. covered with water
.... b. covered with sand
.... c. covered with sticks

7. jar:
.... a. a container made of glass
.... b. a windstorm
.... c. a part of the body

8. stern:
.... a. the middle part of a boat or ship
.... b. the back part of a boat or ship
.... c. the bottom of a boat or ship

9. gull:
.... a. a large fish
.... b. a kind of bird
.... c. a sea lion

10. abandoned:
.... a. left unattended; deserted
.... b. covered; hidden
.... c. twisted; turned

This lesson is to be followed by Chapter 4 of Part II, p. 241: "Nouns with Underlying Verb Forms."

THE OPEN
BOAT

PART 3

The violence of the sea had ceased.[1] The waves now were not so large and dangerous.

In a low voice the correspondent addressed the captain. He was not sure that the captain was awake, although this man of iron seemed to be always awake. "Captain, shall I keep the boat going toward that light in the north?"

The same steady voice answered him. "Yes. Keep going in that direction."

The cook had tied a life-belt[2] around himself in order to get what warmth it would give, and he seemed almost stove-like when the rower, who was always shivering as soon as he finished his work, dropped down to sleep.

The correspondent, as he rowed, looked down at the two men sleeping underfoot. The cook's arm was on the oiler's shoulder. He probably went to sleep at his work, for suddenly a wave hit the side of the boat and water poured in. The cook continued to sleep, but the oiler sat up, rubbing his eyes and shaking with cold.

---

[1] **cease,** stop
[2] **life-belt,** a belt made of cork or other light material which keeps a person from sinking in the water (see picture)

"Oh, I'm very sorry, Billie," said the correspondent.

"That's all right, old boy," replied the oiler; he lay down again and went to sleep.

Presently it seemed that even the captain was no longer awake, and the correspondent felt that he was floating on the ocean all alone.

There was a long sound of something passing through the water very fast. Then all was quiet; the correspondent breathed with an open mouth and looked at the sea. Suddenly there was another sound like the first one and a long flash of bluish light; this time it was alongside the boat. The correspondent saw a big fin [3] speeding like a shadow through the water.

life-belt

The correspondent looked at the captain. His face was hidden, and he seemed to be asleep. The others were certainly asleep. So, being without sympathy, he leaned to one side and swore softly into the sea.

But the thing did not leave immediately. Ahead and astern,[4] on one side or the other, the bluish flame and the fin continued to reappear. The correspondent did not wish to be alone with the thing. He wished one of his companions would wake up and keep him company, but they all remained motionless and from all appearances were all in a deep sleep.

The light in the north was still shining, but it didn't appear to be nearer the boat. Sometimes the sound of the waves at the shore grew louder, and he turned the boat seaward and rowed harder. Southward, someone had built a fire on the beach; it was low and far away. The thing which had followed the boat was no longer to be seen.

Finally the captain, in the bow, moved the water jar and sat up. "Pretty long night," he said.

"Did you see that shark [5] near the boat a while ago?"

---

[3] fin, a wing-like part on the back or sides of a fish
[4] astern, behind or in the back part of a boat or ship
[5] shark, a large fish which eats other fish and sometimes attacks people (see picture)

"Yes, I saw it."

"I didn't think you were awake at the time."

Later the correspondent spoke into the bottom of the boat. "Billie, will you relieve me?" There was a gradual movement.

"Sure," said the oiler.

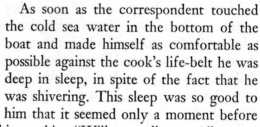

shark

As soon as the correspondent touched the cold sea water in the bottom of the boat and made himself as comfortable as possible against the cook's life-belt he was deep in sleep, in spite of the fact that he was shivering. This sleep was so good to him that it seemed only a moment before he heard a voice speaking to him, "Will you relieve me?"

"Sure, Billie."

The light in the north was gone, but the correspondent took his course from the wide-awake captain.

Later in the night they took the boat farther out to sea, and the captain directed the cook to take an oar at the stern and keep the boat headed toward the sea. He was to call out if he heard the thundering noise of the waves beating on the shore. This plan gave the oiler and the correspondent an opportunity to rest at the same time. "We'll give those boys a chance to regain their strength," said the captain. They lay down and after trembling a little while they slept once more. Neither knew they had left the cook in the company of another shark, or perhaps the same shark.

Water falling into the boat from time to time caused by the waves breaking near the boat gave them fresh soakings, but this did not interrupt their sleep. The wind and water seemed to have no effect on them at all.

"Boys," said the cook, "the boat's pretty close to the shore. I think one of you should take her to sea again." The correspondent, waking up, heard the crash of the waves striking the shore.

As he was rowing, the captain gave him some whisky [6] and water. This made him feel a little warmer and steadier. "If I ever get ashore," he said, "I hope I never see another oar."

Later there was a short conversation: "Billie!—Billie, will you relieve me?"

"Sure," said the oiler.

When the correspondent again opened his eyes, it was day. The morning had appeared with a sky of pure gold, and the sunlight painted the water with gold.

On the distant shore there were many little black houses. But there were no signs of life; no man, nor dog, nor bicycle was seen on the beach. The houses had the appearance of a deserted [7] village. The voyagers looked along the shore as far as they could see. "Well," said the captain, "if no help is coming, I suppose we should try to reach the shore now. If we stay on the water any longer we'll be too weak to help ourselves at all." The others agreed silently. The boat was headed for the beach.

"Now boys," said the captain, "the boat will get full of water from the high waves. All we can do is take her as far as possible, and when she fills up with water, jump out and swim toward the shore. Don't be impatient. Don't jump yet."

The closer they came to the shore, the bigger the waves were. "We won't be able to go very far in this boat," said the captain. The big waves pushed the boat high in the air, and then it fell. Each time a man took his eyes from the waves, he turned his attention toward the shore. The correspondent, observing the others, knew that they were not afraid, but he had no clear idea of their thoughts. As for the correspondent himself, he merely thought that if they should drown, it would be a shame.

There were no hurried words, no shouts, no wild excitement. The men simply looked at the shore. "Now remember," said the captain, "when you jump, move away from the boat quickly."

---

6 **whisky,** a strong alcoholic drink made from grain
7 **deserted,** uninhabited; abandoned

Seaward a big wave fell with a thunderous crash, and a long white sheet of water came rushing toward the boat.

"Wait now," said the captain. The men were silent. They turned their eyes from the shore to the water behind them and waited. The boat rocked and shook, but it did not overturn nor fill up with water.

The next wave crashed also and was followed by a flood of white water which turned the boat around and around. Water came in from all sides. The little boat, made heavier with the weight of the water, sank deeper into the sea.

"Bail, cook!" said the captain.

"All right, Captain," answered the cook.

"Boys, the next one will finish us," said the oiler. "Be sure to jump away from the boat."

The third wave moved forward, bigger than either of the other two. It seemed to swallow the dinghy, and the men went into the sea all at the same time. A piece of life-belt had lain in the bottom of the boat, and as the correspondent jumped he held this to his chest with his left hand.

The January water was icy, and he thought immediately that it was colder than he had expected to find it on the coast of Florida. When he came to the surface he was conscious of nothing but the noisy, cold water. Afterward he saw his companions in the sea. The oiler was ahead of him. He was swimming strongly and rapidly. On the correspondent's left, the cook appeared, with the life-belt holding him above the level of the water. And behind them all the captain was hanging with his one good hand to the overturned dinghy.

The correspondent knew the journey to the shore was a long one, so he did not hurry. The piece of life-belt lay under him, and sometimes the waves seemed to push him along toward the shore.

But finally he reached a place where travel was very difficult. He did not stop swimming to find out what kind of current had caught him, but there his progress ceased.

As the cook passed on the correspondent's left, the captain

was calling to him, "Turn over on your back, cook, and use the oar."

"All right, sir." The cook turned on his back, and, using the oar, he went ahead as if he were in a boat.

Presently the boat also passed to the left of the correspondent with the captain still holding to it with one hand. They went on nearer the shore—the oiler, the cook, the captain—and following them went the water jar floating gaily on the sea.

The correspondent remained caught by this strange new enemy—a current. The shore, with its white slope of sand and its little white houses surrounded by green trees, was spread before him like a picture. It was very near, but at the same time, it was far away. He thought: "I'm going to drown. Can it be possible? Can it be possible?"

But later a wave pushed him away from the current, and he soon found that he was making progress again toward the shore. Later still he heard the captain calling him. "Come to the boat!" he urged.

"All right, Captain."

Presently he saw a man running along the shore. He was undressing with surprising speed. Coat, trousers, shirt, everything seemed to drop off.

As the correspondent swam on he saw the captain leave the boat. An overturned boat near the shore is not a plaything for a swimming man. At that moment a large wave caught the correspondent and hurled [8] him over the boat and far beyond it.

The correspondent arrived in water that reached to his waist, but his condition did not enable him to stand for more than a moment. Each wave knocked him over.

Then he saw the man who had been running and undressing. He dragged the cook ashore, and then went for the captain; but the captain waved him away and sent him to the correspondent. He was naked [9]—naked as a tree in winter, but he was a very welcome helper. He pulled the correspondent's arm, and the

---

[8] **hurl,** throw violently
[9] **naked,** without any clothes

two went on to shallow water and then on to the beach.

The correspondent did not know all that happened afterward. When he had reached the beach he dropped.

It seemed that almost instantly the beach was populated [10] with men bringing blankets, clothes, and whisky, and women with coffee pots and all kinds of home remedies. The welcome of the land was warm and generous.

When night came, the white waves danced in the moonlight, and the wind brought the sound of the great sea's voice to the men on the shore. Whatever the sea had to say, it was probably best understood by the men from the dinghy.

EXERCISES

A. Put a check mark (√) in front of the item (a, b, or c) which best completes each unfinished sentence.

  1. In order to get warmer the cook—
    .... a. built a fire.
    .... b. put on an overcoat.
    .... c. tied a life-belt around himself.

  2. During the night the correspondent saw—
    .... a. a shark's fin.
    .... b. an omnibus.
    .... c. a sailboat.

  3. When the cook was told to steer the boat,—
    .... a. only the correspondent went to sleep.
    .... b. only the oiler went to sleep.
    .... c. both the oiler and the correspondent went to sleep.

  4. When daylight came they were able to see houses on the shore—
    .... a. and many people.
    .... b. but there were no signs of life.
    .... c. so they went to sleep again.

  5. They decided to—
    .... a. go ashore.
    .... b. take the boat to sea again.
    .... c. wait for a lifeboat.

---

[10] **populated,** covered with people; crowded with people

6. When they left the boat—
.... a. the oiler went into the water first.
.... b. they all went into the water at the same time.
.... c. the correspondent went into the water last.

7. When the correspondent jumped he took—
.... a. a towel with him.
.... b. a piece of life-belt with him.
.... c. an oar with him.

8. The men were in the water during the month of—
.... a. July.
.... b. December.
.... c. January.

9. When they reached land they were in the state of—
.... a. New York.
.... b. Florida.
.... c. California.

10. In part, at least, this is a true story. It was probably written by the—
.... a. oiler.
.... b. captain.
.... c. correspondent.

B. Write T for *True* in front of each sentence below which is true according to the story. Write F for *False* in front of the sentence if it is not true.

.... 1. The water in the bottom of the boat was cold.
.... 2. The cook, being tired, slept all night.
.... 3. The captain rowed some of the time so the others could rest.
.... 4. As the men went closer to the shore the waves were larger.
.... 5. Finally they had to leave the boat because it was upset by a wave.
.... 6. The correspondent was caught by a current, but later a wave pushed him away from it.
.... 7. The captain swam ashore holding to a life-belt.
.... 8. A naked man came to help them while they were in the water.
.... 9. When the correspondent reached the beach he danced with joy.

.... 10. Many people came to help them after they reached land.

C. Put a check mark (√) in front of the meaning (a, b, or c) which best fits the numbered word or phrase.

1. **ceased:**   .... a. observed
                     .... b. raised
                     .... c. stopped

2. **naked:**   .... a. without any money
                     .... b. without any clothes
                     .... c. without any food

3. **deserted:**   .... a. at home in the desert
                     .... b. uninhabited
                     .... c. eaten after dinner

4. **shark:**   .... a. a kind of fish
                     .... b. a kind of seaweed
                     .... c. a kind of liquid

5. **whisky:**   .... a. something to smoke
                     .... b. something to wear
                     .... c. something to drink

6. **hurl:**   .... a. throw violently
                     .... b. injure
                     .... c. undress quickly

7. **fin:**   .... a. part of a fish
                     .... b. wing of a bird
                     .... c. edge of a knife

8. **life-belt:**   .... a. a belt made of light material
                     .... b. a belt made of sea shells
                     .... c. a belt used for carrying money

9. **astern:**   .... a. toward the front of a boat or ship
                     .... b. toward the back of a boat or ship
                     .... c. toward the left side of a boat or ship

10. **beach:**   .... a. sandy part of a seashore
                     .... b. foamy part of a wave
                     .... c. top part of a sail

This lesson is to be followed by Chapter 5 of Part II, p. 246: "More Nouns with Underlying Verb Forms."

SELECTION 6

A WHITE HERON

Sarah Orne Jewett

PART 1

It was a June evening about eight o'clock. The woods were already filled with shadows, and the sun was just setting. A little girl was taking her cow home—a slow-moving, weary-looking [1] animal, but nevertheless [2] a valued companion. They were going away from the sunlight into the dark woods, but their feet were familiar with the dirt road, and it didn't matter whether their eyes could see it or not.

---

[1] **weary**, tired; in need of rest
[2] **nevertheless**, inspite of that; still; even so

51

Almost every night during the summer Sylvia had to come and look a long time before she found the cow. It was one of the cow's greatest pleasures to hide among the high bushes; the bell at her neck seldom gave a sign of her presence, for this creature had discovered that if she stood perfectly still, the bell would not ring. So Sylvia had to hunt until she found her—the search often exhausting [3] the child's patience. Since the cow gave good milk and plenty of it, her owners felt that she deserved a reasonable amount of care. Besides, Sylvia had lots of time and very few ways to use it. Sometimes when the weather was pleasant, Sylvia thought of her search for the cow as a kind of game. As she had no children to play with, she entered into the game with a great deal of amusement. This day she had wandered slowly through the fields and woods until the animal had somehow given a signal of her whereabouts,[4] and Sylvia came upon her near the swamp. Sylvia laughed and then urged the cow homeward [5] using a small stick. Leaving the grassy field, they stepped along the road toward the farmhouse; the cow was now ready to be milked.

Sylvia wondered what her grandmother would say because they were so late. She had left home at five thirty, but, of course, everybody knew the difficulty of finding the cow within a short time. Mrs. Tilley, the grandmother, had gone to look for the old cow many summer evenings herself, and she did not want to scold Sylvia for returning home late; in reality, she was glad that she had Sylvia to help her with the many things to be done on the farm. The good woman suspected that Sylvia's late arrivals were not always on account of the cow, but because Sylvia liked to wander in the woods. There never was a child who loved the out-of-doors so much! Everybody said that the change from a crowded manufacturing city was good for the little girl; as for Sylvia herself, it seemed as if she had never been alive at all before she came to live at the farm. "Afraid

---

[3] **exhaust,** use up completely
[4] **whereabouts,** position; place where someone or something is
[5] **homeward,** toward home

of people," said old Mrs. Tilley, who had decided to leave the
city and return to the farm. She had chosen Sylvia from her
daughter's houseful of children to go with her. "If she's afraid
of people," Mrs. Tilley continued, "she should go to the farm.
She won't see people there." When they had reached the lonely
farmhouse after their long trip from the city, Sylvia had whis-
pered, "This is a lovely place to live. I'll never want to return
to the city."

Sylvia and the cow now followed the shady road, the cow
taking slow steps, and the child fast ones. While the cow stopped
at the stream for a drink, Sylvia stood still and waited, letting
her bare feet cool themselves in the water. She walked around
in the water, scarcely noticing when the cow moved on. She
listened with interest to the noises in the big branches overhead.[6]
The trees were full of birds and beasts that seemed to be wide-
awake and moving about or else saying good night to each other
before retiring for the night. Finally she hurried after the cow;
she was getting sleepy as she walked along the road. However,
it was not much farther to the house, and the air felt fresh and
clean. She had not often been in the woods as late as this, and
at this time of day she thought of herself as part of the gray
shadows and the moving leaves. She remembered that she had
come to the farm a year ago, and she wondered if everything
in the noisy city was just the same as when she lived there. She
remembered a red-faced boy in the city who used to follow her
and frighten her.

Suddenly she heard a loud, clear whistle not far away. It was
not a bird's whistle, which always had a friendly sound, but a
human whistle—the kind she used to hear in the city. Sylvia
left the cow and stepped quickly into the bushes. But too late;
she had been seen. A cheerful voice called out, "Hello, little
girl! How far is the main road?" and trembling Sylvia answered,
"It's rather far."

She did not dare to look directly at the tall young man who

---

[6] **overhead,** above one's head

had asked the question, but she came out of the bushes and again followed the cow, while he walked beside her. The young man, she noticed, was carrying a gun over his shoulder.

"I've been hunting some birds," the stranger said kindly, "and I think I'm lost. Don't be afraid," he added, "I need a friend right now. Won't you be my friend?" Sylvia did not answer, so the stranger continued talking, "Can I spend the night at your house, and go hunting again tomorrow morning?" Still no answer, so he tried once more, "Won't you tell me your name?" Sylvia became more and more frightened, but she finally replied "Sylvy" very softly.

Mrs. Tilley was standing in the doorway when the three—Sylvia, the cow, and the young man—came into view. The cow gave a loud moo as they reached the house.

"Yes, I can see you are home finally," she said to the cow. "Where did you find her this time, Sylvy?" Sylvia kept silent; she believed her grandmother did not understand the seriousness of the situation; her grandmother probably thought the stranger was one of the farm boys of the neighborhood.

The young man placed his gun beside the door and dropped a heavy bag beside it. Then he said good evening to Mrs. Tilley, repeated his story about becoming lost in the woods, and asked if he could spend the night there.

"Put me anywhere," he said. "I have to leave early tomorrow morning, before daylight; right now I'm very hungry. Maybe you can let me have some milk . . ."

"Yes, of course," said Mrs. Tilley. "You would find a better place to stay on the main road a mile or so from here, but you're welcome to what we have, if you want to stay. I'll milk the cow right away, and you can make yourself at home. Set a place at the table for the gentleman, Sylvy." Sylvia promptly obeyed. She was glad to have something to do, and she was hungry herself. Her fear decreased as she saw that her grandmother was not afraid of the stranger.

The young man was surprised to find such a clean and comfortable little house in this wild part of New England. He had

known the difficulties of housekeeping without modern con-
veniences, and he respected that level of society which does not
despise [7] the companionship of chickens. He listened attentively
to the old woman's description of their life in the "back" country; he watched Sylvia's pale face and shining gray eyes with
ever-growing interest, and he insisted that this was the best
supper he had eaten for a month; then, afterwards, the new-
made friends sat down near the doorway and talked while the
moon came up.

Soon it would be berry-time, the grandmother said, and
Sylvia was an excellent berry-picker. The cow was easy to milk,
and they had no complaints about the quantity or quality of
her milk. Mrs. Tilley said that four of her children had died,
so that Sylvia's mother, and a son (who might be dead) in California were all the children she had left. "Dan, my son, used to
go hunting in these woods," she explained sadly. "We always
had plenty of partridges [8] and gray squir-
rels to eat while he was at home. Dan was
the wanderer of the family, and he never
wrote letters. I never objected when he left
home for long periods of time. In fact, I'd
have gone to see the world myself, if it had
been possible."

partridge

"Sylvia is like Dan," the grandmother
went on, after a moment's pause. "She knows every foot of
ground in the woods as well as the wild creatures that live there.
Squirrels come and eat from her hand, and birds too. Last winter
she took care of some jay birds. If I hadn't watched her, she
would have gone without food herself in order to feed them.
Anything but crows, I tell her; I'm willing to feed anything
but crows! Dan tamed a crow one time, and it stayed around
even after he left; we thought it would never leave. Dan and
his father didn't get along well together; finally Dan went away
and didn't come back."

---

[7] **despise**, hate; look down on
[8] **partridge**, a kind of bird (see picture)

The guest did not notice the sound of sorrow in the old woman's voice; he was thinking about something else.

"So Sylvy knows all about birds, does she?" he said, as he turned to look at the little girl who sat very still in the moonlight and was becoming increasingly sleepy. "I'm making a collection of birds myself. I started the collection when I was a little boy. (Mrs. Tilley smiled.) There are two or three very rare ones I've been hunting for five years."

"Do you put them in cages?" asked Mrs. Tilley.

"Oh, no, they are stuffed [9] and preserved, dozens and dozens of them," he answered, "and I've shot or caught every one of them myself. I saw a white heron [10] for an instant about three

miles from here last Saturday, and I've followed it in this direction. Herons have never been found in this part of the country," and he turned again to look at Sylvia with the hope of discovering that the rare bird was one of her feathered friends.

But Sylvia didn't seem to hear what the young man was saying.

"You would know the heron if you saw it," the young man continued eagerly. "A strange-

heron

looking tall white bird with soft feathers and long thin legs. It always has a nest made of sticks in the top of a high tree.

Sylvia's heart began to beat faster; she knew that strange white bird. Once she had crept near it over on the other side of the woods, as it stood in some bright green swamp grass. There was an open place where the sunshine seemed strangely yellow and hot, where tall grass-like plants grew, and her grandmother had warned her that she might sink into the soft black mud and not be able to get out. Beyond this place was the sea— the sea which Sylvia wondered and dreamed about, but which she had never seen. But on stormy nights she had heard great noises from the sea, and she knew it was not far away.

---

[9] **stuffed,** the skin of a dead animal or bird filled with wool and other material, so that it will look the same as it did when living

[10] **heron,** a large white bird with very long legs and a long neck (see picture)

"I would certainly like to find that heron's nest," the stranger said. "I would give ten dollars to anybody who could show it to me," he added; "if necessary I'll spend my whole vacation looking for it."

Mrs. Tilley gave her undivided attention to all this, but Sylvia still gave no signs of interest in talking about birds. Nevertheless, she had heard every word the stranger had said, and that night she thought over and over about the many wonderful things that ten dollars would buy.

EXERCISES

A. Put a check mark (√) in front of the item (a, b, or c) which best completes each unfinished sentence.

1. Sylvia was Mrs. Tilley's—
.... a. grandmother.
.... b. daughter.
.... c. granddaughter.

2. At the time of this story Mrs. Tilley and Sylvia lived—
.... a. on a farm.
.... b. in a manufacturing city.
.... c. in a small town.

3. Every evening Sylvia was sent to—
.... a. feed he chickens.
.... b. shoot some birds.
.... c. look for the cow.

4. Returning home one evening she met a—
.... a. stranger with a dog.
.... b. stranger with a gun.
.... c. stranger with a heron.

5. The stranger wanted—
.... a. to spend the night at Sylvia's house.
.... b. to spend the night in the woods.
.... c. to spend the night at the seashore.

6. Mrs. Tilley told the stranger—
.... a. that Sylvia disliked the wild creatures in the woods.
.... b. that Sylvia knew the woods as well as the wild creatures living there.
.... c. that Sylvia played with other children in the woods.

7. The stranger said he had a—
.... a. collection of insects.
.... b. collection of animals.
.... c. collection of birds.

8. He was very anxious to find a—
.... a. heron.
.... b. crow.
.... c. sea gull.

9. When the stranger mentioned a strange-looking white bird with long thin legs,—
.... a. Sylvia did not think that she had seen it.
.... b. Sylvia remembered that she had seen it.
.... c. Sylvia said her grandmother had seen it.

10. If Sylvia showed the stranger a heron's nest, she would receive—
.... a. two dollars.
.... b. ten cents.
.... c. ten dollars.

B. Write T for *True* in front of each sentence below which is true according to the story. Write F for *False* in front of the sentence if it is not true.

.... 1. Sylvia always found the cow easily.
.... 2. The cow gave good milk and plenty of it.
.... 3. Sylvia never went into the woods without her grandmother.
.... 4. She had lived on the farm for two years.
.... 5. Mrs. Tilley was older than Sylvia.
.... 6. The young man Sylvia met on the way home was one of the farm boys of the neighborhood.
.... 7. The young man had supper with Mrs. Tilley and Sylvia.
.... 8. Mrs. Tilley did not like to feed crows.
.... 9. A heron always builds its nest on the ground.
.... 10. Sylvia was not interested in receiving ten dollars.

C. Put a check mark (√) in front of the meaning (a, b, or c) which best fits the numbered word.

1. **homeward:** .... a. away from home
.... b. toward home
.... c. at home

2. **partridge:**
.... a. a kind of bird
.... b. a kind of house
.... c. a kind of tree

3. **despise:**
.... a. pass slowly
.... b. hate
.... c. be quiet

4. **overhead:**
.... a. above one's head
.... b. beside one's head
.... c. below one's ears

5. **exhaust:**
.... a. break
.... b. deserve
.... c. use up completely

6. **swamp:**
.... a. soft, wet land
.... b. red-faced person
.... c. dark woods

7. **nevertheless:**
.... a. in spite of that
.... b. familiar with that
.... c. with plenty of that

8. **weary:**
.... a. sunny
.... b. tired
.... c. late

9. **whereabouts:**
.... a. whomever one can find at this time
.... b. whenever one moves too fast
.... c. place where something or someone is

10. **crow:**
.... a. a large green insect
.... b. a large black bird
.... c. a tall white bird

This lesson is to be followed by Chapter 6 of Part II, p. 251: "Review: Formal Contrasts and Derivation."

A WHITE
HERON

PART 2

The next day the young sportsman returned to the woods, and Sylvia went with him. She had completely lost her fear of this friendly fellow, who proved to be very kind and generous. He told her many things about the birds: where they lived, what they knew, and what they were able to do. And he gave her a pocket knife. All day long he did not once cause her to worry or be afraid, except when he shot some unsuspecting creature with his gun. Sylvia would have liked him much better without that gun. One thing puzzled her especially: he seemed to be very fond of birds, so why did he want to kill them? But as the day wore on,[1] she still watched the young man with loving admiration. She had never seen anyone so charming and delightful. At times they stopped to listen to a bird's song; then they walked on, parting the branches,—speaking to each other rarely and in whispers. The young man went first and Sylvia followed a few steps behind, with her gray eyes dark with excitement.

She was sorry that the white heron was hard to find, but she did not lead the guest, she only followed, and she never spoke

---

[1] **wore on,** passed slowly

first. The sound of her own voice would have frightened her,—
it was hard enough to answer yes or no when the need arose.
At last evening came, and they took the cow home together.
The young man decided to spend one more night at Mrs. Tilley's
house. Sylvia smiled with pleasure when they passed the place
where she had heard the stranger's whistle the evening before.

Half a mile from home, at one edge of the woods where the
land was highest, there was a great pine tree,[2] the last of its kind
still growing there. Why a single pine tree stood at this place
no one could say. The woodcutters who had cleared away the
surrounding trees were dead and gone long ago, and a whole
forest of other trees had grown up in their place. The top of this
great pine tree stood above the rest, and it could be seen from
miles away. Sylvia knew it well. She had believed that anyone
who climbed to the top of it could see the ocean. Many times
she had put her hand on its rough trunk and looked up at those
dark branches that waved in the wind, no matter how hot and
still the air was below. Now she thought of the tree with a new
excitement, for if she climbed it at daybreak, why couldn't she
see all the world and easily discover where the white heron
had its nest? According to her new companion, the heron left
its nest early in the morning, at the first signs of day.

What an adventure! What excitement! What a wonderful
plan—to discover the secret of the white heron's nest! Long
after the young sportsman and his old hostess were asleep that
night, Sylvia was still wide awake. She forgot to think of sleep.
The short summer night seemed as long as the winter darkness.
At last she realized it was time to go. She quietly went out of the
house and hurried through the woods toward the open place
beyond.

She was afraid for a while that morning might come too soon,
and the bird would be gone; but as the great tree came in view,
the pale moon showed no signs of disappearing yet. Reaching

---

[2] **pine,** an evergreen tree with needle-like leaves

the base of the tree she thought of her climb to its top; her bare feet and fingers would be like bird's claws [3] holding to a ladder that reached up, up, almost to the sky itself. First she had to climb the white oak tree [4] that grew alongside the pine. She made her way through the dark branches and the green leaves which were heavy and wet with dew.[5] She frightened a bird from its nest, and a surprised red squirrel hurried out of sight to escape from a possible enemy. Sylvia felt her way easily. She had often climbed there, and she knew that high in the tree one of the oak's upper branches touched the trunk of the big pine. There, when she made the dangerous pass from one tree to the other, her great adventure would really begin.

claws

She crept out along the oak limb [6] at last and took the daring step across into the old pine tree. Climbing in the pine was harder; she had to reach far and hold tight. The short limbs sometimes caught her clothes and hair and scratched her like thorns. The sparrows [7] and robins [8] in the woods below were beginning to wake up and move about in the trees. The child realized she must hurry. The tree seemed to become higher as she went up, but she continued to climb as quickly as possible round and round the trunk and farther and farther upward.

Sylvia's face was like a pale star when the last thorny branch was past, and she stood trembling and tired, high in the treetop. Yes, there was the sea and on it the reflection of the rising sun, and toward the east also she could see two hawks [9] which seemed to be floating in the air. How low they looked from where she stood! Westward, the woodlands and farms reached for miles

---

[3] **claws,** the hard, sharp, and pointed nails on the feet of some birds and animals (see picture)
[4] **oak,** a kind of tree
[5] **dew,** water which forms on plants at night
[6] **limb,** a branch of a tree
[7] **sparrow,** a small, brownish-gray bird
[8] **robin,** a small, brownish bird with a red breast
[9] **hawk,** a strong, swift, meat-eating bird

and miles; here and there she could see little churches and an occasional village.

The birds sang louder and louder. At last the sun came into full view with extraordinary brightness. Sylvia could see the white sails of boats at sea, and the clouds which at first were purple and red and yellow began to fade away. Where was the heron's nest in that mass of green branches below? Was this wonderful view of the world the only reward for having climbed to such a height? She looked long and hard and finally, where she had seen the white heron once before, she now saw a white spot like a floating feather. It began to rise and come closer. Then it passed the pine tree, with outstretched [10] wings and neck. An instant later she saw the heron returning; it stopped to rest on a branch not far below her. Sylvia remained completely motionless, not moving a foot or even a finger. Then other birds came to the tree, and the heron, becoming tired of the noise, soon went away. Sylvia watched the wild, light bird floating back to its home in the green world beneath her. Now she knew the heron's secret, and being well satisfied with this knowledge, she started down. She wondered over and over what the stranger would say to her and what he would think when she told him how to find the heron's nest.

"Sylvy, Sylvy!" called the busy old grandmother, but nobody answered; the small bed was empty, and Sylvia had disappeared.

The guest, waking from a dream, remembered the day's pleasure ahead of him and hurried to dress himself. "Surely this shy little girl has seen the white heron," he thought. "She knows the woods as well as any wild creature living there. I must persuade her to tell me." Then he saw her, paler than ever, her old dress torn in several places, and her arms and legs covered with scratches. The grandmother and the sportsman stood in the doorway and questioned her; now was the moment to speak.

But Sylvia did not speak after all, although the old grandmother scolded, and the young man's kind eyes looked straight

---

[10] **outstretched,** stretched or spread out; extended

into her own. He could make them rich with money; he had promised it, and they were poor. The story she could tell would make him very happy.

No, she must keep silent! She couldn't say a word. The sound of the pine's green branches was still in her ears; she remembered how the heron came flying through the golden air and how they watched the sea and the sunrise together; and Sylvia could not speak; she could not tell the heron's secret and give its life away.

Later in the day the guest went away disappointed. Loyalty to her wild friends in the woods had outweighed her love and admiration for the young man. But parting was the saddest experience in all the nine years of her life; she wanted to serve and follow him and love him as a dog loves its master. Many a night Sylvia remembered his whistle on the road as she came home slowly with the old cow. She even forgot the sorrow she had felt when she had heard shots from his gun and had seen birds dropping silently to the ground, their songs hushed and their pretty feathers stained with wet blood. Were the birds better friends than the hunter? Who can tell?

Oh, woodlands! Wild creatures of the woodlands! Bring your gifts and tell your secrets to this lonely country child!

EXERCISES

A. Put a check mark (√) in front of the item (a, b, or c) which best completes each unfinished sentence.

1. The next day Sylvia—
.... a. was still afraid of the stranger.
.... b. had lost her fear of the stranger.
.... c. did not go into the woods with the stranger.

2. She found the young man—
.... a. dull and uninteresting.
.... b. frightening.
.... c. charming and delightful.

3. Sylvia could not understand—
.... a. why the stranger wanted to climb trees.
.... b. why the stranger wanted to kill birds.
.... c. why the stranger wanted to eat all the time.

4. According to the stranger, the heron always left its nest—
.... a. at nightfall.
.... b. at daybreak.
.... c. at noon.

5. Sylvia decided to climb to the top of a pine tree in order to—
.... a. discover the heron's nest.
.... b. catch the heron.
.... c. shoot the heron.

6. While climbing in the tree she—
.... a. found a bird's claw.
.... b. sat down on a branch and went to sleep.
.... c. scratched her arms and legs.

7. After Sylvia reached the top of the tree,—
.... a. she could see the ocean.
.... b. she could see the stranger in the woods.
.... c. she could see a cow.

8. When Mrs. Tilley called Sylvia,—
.... a. she was still asleep in her bed.
.... b. she was feeding some birds.
.... c. she was not in the house.

9. The grandmother and the stranger wanted to know where she had been,—
.... a. but Sylvia did not tell them.
.... b. so Sylvia told them.
.... c. but Sylvia could not remember.

10. The stranger went away disappointed because—
.... a. Mrs. Tilley talked too much.
.... b. he was unable to find the heron's nest.
.... c. Sylvia did not want him to stay.

B. Write T for *True* in front of each sentence below which is true according to the story. Write F for *False* in front of the sentence if it is not true.

.... 1. Sylvia was thirteen years of age.
.... 2. In the woods Sylvia always walked ahead of the stranger.
.... 3. The stranger climbed the pine tree.
.... 4. Mrs. Tilley had seen the heron many times.
.... 5. The stranger spent two nights at Mrs. Tilley's house.
.... 6. Sylvia began to climb the pine tree after daybreak.

.... 7. She never discovered the whereabouts of the heron's nest.

.... 8. Sylvia tore her dress in the tree.

.... 9. Sylvia did not want the stranger to leave.

.... 10. The heron's nest was only a few yards from Mrs. Tilley's house.

C. Put a check mark (√) in front of the meaning (a, b, or c) which best fits the numbered word or phrase.

1. **pine:**
    .... a. a kind of tree
    .... b. a kind of grass
    .... c. a kind of bird

2. **The day wore on:**
    .... a. The day ended quickly.
    .... b. The day seemed short.
    .... c. The day passed slowly.

3. **dew:**
    .... a. water on the brain
    .... b. water on plants
    .... c. water in the lake

4. **daybreak:**
    .... a. beginning of day
    .... b. beginning of night
    .... c. beginning of the afternoon

5. **claws:**
    .... a. sharp-pointed nails on the feet of some birds
    .... b. loud, clear whistles
    .... c. feet of a cow

6. **limb:**
    .... a. leaf of a tree
    .... b. branch of a tree
    .... c. trunk of a tree

7. **hushed:**
    .... a. hurried
    .... b. silenced
    .... c. discovered

8. **stuffed:**
    .... a. filled
    .... b. covered
    .... c. promised

9. **outstretched:**
    .... a. shortened
    .... b. extended
    .... c. frightened

10. **robin:**
    .... a. a small brownish bird with a red breast

.... b. a large white bird with long legs
.... c. a black meat-eating bird

This lesson is to be followed by Chapter 7 of Part II, p. 255:
"Verbs with Underlying Noun Forms; Contrasts in Stem Forms."

SELECTION 8

TAPPAN'S BURRO

Zane Grey

PART 1

Tappan looked down at the newly-born burro [1] with pity and wonder. It was not a healthy little burro, although its mother was the strongest and toughest of all the burros he had owned during his years of prospecting [2] in the desert. He could not leave it there to die. Surely it was not strong enough to follow its mother. And he certainly did not want to kill it.

"Poor little creature," thought Tappan. "Neither Jennie nor I wanted it to be born. We'll have to stay here a few days. One

---

[1] **burro,** a small donkey used as a pack animal (see picture)
[2] **prospecting,** exploring in the hope of finding gold or other valuable minerals

never knows what to expect of a burro. It may gain enough strength to go with us."

So Tappan left Jennie and her tiny, long-eared baby and began to make a permanent camp. He did not like the water at this oasis [3] very well, but it was drinkable. In other respects the oasis was desirable enough as a camping place. Desert wanderers like Tappan preferred to camp at lonely spots where water was not difficult to find. This one was at the foot of the Chocolate Mountains, where a rocky slope met the desert sand, and some green grass and a few trees proved the presence of water. Opposite these mountains there were miles of sand and desert plants, then a belt of green and a strip of red that marked the Colorado River, and then the higher Arizona land rising upward until one could see the tops of the distant mountains against the blue sky.

burro

Buried in these desert mountains was gold. Tappan was a prospector.[4] But the desire for gold did not tie him to this wandering life any more than the freedom it offered. He had never found a lot of gold in one place. About the best he had done was to dig enough gold to buy supplies for another prospecting trip into some far corner of the American Desert. Tappan knew the dry Southwest from San Diego to the Pecos River and from Picacho on the Colorado River to the Tonto Basin. Few prospectors had the toughness and ability of Tappan. He was tall and heavy, and at thirty-five he had still not reached the limit of his growth in size and force.

With hammer and pick [5] and magnifying glass [6] Tappan climbed the bare mountains. He was not skilled in testing min-

---

[3] **oasis,** a place in the desert where there are trees and water
[4] **prospector,** one who explores in the hope of finding gold or other valuable minerals
[5] **pick,** a heavy tool used for breaking ground (see picture)
[6] **magnifying glass,** a piece of glass which makes objects appear larger than they really are

erals. He knew that he might easily overlook valuable ore [7] in many places. But he did his best, sure at least that no other prospector could do better, in his search for gold. Tappan was more like a naturalist than a prospector, and more like a dreamer than either. At many idle moments he sat looking at the great desert

pick

valleys, or watching some desert insect or animal, or admiring the colors of some desert flowers.

Tappan waited two weeks at this oasis for Jennie's baby burro to grow strong enough to walk. And the day that Tappan decided to break camp he found signs of gold near the oasis. Quite accidentally as he was looking for the burros, he dropped his pick into a place no different from thousands of others there, and found a pocket of gold. He cleaned out the pocket before sunset, becoming richer by several thousand dollars.

"You brought me luck," said Tappan to the little gray burro who was making an effort to stand alongside its mother. "Your name is Jenet. You're Tappan's burro, and I'm going to take you with me."

Jenet differed from what Tappan expected at her birth. Like a weed in good soil she grew and grew. Winter and summer Tappan wandered across the desert from one edge to another, and his burros traveled with him. Jenet received especially good training. Her mother was an excellent burro even before Tappan bought her. And Tappan had patience; he found time to teach his burros, and he became proud of Jenet. Whenever he stopped in Ehrenberg or Yuma, or any town near the desert, other prospectors always tried to buy Jenet. She grew as large as a middle-size horse, and a three-hundred-pound pack was not an uncomfortable load on her back.

Tappan, like most lonely wanderers of the desert, talked to his burro. As the years passed this habit grew, until Tappan would

---

[7] **ore**, rock from which metal is obtained

talk to Jenet just to hear the sound of his own voice. Perhaps that was all that kept him human.

"Jenet, you deserve a happier life," Tappan would say, as he unpacked her after a long day's walk over the bare wasteland. "You're like a ship on the desert. Here we are, with food and water, a hundred miles from any camp. And only you could bring me here. No horse! No man! Nothing but a burro or a camel,[8] and so I call you a ship of the desert. If we had no animals like you, there would be no prospectors and few gold mines. I suppose the desert would still be an unknown wasteland. You're the greatest beast of burden,[9] Jenet, and no one praises you."

camel

And at sunrise, when Jenet was packed and ready to face the cool, bright desert, Tappan would say:

"Go along, Jenet. The morning's fine. Look at those mountains ahead. They seem to call us. And look below at the desert— all purple and pretty. Ah, this is the life for us, my burro, and Tappan's the richest man alive!"

But sometimes, at sunset, when the day had been long and hot, Tappen would bend over Jenet's head and talk differently.

"Another day gone, Jenet, another journey ended—and Tappan is older and wearier. There's no reward for your faithfulness. I'm only a desert rat. No home! No face to see. . . . Some day, Jenet, we'll die here in the desert. Our bones will lie on the sand. And no one will know or care!"

When Jenet was two years old she would have taken the prize in any competition with other burros of the Southwest. She was unusually large and strong, her entire body in perfect condition, and practically tireless. But there was another thing

8 **camel**, an animal used in the desert (especially in Asia and Africa) for riding and carrying things (see picture)
9 **beast of burden**, an animal used for carrying things, such as a horse, donkey, or camel

about Jenet which made other prospectors envious of Tappan. She had sense—as much as an animal could possibly have.

During these years Tappan crossed the mineral region [10] of the Southwest many times. But, as usual, he found little gold. Jenet knew the trails [11] and water holes better than Tappan. She could follow a trail hidden by deep sand or made unrecognizable to Tappan by running water. At a long distance she could smell a new spring on the desert or a strange water hole. She never wandered far from camp so that Tappan could always find her easily. Wild burros held no charm for Jenet. And she had never shown any special liking for a tame burro either. This also made her different from other burros that Tappan had owned. Burros were noted for their habits of forming friendships with one or more of their own kind.

Tappan scarcely realized how much he depended on this big, gray, quiet beast of burden. Of course, when he was among other prospectors he frequently boasted about her. But he really never thought about how important Jenet was. When he boasted it was only her good qualities that he talked about. But what he really liked best about her were the little things of everyday life.

During the earlier years of her training Jenet had been a thief. She would pretend to be asleep and then try to steal something from the camp. Tappan had broken this habit at its beginning. But he never trusted her completely. After all, she was a burro.

Jenet ate anything offered to her. She could find food for herself or go without. What Tappan had left from his own meals was certain to be something that Jenet liked. Every meal time she would stand near the camp fire, with one great long ear straight up and the other hanging to one side. Her expression was one of timidness, but she had unending patience. Jenet's behavior was about the same on all occasions. It did not seem to matter whether the trail she followed was long, hard, and bare or there were water holes and green grass. She did not need

---

[10] **region**, a part of some larger land surface
[11] **trail**, a path through a rough part of the country

to have grass or grain. Desert plants of all kinds provided suitable food. She could even eat cactus.[12]

Climbing or descending steep slopes was never too hard or dangerous for Jenet, provided it was possible for a burro to do. She would refuse to follow a trail that was impassable and she seemed to know what was beyond a burro's ability. Swift streams of water, always difficult for burros, did not stop Jenet. When she stepped onto ice or wet sand, Tappan would know it was safe; if not, Jenet would turn back. Thunder and lightning,[13] extreme heat or extreme cold, the sand storm of the desert—these gave Jenet no trouble at all.

cactus

One August, the hottest and driest of his desert experience, Tappan was working in the Panamint Mountains—on a northern slope above Death Valley. It was difficult to work there during the best season of the year; in August it was terrible.

Several groups of outlaws [14] lived in these mountains. The outlaws robbed prospectors and sometimes killed them, if necessary, to get their gold.

Tappan's friends warned him not to go into this region alone. But he never paid any attention to warnings. And the idea that he would ever find enough gold to attract outlaws was unthinkable. Much to his surprise he did discover gold—lots of gold—in the Panamint Mountains, and he spent several days digging it with his pick and shovel.[15] He forgot about the outlaws until one day he saw Jenet's long ears standing straight up—a habit she had when she saw strangers. Tappan was watchful during the rest of the day, but he saw no living thing. It was a lonely, out-of-the-way place, surrounded by rocky slopes, hot, and silent.

shovel

---

12 cactus, a desert plant with many tiny thorns (see picture)
13 lightning, a flash of light caused by electricity passing between clouds or between a cloud and the ground
14 outlaw, a person living outside the protection of the law; a lawless person
15 shovel, a broad blade fixed in the end of a handle, used for moving earth, snow, coal, etc. (see picture)

Not long afterwards Tappan discovered boot [16] tracks of several men near his camp. This persuaded him that some outlaws were watching him. They were probably going to let him dig the gold and then steal it. Tappan was not afraid. He sometimes grew angry or worried, but never afraid. He had six small bags of gold and did not intend to lose them.

boot

"Now, what's best to do?" he wondered. "I must act natural, as if I didn't know they were watching me. But I can't stay here any longer. I've dug almost all the gold. I suppose they know this too. I'll have to leave tonight."

Tappan did not want to bury the gold, for in that case, of course, he would have to return for it. Still, he finally admitted that this was the best way to save it. The outlaws were probably watching him day and night. It would be very unwise to try to travel over the mountains.

"If I expect to escape I'll have to go down into Death Valley," Tappan thought sadly.

Crossing Death Valley was always dangerous. No one ever attempted it during the heat of the day. And at this season, the midnight wind blowing the sand was almost as bad as the day's heat. Even if he did reach the other side of the valley, he would find himself in the region of the Funeral Mountains—a place not much more desirable than his present location.[17]

EXERCISES

A. Put a check mark (√) in front of the item (a, b, or c) which best completes each unfinished sentence.

    1. Tappan was a—

    .... a. seaman.

    .... b. farmer.

    .... c. prospector.

---

[16] **boot,** a leather covering for the foot and part of the leg (see picture)
[17] **location,** position

2. He spent most of his time in—

.... a. the city.

.... b. the desert.

.... c. the forest.

3. When Jenet was born she was—

.... a. strong and tough.

.... b. carrying six bags of gold.

.... c. not a healthy burro.

4. While waiting for the baby burro to grow strong enough to walk—

.... a. Tappan went to Yuma.

.... b. Tappan looked for desert rats.

.... c. Tappan found a pocket of gold.

5. Tappan sometimes called Jenet a—

.... a. ship of the desert.

.... b. worthless beast of burden.

.... c. camel in the wasteland.

6. Tappan's age—

.... a. was not mentioned in the story.

.... b. was mentioned in the story.

.... c. was fifty-seven.

7. Unlike most burros, Jenet—

.... a. did not form friendships with other burros.

.... b. liked other burros.

.... c. formed friendships only with wild burros.

8. When Jenet was two years old—

.... a. she was an excellent beast of burden.

.... b. Tappan sold her.

.... c. she would eat only grass and grain.

9. One August Tappan discovered gold in—

.... a. the Funeral Mountains.

.... b. Death Valley.

.... c. the Panamint Mountains.

10. Because of his discovery he expected to have trouble with—

.... a. burros.

.... b. outlaws.

.... c. swift streams of water.

B. Write T for *True* in front of each sentence below which is true according to the story. Write F for *False* in front of the sentence if it is not true.

.... 1. Tappan liked his wandering life because of the freedom it offered.

.... 2. Jenet's mother was called Jessie.

.... 3. Tappan was tall and heavy.

.... 4. Other prospectors wanted to buy Jenet.

.... 5. A three-hundred-pound pack was too heavy for Jenet.

.... 6. Jenet often talked to Tappan.

.... 7. Desert plants provided suitable food for Jenet.

.... 8. Several groups of outlaws lived in Death Valley.

.... 9. In order to escape from the outlaws Tappen decided he would have to travel over the mountains.

.... 10. When Jenet saw a stranger her ears stood straight up.

C. Put a check mark (√) in front of the meaning (a, b, or c) which best fits the numbered word or phrase.

1. **pick:**
.... a. a rocky slope in the desert
.... b. a heavy tool used for breaking ground
.... c. a flower which grows near an oasis

2. **beast of burden:**
.... a. an animal used for carrying things
.... b. an animal that lives in trees
.... c. an animal that can't walk

3. **ore:**
.... a. oil
.... b. a small donkey used for food
.... c. rock from which metal is obtained

4. **trail:**
.... a. a path
.... b. a mineral
.... c. a load

5. **cactus:**
.... a. a kind of desert insect
.... b. a kind of desert plant
.... c. a kind of desert animal

6. **lightning:**
.... a. a flash of light in the sky
.... b. a burro's mother
.... c. a trail hidden by deep sand

7. **prospector:**   .... a. an explorer
                        .... b. a reward
                        .... c. a tame animal

8. **tiny:**   .... a. extremely hot
                        .... b. very small
                        .... c. entirely safe

9. **outlaw:**   .... a. a lawless person
                        .... b. a lawyer
                        .... c. a policeman

10. **location:**   .... a. attention
                        .... b. season
                        .... c. position

This lesson is to be followed by Chapter 8 of Part II, p. 260: "Prefixes and More Noun Suffixes."

TAPPAN'S
BURRO

Tappan was certain now that the outlaws were watching him. Thinking and planning, he continued his work, trying his best to act natural. But he did not succeed. It was impossible, while expecting to hear a gun shot at any moment, to act as if there was nothing to worry him. His camp lay at the bottom of a rocky slope. There was a tiny spring, some green grass, and a few bushes and trees. His little gold mine lay behind a rocky wall and had two advantages—one that it was hidden from the sun, and the other that no one outside the camp could see it. He still did not feel entirely safe, however. The heat seemed to be increasing. Every few minutes Tappan would stop his work and look toward the camp. On the last of these occasions he saw Jenet with her ears standing straight up. His sharp eyes searched for signs of movement. And at last he saw two men in the distance, crawling [1] over the rocks toward his camp.

Tappan's excitement grew. These visitors were probably planning to hide behind the rocks and kill him when he returned to camp.

Tappan left his tools and crawled away from the mine. He

---

[1] **crawl,** move along slowly with the body close to the ground

had a pistol [2] with him, but he had left his rifle [3] in camp. Tappan
had seen only two men but he guessed there were others not
far away. His only chance to protect himself was to reach the
camp and get his rifle. If he crawled perhaps the men would not
see him.

He had already decided to pack and
hurry away. At that moment Death Valley worried him less than the probability
of being killed by the outlaws. Crawling
and sliding on the ground was hard work,
and it was difficult to stay out of sight

pistol

because of his great size. He was too big to hide behind a little
bush or rock. And he was not accustomed to moving silently.
He could not place his boots noiselessly on the stones. Besides,
he could not make progress without moving bits of rock all
around him. He was sure that sharp ears
not far away could hear him. But he continued, making fair progress. The sun had
gone behind the mountain but it had left
the rocks so hot that Tappan could not
touch them with his bare hands.

He decided to run the rest of the way.
Then he saw the men headed toward his
camp on the opposite side. They looked
in his direction. Surely they had heard

rifle

him or seen him; perhaps not. Tappan
noticed that he was closer to the camp than they. Without a
moment's hesitation he left his hiding place and ran. The men
saw him and began to shoot. He felt the wind of a heavy bullet [4]
before he heard it strike the rocks beyond. Bending low he
raced over the rough ground scarcely hearing the rapid shots
that followed.

It had been Tappan's habit to pile his boxes of supplies and

---

[2] **pistol,** a short gun held and fired with one hand (see picture)
[3] **rifle,** a long gun fired from the shoulder (see picture)
[4] **bullet,** a piece of lead or steel fired from a rifle or pistol

roll of bedding together. His rifle was leaning against this pile
of things. As Tappan reached the camp he dove for the rifle.
One of the outlaws—the one nearest the camp—had his gun
aimed at this pile and was waiting for Tappan to show his face.
But Tappan did not get up. He put his rifle between two boxes,
took careful aim, and shot the outlaw.

Then, jumping up, he ran forward in an effort to see where
the second outlaw was. This man was running for safety behind
some high rocks nearby. Tappan fired rapidly at him. The third
shot knocked the fellow down, but he got up and ran on. Tappan shot again before the man disappeared.

He went back and looked at the fallen outlaw. His bullet
had gone through the man's head, and he lay there lifeless. Tappan thought it would be better to use his time for packing
instead of following the other outlaw.

Reloading the rifle, he hurried out of the camp to find Jenet.
"You're a real treasure, old girl," said Tappan to the burro.

Never in his life had he packed Jenet, or any other burro, so
quickly. His last act was to drink all the water he could, fill his
two water containers, and force Jenet to take a drink. Then,
rifle in hand, he and Jenet went down into Death Valley.

Tappan looked behind him more than he looked ahead. After
he had traveled a mile or two he began to feel safe again. He
had escaped from the outlaws. Even if they tried to follow him,
they would never catch him. Tappan believed he could travel
faster and farther than any man alive. But the outlaws did not
appear. Perhaps the wounded man died before he was able to
reach his companions. More likely, however, the group had no
desire to follow anyone in the terrible heat of Death Valley.

Tappan began to walk slower. The sweat rolled down his
face. His entire body was wet, as if he had fallen into the spring.
He also found breathing difficult. But he did not stop until he
reached the shade of a rocky wall. The heat was terrible. He
knew he was safe from the outlaws. But he knew too that he
faced a greater danger than the outlaws. He could fight evil men,
but he could not fight this heat.

So he rested there. Already he felt thirsty. Jenet stood nearby, watching him. Tappan, with his habit of thinking of Jenet as human, imagined that Jenet looked serious. A moment's thought was enough for Tappan to realize the seriousness of his situation. He was about to go into the upper end of Death Valley—a part of the country unfamiliar to him. He must cross it, and also the Funeral Mountains, at the worst season of the year. He had no choice.

His rifle was too hot to hold, so he put it on Jenet's pack; and, carrying only a water container, he started his journey with the burro walking ahead. Back at his camp the mountains gave him some protection from the sun, but here in this valley the sun's rays were fierce. There was no movement of anything. No life. No wind. The valley was as still as death.

He went on, mindful that Jenet had opinions of her own. She did not want to go straight ahead nor to the left or right; she wanted to go back. That direction, unfortunately, was impossible. He finally had to beat Jenet to keep her moving.

When Tappan stopped sweating and his skin became dry, he took a big drink of water and began to walk slower. The sun seemed to burn him through his clothes. Although he was accustomed to life in the desert, he could not endure [5] the heat of this valley very long. Jenet showed no signs of weakening; what she did show, however, was an increasing nervousness. It almost seemed that she was going to face an enemy. Tappen never before had such faith in her. Jenet was equal to the task.[6]

With the hot sun shining on his back, Tappan felt that he was being followed by a ball of fire. He drank some more water. Sunset would save him. Two more hours of such heat would finish him.

The glare [7] of the valley became reddish and it soon blinded him. The time came when he walked beside Jenet with a hand on her pack, for his eyes could no longer endure the glare. Even

---

[5] endure, bear
[6] task, a piece of work that must be done
[7] glare, brightness of the sun shining on the sand

with his eyes closed he knew when the sun sank behind the Panamint Mountains. That ball of fire no longer followed him. And the red left his eyelids.

With the setting of the sun the world of Death Valley changed. The change was so great that it seemed to have brought coolness. Night came. A night without stars or sky or sound— still hot and still no fresh air to breathe. Tappan now thought of the midnight winds of Death Valley. He had heard prospectors say that any man caught in Death Valley when these winds began to blow would never get out of the valley alive. And Jenet seemed to have something on her mind. She certainly knew now which way she wanted to travel. He had to move faster or she would leave him behind. Ten steps beyond him she was out of sight. Tappan had ceased trying to keep directions in mind. North, south, east, and west were all the same to him. The night was black—the darkness like a wall. It was no place for a man.

Tappan was now more than three hundred feet below sea level, after a day of one hundred and forty-five degrees of heat. After hours of walking he knew that little by little he was beginning to lose balance and control, and he struggled to keep his sense of sight and feeling.

Suddenly it seemed that the air, heavy with heat, began to move. It had weight; it moved soundlessly and swiftly. Tappan realized what was happening. The low pressure caused by the heat during the day was now yielding to higher pressure from outside. Something had started a movement of hotter air that must find its way upward, to give place for cooler air that must find its way down.

Tappan heard a low, distant moan [8] of the wind, and he became more and more worried. It did not have an earthly sound. After that moan came others, growing louder and longer until there was a continuous sound. Then the wind moved faster and began to carry a fine dust. Dark as the night was, it did not hide

---

[8] **moan**, a long, low sound, usually expressing pain or sorrow

the pale sheets of dust that moved along the level plain. Tappan's feet felt the floor of the valley rise slowly.

The moan increased to a roar, coming like a storm through a forest. It seemed to Tappan that a million needles of fire were striking his body. The flying sand made him cough continually. But hardest to endure was the moving heat. Tappan grew blind again so that he had to hold to Jenet and follow her along. This was a real test of his endurance, and he was almost conquered.

Tappan's sense of sight and smell and hearing failed him. There was left only the sense of touch—a feeling of rope and burro and ground—and a terrible pressure on his entire body. His feet then felt a change from the sandy plain to a rocky slope. The pressure lessened: the difference in air made life possible; the feeling of being dragged endlessly by Jenet ceased. Tappan fell to the ground unconscious.

When he came to, his body was full of aches and pains. Sight was almost impossible, but he could see walls of rocks, trees, bushes, and grass. Jenet was lying down, with her pack resting on the ground beside her. Tappan's dead ears came back to life with the sound of running water. Then he realized what had happened. Jenet had led him across Death Valley, up into the mountains, straight to a spring.

Tappan crawled to the edge of the water and drank little by little. It was an effort to control his terrible thirst and keep from drinking gallons. Then he crawled to Jenet; loosening the ropes of her pack, he freed her from the load. Jenet got up and looked at Tappan mildly, as if to say: "Well, I brought you out of that hole."

Tappan tried to speak: "Jenet, you—saved—my life—I'll never—forget."

EXERCISES

A. Put a check mark (√) in front of the item (a, b, or c) which best completes each unfinished sentence.

   1. In order to escape from the outlaws, Tappan decided he would have to cross—

.... a. the mineral region of the desert.

.... b. Death Valley.

.... c. the Pecos River.

2. He discovered that two men were crawling toward his camp after—

.... a. he saw Jenet's ears standing straight up.

.... b. he finished digging all the gold.

.... c. sunset.

3. Tappan had a pistol with him, but his rifle was—

.... a. at the mine.

.... b. buried near the camp.

.... c. in camp.

4. Before Tappan reached his camp—

.... a. a bullet hit him.

.... b. the outlaws began to shoot at him.

.... c. he found his rifle.

5. Tappan's bullets hit both of the outlaws, but one of them—

.... a. escaped.

.... b. stole Jenet.

.... c. reached the camp.

6. Before going into Death Valley, Tappan and Jenet—

.... a. rested a while.

.... b. drank some water.

.... c. ate some food.

7. None of the outlaws followed Tappan into Death Valley, probably because—

.... a. Tappan could run faster than they could.

.... b. they would not be able to find Tappan.

.... c. they had no desire to follow anyone in the terrible heat.

8. When his rifle became too hot to hold, Tappan put it—

.... a. on his shoulder.

.... b. on the ground.

.... c. on Jenet's pack.

9. Tappan knew when the sun sank behind the mountains, because—

.... a. he could see stars in the sky.

.... b. he no longer felt the sunshine on his back.

.... c. it began to rain.

10. Besides the terrible heat in Death Valley, Tappan faced another danger:—

.... a. the midnight winds.

.... b. wild animals.

.... c. a snowstorm.

B. Write T for *True* in front of each sentence below which is true according to the story. Write F for *False* in front of the sentence if it is not true.

.... 1. Tappan felt safe as soon as he started into Death Valley.

.... 2. During most of the journey Jenet walked ahead of Tappan.

.... 3. Jenet frequently showed signs of being thirsty.

.... 4. Tappan was blinded only once during the journey.

.... 5. At one place in Death Valley Tappan was more than 300 feet below sea level.

.... 6. The midnight winds started to blow at sunset.

.... 7. Jenet led Tappan to a spring in the mountains.

.... 8. The heat of Death Valley never reached 145 degrees.

.... 9. There was no noise when the midnight winds began, but later there was a moan and then a roar.

.... 10. When Tappan was blinded he had to hold to Jenet and follow her along.

C. Put a check mark (√) in front of the meaning (a, b, or c) which best fits the numbered word or phrase.

1. **pistol:**
.... a. a stranger with no burros
.... b. a short gun fired with one hand
.... c. a place where outlaws live

2. **boot:**
.... a. a covering for the foot only
.... b. a covering for the leg only
.... c. a covering for the foot and part of the leg.

3. **glare:**
.... a. a lonely, out-of-the-way place
.... b. brightness of the sun shining on the sand
.... c. an impassable trail

4. **bullet:**
.... a. a piece of lead or steel fired from a gun

.... b. a swift stream of water

.... c. a pocket of gold

5. **endure the heat:**   .... a. cook with heat

.... b. bear the heat

.... c. make a fire

6. **task:**   .... a. a piece of work that must be done

.... b. something with an agreeable sound

.... c. an angry or worried expression

7. **rifle:**   .... a. a hot stone that burns the hands

.... b. an oasis with no trees

.... c. a long gun fired from the shoulder

8. **swift:**   .... a. fast; quick

.... b. bare; uncovered

.... c. rocky; hard

9. **oasis:**   .... a. a place in the desert where there are water and trees

.... b. a path through a rough part of the country

.... c. a place in the desert where there is always some bird life

10. **moan:**   .... a. a kind of desert plant

.... b. a kind of sound

.... c. a kind of rock

This lesson is to be followed by Chapter 9 of Part II, p. 265: "How We Recognize Nouns."

TAPPAN'S
BURRO

PART 3

As Tappan grew older he became less and less interested in living on the desert. Something changed him. The green fragrant[1] forest and the cold spring water of the mountains began to seem much preferable to the heat and dust and glare and emptiness of the wasteland. So from a prospector searching for gold Tappan became a hunter, searching only for food to keep himself alive. All he cared about was his faithful burro Jenet, and the loneliness and silence of the forest land.

He was to learn that the mountain forest, although not many miles from the desert, was a difficult place to live, especially in winter. Down near the desert the winter was mild—the snow did not stay long and ice seldom formed. But up near the tops of the mountains, where Tappan always lingered[2] as long as possible, the storms were often dangerous. Fifteen feet of snow and zero weather were not unusual. An old native once warned Tappan: "Be sure to come down before cold weather begins. If a big storm comes while you're up in those mountains, you'll never get out alive."

---

[1] fragrant, pleasant-smelling
[2] linger, stay at a place after the proper time for leaving

Tappan seldom took anyone's advice. He had lived through the terrible midnight storm in Death Valley. Why should he be afraid of snow and cold? Late autumn on the mountaintops was the most perfect and beautiful season of the year. He had seen the forest land brown and dark green one day, and the next day it was covered with white snow. What a remarkable change! Then the sun began to melt the snow, it fell from the branches leaving the woodlands with a white floor, and the great brown tree trunks on the distant mountainsides looked thicker and taller than ever.

The years seemed to speed by. His mind grew old faster than his body, and every season he felt lonelier. He now believed that some day his bones would rest among the pine trees and soft fragrant moss[3] rather than on the hot sand of the desert. The idea was pleasant to Tappan.

One afternoon in November he was camped on a mountainside not far from the top. The fall season had been beautiful, with not a single snowstorm. A few natives passing the camp had remarked that such autumns are sometimes deceiving. This late afternoon was one of beauty and warmth. The smoke from Tappan's campfire gave the air a bluish color. Near the camp Jenet was grazing[4] peacefully with some deer. Other wild animals lingered there, knowing full well that they should be looking for winter homes farther down. Gray squirrels and red squirrels jumped around in the trees playfully.

Before dark a stranger arrived at Tappan's camp—a big middle-aged fellow. He was a bearded man, wide-eyed, with a pleasant face. He had no horse, no baggage, not even a gun.

"Lucky for me I smelled your smoke," he said. "I've had nothing to eat for two days."

"Hello, stranger," was Tappan's greeting. "Are you lost?"

"Well, yes and no. I could find my way down the mountain, but it's not healthy for me down there. So I'm going north."

---

[3] **moss,** small green, brown, or yellow plants growing in thick, soft masses on trees and on the ground

[4] **graze,** eat growing grass

"Where's your horse and pack?"

"A gang[5] of outlaws took them."

"Well, you're welcome here, stranger," said Tappan. "My name is Tappan."

"I've heard of you. I'm Jess Blade. And I'll tell you, Tappan, I was an honest man until I came into these mountains."

"Come and eat. My supplies are getting low, but there's plenty of meat."

Blade ate like a starved man[6] and did not seem to care if Tappan's supplies were low. He did not talk. After the meal he lighted his pipe and smoked in silence. The light from the campfire shone on his strong face. Tappan guessed he was a wanderer, a drinker, a fighter, a man who would be a good friend and a bad enemy. The wind moaned in the tall pines on the slope.

"That wind sounds like a storm," observed Blade.

"I've heard it for weeks," replied Tappan.

"Are you a woodsman?"

"No, I'm a desert man."

"Well, I'd advise you to start for the low country."

This was probably good advice, but it irritated[7] Tappan. He had liked this stranger. But his mind was getting old, and he really did not care about other people. The only living creature he loved was a long-eared, lazy burro, also growing old in contentment. Nevertheless, that night Tappan shared one of his blankets.

The following morning was gray, and the sun rose without its usual brightness. The air seemed thick and heavy. Thin, swiftmoving clouds began to appear in the southwest. The wind was cold, the forest was dark, and the birds and squirrels were silent.

"Well, I suppose you'll break camp today," said Blade.

"No. I'll stay here a while longer," returned Tappan.

"But man, if it starts to snow while you're up here—that's dangerous."

"Well, it won't bother me. But you can go if you want to."

---

[5] **gang**, a group of persons
[6] **starve**, suffer from hunger
[7] **irritate**, annoy; make angry

"Tappan, it's four days' walk out of this forest. If a big snow-storm comes, it'll bury me."

"Then you should go down the mountainside," suggested Tap-pan.

"No. I'll have to go the other way. But if you prefer not to have me with you, I'll leave."

Tappan did not know what to say. He thought it advisable to tell the man to go. Not empty-handed, but to go. But this was selfish, and entirely unlike Tappan. Finally he spoke.

"You're welcome to half my supplies—go or stay."

"That's very good of you, Tappan," replied the other. "Do you have a burro you can give me?"

"No, I only have one."

"Well, then. I'll stay with you till you leave."

No more was said. They had breakfast in silence. The wind began to blow hard in the treetops. Tappan's burro came into camp, and the stranger noticed her.

"That's certainly a fine burro," he observed. "I've never seen one like that."

Tappan performed his camp duties. And then there was nothing to do but sit by the fire. Blade expected the threat of a coming storm to stir Tappan into action. But the graying sky and the increased force of the wind did not affect him. What was Tappan waiting for? Jenet remained in camp. She was wait-ing to be packed, for she knew they should go. The wind brought a cold mist,[8] then some wet snow. Tappan gathered firewood—a great quantity of it. Blade saw this and suggested again that they leave. Tappan paid no attention. By nightfall snow was falling steadily. The men made a shelter of tree limbs, ate their supper, and went to bed early.

It worried Tappan that Jenet stayed in camp. He stayed awake a long time. The sound of the wind grew louder. Finally he fell asleep. When he woke up the forest was all white. The trees were covered with blankets of wet snow, and on the ground it was about two feet deep. But the clouds were gone, the sky blue

---

[8] mist, rain in tiny drops

once again, the storm over. The sun came up warm and bright.

"The snow will all melt today," said Tappan.

"If this was early October I'd agree with you," replied Blade. "But another storm will come soon. Can't you hear that wind blowing?"

The snow began to drop from the south branches of the trees, and by mid-afternoon it was falling everywhere. All of the snow, except in shaded places on the north sides of the trees, melted that day, and half of that on the ground. The next day more snow disappeared, until Jenet was finding grass and moss again. That afternoon the thin clouds appeared again in the southwest, and the wind moaned once more.

"Tappan, let's pack up and leave," said Blade anxiously. "I know these mountains. Maybe I'm wrong, but I think another storm's coming."

"Let it come," replied Tappan calmly.

"Say, do you want to be trapped by the snow," asked Blade, losing his patience.

"I might like it for a while. It would be new to me," replied Tappan.

"But man, if a heavy snow comes you can't get out."

"That burro of mine can take me out."

"You're crazy.[9] That burro couldn't go a hundred feet. Besides, you'd have to kill and eat her."

Tappan gazed [10] at his companion but made no reply. Blade began to pace [11] back and forth alongside the campfire. He was very worried. That day he seemed to change, and so did Tappan. Blade's thoughts were on self-preservation. Tappan became more indifferent [12] than ever.

Later in the day Blade started again—trying to persuade Tappan they should leave. Finally he swore at Tappan and called him a nature-loving idiot.[13]

---

9 **crazy,** mad; foolish
10 **gaze,** look long and steadily
11 **pace,** walk with slow, steady steps
12 **indifferent,** not interested; not caring
13 **idiot,** a stupid person; fool

"I tell you what I'm going to do," he said. "When morning comes I'll take some of your food and go—storm or no storm."

But long before daybreak Blade had to change his mind. The roar of a new storm waked both of them; then there was a crash. By the light of the campfire Tappan saw snow falling again, great flakes [14] as large as feathers. It was a fierce mountain storm, and by morning there was two feet of snow already on the ground.

"I was wrong," Tappan said to his companion. "What's best to do now?"

"You fool!" shouted Blade. "Now we'll have to keep from freezing and starving till the storm ends and a crust [15] forms on the snow."

For three days and three nights the storm continued. It took the men hours to keep a space cleared for their camp, which Jenet shared with them. On the fourth day the storm ended, the clouds went away, and the sun shone again. The temperature dropped to zero. The snow was as high as Tappan's head, and in drifts [16] it was ten and fifteen feet deep. The forest was a solemn, still, white world. But now Tappan had no time to dream. Dry firewood was hard to find under the snow. It was possible to cut down one of the dead trees on the slope, but impossible to carry enough wood to the camp. They had to burn green wood. Then the making of snowshoes took a lot of time. Tappan had no knowledge of such footwear. He could only help Blade. The men were encouraged by the extreme cold which was forming a crust on the snow. But just as they were about to pack and try to leave, the weather became milder, and the crust would not hold their weight. Then another foot of snow fell.

"Why didn't you kill a deer?" asked Blade in a loud voice. He had become very unhappy, and at times was angry. He knew they were in danger, and he was not ready to die. "Now

---

[14] flake, a small, thin, flat piece of something
[15] crust, a hard outside covering or surface
[16] drift, heap; pile

we'll have to kill and eat your burro. And maybe she won't furnish enough meat till we're able to travel."

"Blade, don't talk about killing and eating Jenet," returned Tappan in a still louder voice.

The two men became enemies then and there. Blade thought only of himself. Tappan would die, if necessary, to protect his burro; he had no thoughts of his own preservation.

Tappan's supplies were lower than ever. All the meat and coffee were gone. There was a bag of beans, a sack [17] of flour, and a small quantity of salt left.

"If a crust forms on the snow and we can carry that flour, we'll get out alive," said Blade. "But we can't take the burro."

Another day of bright sunshine softened the snow, and a night of freezing cold made a crust that would hold a man walking fast.

"It's our only chance—and not a very good one," declared Blade.

Tappan allowed Blade to choose the time and method and supplies. They cooked all the beans and divided them in two sacks. Then they baked about five pounds of bread for each of them. Blade chose the small bag of salt for himself and let Tappan take the tobacco. Blade declared that this quantity of food and a blanket for each was all they could carry. They argued about the guns, and in the end Blade agreed that Tappan should carry the rifle, in case he had a chance to kill a deer. When this matter was decided, Blade began to put on his snowshoes which they had made from old boxes, straps, and sacks.

"They won't last long," said Blade looking down at the snowshoes.

Meanwhile Tappan fed Jenet some bread and he began to tie a tarpaulin [18] on her back.

"What are you doing?" asked Blade suddenly.

"Getting Jenet ready," replied Tappan.

"Ready for what?"

---

[17] **sack,** a bag made of cloth
[18] **tarpaulin,** a sheet of coarse, strong cloth made waterproof

"To go with us."

"You idiot!" shouted Blade. "You can't take that burro."

"I can't go without her. Jenet's mother was a good faithful burro. I saw Jenet born down near the Colorado River. She wasn't a healthy burro; I had to wait there until she was strong enough to walk. And when she grew up and after her mother died, Jenet and I wandered across the desert alone—year after year. She wasn't an ordinary burro. She learned quickly. She was different. But I treated her the same as any burro. And she grew big and strong as the years went by. Desert men said they had never seen such a burro as Jenet. They called her Tappan's burro, and tried to borrow or buy or steal her. . . . I can't remember how many times she helped me in difficult situations. She saved my life once. She dragged me out of Death Valley. . . . I'll not leave her. It may seem strange to you, Blade. Jenet's only a burro, but I won't leave her."

"Man, you talk as if that lazy old burro was a woman," declared Blade in disgust.

"I don't know women, but I believe Jenet's more faithful than most of them."

"Well, you're the worst fool I've ever known."

"Fool or not, I know that I won't leave her," replied Tappan.

EXERCISES

A. Put a check mark (√) in front of the item (a, b, or c) which best completes each unfinished sentence.

    1. After years of being a prospector, Tappan became a—
    .... a. trapper.
    .... b. hunter.
    .... c. farmer.

    2. A native warned Tappan that winters in the mountain forest were—
    .... a. always pleasant and mild.
    .... b. like winters on the desert.
    .... c. dangerous.

    3. One day a stranger named Blade arrived at Tappan's camp—
    .... a. empty-handed.

.... b. with a burro loaded with supplies.

.... c. riding a horse.

4. Tappan invited Blade to—

.... a. go down the mountain with him.

.... b. eat with him.

.... c. shoot squirrels with him.

5. Blade advised Tappan to—

.... a. break camp and leave.

.... b. spend the entire winter in the forest.

.... c. build a log house.

6. When the first snow came,—

.... a. Tappan decided to leave.

.... b. Tappan stayed at the camp.

.... c. Blade and Jenet disappeared.

7. After the big snowstorm they could not leave immediately because—

.... a. they had to kill a deer.

.... b. there was no crust on the snow.

.... c. it was raining.

8. Blade said it was impossible to take Jenet with them,—

.... a. so they decided to kill her.

.... b. and Tappan agreed.

.... c. but Tappan refused to go without her.

9. After an argument about the guns, they agreed that—

.... a. Blade should carry the rifle.

.... b. Tappan should carry the rifle.

.... c. the rifle was too heavy to carry.

10. When they divided the food, each had—

.... a. beans and bread.

.... b. meat and salt.

.... c. cheese and rice.

B. Write T for *True* in front of each sentence below which is true according to the story. Write F for *False* in front of the sentence if it is not true.

.... 1. As Tappan grew older he liked living in the forest better than living on the desert.

.... 2. Near the tops of the mountains deep snow and cold weather were unusual in winter.

.... 3. When Blade reached Tappan's camp he was not hungry.

.... 4. Tappan told Blade he was a woodsman.

.... 5. Blade said Jenet was a fine burro.

.... 6. After the snowstorm dry firewood was easy to find.

.... 7. Blade suggested killing and eating Jenet.

.... 8. They made snowshoes from old boxes, straps, and sacks.

.... 9. Tappan called Blade a nature-loving idiot.

.... 10. When they were ready to leave, they decided to carry the
flour and leave the beans and salt behind.

C. Put a check mark (√) in front of the meaning (a, b, or c)
which best fits the numbered word.

1. **graze:**
.... a. search for spring water
.... b. eat growing grass
.... c. lift slowly

2. **drift:**
.... a. heap; pile
.... b. valley; low land
.... c. thick; fat

3. **indifferent:**
.... a. not the same
.... b. similar
.... c. not interested

4. **sack:**
.... a. bag
.... b. season
.... c. flour

5. **fragrant:**
.... a. empty-handed
.... b. pleasant-smelling
.... c. good-humored

6. **starve:**
.... a. suffer from blows on the head
.... b. suffer from the lack of sleep.
.... c. suffer from hunger

7. **irritate:**
.... a. annoy
.... b. warn
.... c. remain

8. **mist:**
.... a. snow in tiny flakes
.... b. gray smoke from the campfire
.... c. rain in tiny drops

9. **pace:**
.... a. walk with slow steps
.... b. cover with a blanket
.... c. warm by the fire

10. **tarpaulin:** .... a. sheet of ice
.... b. sheet of waterproof cloth
.... c. sheet of metal

This lesson is to be followed by Chapter 10 of Part II, p. 270: "How We Recognize Verbs."

TAPPAN'S
BURRO

PART 4

Blade and Tappan continued their argument about taking Jenet with them.

"Don't you have enough sense to see that we can't travel with a burro?" asked Blade, patiently controlling his temper. "She has little hoofs,[1] as sharp as knives. She'll cut through the crust. And we'll have to stop and pull her out—maybe break through the crust ourselves. It'll take us a long time to get out of the forest with her."

"Long or short we'll take her."

Blade's patient explanation meant nothing. He would never attempt to take Jenet out of the forest while the snow was so deep.

"Traveling is going to be hard work for us. And working men in winter must have meat to eat."

"What do you mean?"

For an answer Blade jerked[2] his hand backward and downward, and when it came in sight it held Tappan's worn and shining rifle. Then he took a shell and put it into the rifle. All

---

[1] **hoof,** the hard, solid part of the foot on animals like horses, cows, donkeys, etc. (see picture)
[2] **jerk,** pull suddenly and quickly

the time his eyes were fixed on Tappan. His face seemed that of
another man, evil, determined to preserve his own life at any
cost.

"I'm going to kill your burro," he said in a tone
that suited his look and manner.

"No!" shouted Tappan, shocked by Blade's
remark.

"Yes, I am. And before we get out of this
forest, you'll be glad to eat some of her meat!"

"I'd starve to death before I'd kill that burro."

"Starve then!" answered Blade angrily.

hoof

Jenet stood behind Tappan—peaceful as usual
—with one long ear straight up and the other hanging to one
side.

"You'll have to kill me first," said Tappan sharply.

"I'll do that too, if I have to," returned Blade.

As Blade stepped aside in order to aim at Jenet, Tappan
leaped [3] forward and pushed the rifle upward as it was fired.
The bullet sped harmlessly over Jenet's back. Tappan heard it
strike a tree. Blade swore, and as he lowered the rifle Tappan
took hold of the barrel with his left hand. Then, with his right
fist [4] he struck Blade squarely in the face. Only Blade's hold on
the rifle prevented him from falling. Blood streamed from his
nose and mouth.

"I'll kill you for that!" yelled Blade.

"No, Blade," answered Tappan, "you're not man enough."

There was a struggle for possession of the rifle. Tappan beat
Blade's face with his hammerlike fist. Then he had to use both
hands to keep his hold on the rifle. Pulling and pushing, the men
fought there in the snowy camp, scattering the campfire and
knocking down the shelter. Tappan felt he was the stronger of
the two, in spite of Blade's larger size. Suddenly he put all of his
force into one great jerk. The rifle broke, leaving the steel barrel

---

[3] **leap,** jump
[4] **fist,** the hand when closed **tightly**

in his hands and the wooden stock [5] in Blade's. The faster-think-
ing Blade used his weapon to knock Tappan down. As he was
about to strike again, Tappan knocked the other's feet from
under him. Blade fell in the snow but was up as quickly as
Tappan. They started again, Tappan waiting to strike, and Blade
raining blows on Tappan. These were heavy blows aimed at his
head, but somehow he managed to receive most of them on the
arms and on the rifle barrel he was holding. For a few moments
Tappan was able to endure this beating. His own blood soon
blinded him. Then he swung his heavy weapon. The blow broke
Blade's left arm. Like a wild beast he screamed [6] in pain; and
then he rushed toward Tappan too angry for further caution.
Watching his chance, Tappan swung the rifle barrel again. This
time, the blow was so powerful it beat down Blade's arm and
crushed his skull.[7] He died on his feet; falling backward into a
wall of snow he went out of sight, except for his boots, one of
which still had a snowshoe fastened to it.

Tappan stared,[8] slowly realizing what had happened.

"So, stranger Blade!" he said, breathing hard and looking at
the hole in the snowbank where his enemy had disappeared.
"You were going to—kill and eat—Tappan's burro!"

Then he saw the bloody rifle barrel and threw it away. He
became conscious of injuries which needed attention. But he
could do little more than wash off the blood and wrap a piece
of cloth around his head. Both arms and hands were bruised [9]
and beginning to swell. But fortunately no bones were broken.

Tappan finished tying the tarpaulin on the burro; and picking
up both his and Blade's supply of food he said, "Come on, Jenet."

Which way should he go? There was no more choice for him
than there had been for Blade. Toward the top the snowdrift
would be deeper and impassable. Tappan realized that the only

---

[5] **stock,** the wooden part of a rifle (see picture, p. 79)
[6] **scream,** give a loud, sharp cry
[7] **skull,** the bony frame of the head
[8] **stare,** look steadily
[9] **bruised,** having the skin discolored in places by a blow or fall

possible chance for him was downhill. So he led Jenet from the camp without looking back once. What had actually happened to him? He seemed a different man from the one who had come into this woodland.

A path in the snow had been made by the men carrying firewood into camp. At the end of this path the wall of snow stood higher than Tappan's head. To get on top of the snow without breaking the crust presented a problem. He lifted Jenet up and was relieved to see that the crust did not break. But he found a different task in his own case. Returning to camp, he gathered several of the long branches that had been part of the shelter; carrying them out he laid them against the slant of snow he had to climb, and with their aid he reached the top. The crust held him.

With fresh hope he and Jenet started their journey. Walking with his snowshoes was awkward. He had to go slowly, sliding them along the crust. But he made progress. Jenet's little steps kept her even with him. Now and then one of her sharp hoofs cut through the crust, but she did not fall. At the start Tappan observed something about Jenet. This was the first time she had ever been dependent on him. She knew it. She realized that if she got out of this snow-covered forest it would be due to the strength and skill of her master.

Travel was slow. He and Jenet had to proceed [10] with extreme care. Jenet appeared to be absolutely unable to sense either danger or safety. Her experience had been limited to walking on rocks and sand of the desert. She walked wherever Tappan led her. She had to trust him completely.

"Well, old girl," said Tappan, "this time you have to depend on me."

Eventually [11] they came to a long gradual slope which they had to climb before continuing downhill. Small pine trees dotted the slope. This appeared to be fortunate, and proved to be so, for when Jenet broke through the crust Tappan had trees and

---

[10] **proceed,** advance; progress
[11] **eventually,** at last; finally

branches to hold while he lifted her out. The labor of climbing that slope caused him to remember Blade's absolute refusal to take Jenet with them. By nightfall they had not traveled far from camp, and this fact worried him a good deal.

To go on in the dark would be foolish. So Tappan selected a thick tree under which the snow was not deep and made preparations to spend the night. Untying the tarpaulin he spread it on the snow. All the lower branches of the trees were dead and dry. Tappan broke off several and soon had a fire. Jenet found some moss to eat on the trunk of the tree. Tappan's meal was beans, bread, and a ball of snow which he softened by holding it over the fire. He made sure that Jenet had as much to eat as he. Soon it was dark and terribly cold. Tappan needed the fire. Gradually it melted the snow and made a hole down to the ground. Tappan rolled himself in the tarpaulin and soon fell asleep.

In three days Tappan traveled about fifteen miles, gradually descending, until the snow crust would no longer hold Jenet. Whatever his difficulties had been before, they were now a hundred times worse. As soon as the sun came into the sky, somewhat softening the snow, Jenet began to break through the crust. And often when Tappan tried to lift her out he broke through himself. This exercise was back-breaking even for a man of Tappan's strength and endurance. Although he had learned years before to resist heat and flying sand on the desert, working in the snow and cold was a different matter. The way out of the forest seemed endless. Cold, lonely, white—he felt trapped by the snow which surrounded him on all sides. He loved the sun—the open spaces. As he continued his slow, difficult journey he was more determined than ever to save Jenet. In some places he carried her.

The fourth night he was dangerously near the end of his stock of food. He had been generous with Jenet. But now, considering that he had to do more work than she, he reduced her share. On the fifth day Jenet broke through the snow crust so often that they made almost no progress. Tappan realized it was impossible for her to get out of the woods by her own efforts. He made her lie on the tarpaulin, so he could drag her. All the rest of·that day she rode on the tarpaulin while Tappan pulled it. All the next day he continued the same way, hands behind him, holding the edge of the tarpaulin, head and shoulders bent forward, like a man who could not be defeated. That night he was too weary to build a fire, and too worried to eat the last of his food.

The next day Tappan did not even notice the changing character of the forest. He had come down from the mountain heights; the pines were less numerous and smaller in size; oak trees began to appear. The snow was still four feet deep, and the crust held Tappan only about half of the time. The long descending slope had come to an end. There were small hills and valleys now.

When the crust broke, he put his snowshoes on Jenet's back, and with his feet he made a path in the snow for her to follow. Two days of this, without food or fire, broke Tappan's endurance. But not his spirit! He dragged and carried Jenet over the snow, and through the snow, down the hills and up the slopes, knowing that soon—perhaps over the next hill—there would be safety. Deer tracks were more numerous now. He saw an occasional pine tree here and there. At last he was leaving the forest land. Only such hope as that kept him on his feet.

He fell often, and each time it was harder to get up and go on. The time came when the crust failed altogether to hold Tappan, and he had to stop dragging Jenet. It was necessary to make a road for her. How weary, cold, and miserable he felt! Yard by yard Tappan made his way. He no longer sweat. There was no feeling in his feet and legs. Hunger ceased to bother him. His thirst was satisfied with snow—soft snow, instead of the hard icy snow farther up the mountain. He felt terrible pains in his chest and the dull ache of an overworked heart.

Tappan came to an opening where he could see for several miles ahead. Another long slope was in front of him. It went down and down to the open country. His desert eyes, sharp as those of an eagle, saw the flat land far below, almost without snow, and black dots that were cows. The last slope! Three feet of snow, except in drifts; down and down he went, making way for Jenet. Sometimes they walked; sometimes they fell and rolled, always downward.

Finally Jenet was able to travel unaided. At the end of the day they were at the edge of the woods where here and there the wind had blown away the snow and left bunches of grass uncovered. Jenet started grazing.

As for Tappan, he fell with the tarpaulin and tried with strengthless hands to spread it in order to cover himself. He looked for Jenet. She was there; he could see her but not clearly. Tappan lay down and slowly drew the tarpaulin over him.

A very cold wind came down from the snowy heights. It pushed the few scattered trees back and forth. Yet the night seemed silent. The stars shone white in a cloudless sky, like cold watchful eyes looking down without pity or hope. All night the winter wind blew down, colder and colder. Then dawn came, with a bright sunrise in the east.

Jenet came back to the place where she had left her master. She had grazed all night. Her sides that had been flat were now full. She stood for a while, with one ear hanging down over her face. Jenet was waiting for Tappan.

But he did not get up. Jenet waited. The winter sun rose into the sky, and the snow reflected its rays like diamonds. Somewhere in the distance there was a long bray.[12] Jenet's ears stood straight up. She listened. She recognized the call of one of her kind. Lifting her gray head she returned the call: "Hee-haw hee-haw-haw—hee-haw how-e-e-e!"

Her bray started echoes.[13] They sounded down the slope and over the open country loud enough to awaken any living thing. But this morning Tappan did not wake up.

---

[12] bray, the noise made by a donkey
[13] echo, the repetition of a sound caused by the reflection of sound waves

EXERCISES

A. Put a check mark (√) in front of the item (a, b, or c) which best completes each unfinished sentence.

1. According to Blade, it was impossible to travel with Jenet because—

.... a. she was too old.

.... b. her hoofs would cut through the crust.

.... c. her ears did not stand up straight.

2. When Blade fired the rifle, the bullet—

.... a. hit Tappan's arm.

.... b. struck the crust on the snow.

.... c. sped over Jenet's back.

3. While Tappan and Blade were struggling for possession of the rifle,—

.... a. the rifle was fired a second time.

.... b. the rifle broke.

.... c. both men fell on the ground.

4. Using the barrel of the gun as a weapon, Tappan—

.... a. broke Blade's left arm and crushed his skull.

.... b. rained blows on Blade's knees.

.... c. broke Blade's back and his right arm.

5. Tappan climbed on top of the snow with the aid of—

.... a. some branches.

.... b. the tarpaulin.

.... c. the bloody rifle.

6. When they started their journey,—

.... a. Jenet was wearing snowshoes.

.... b. Tappan was wearing snowshoes.

.... c. neither Tappan nor Jenet was wearing snowshoes.

7. At the end of three days they had traveled—

.... a. two miles.

.... b. fifteen miles.

.... c. twenty-five miles.

8. Sometimes, when Jenet broke through the snow crust,—

.... a. Tappan rode her.

.... b. Tappan kicked her.

.... c. Tappan carried her.

9. Finally they reached the last slope, at the bottom of which Tappan could see—

.... a. outlaws on horseback.

.... b. flat land and cows.

.... c. a village.

10. At the end of the day they were at the edge of the woods where—

.... a. Jenet found nothing to eat.

.... b. Tappan lay down but never got up.

.... c. the snow was fifteen feet deep.

B. Write T for *True* in front of each sentence below which is true according to the story. Write F for *False* in front of the sentence if it is not true.

.... 1. Blade attempted to shoot Jenet with Tappan's rifle.

.... 2. Tappan said he was going to kill Blade.

.... 3. In spite of Blade's larger size, Tappan felt that he was the stronger of the two.

.... 4. After the fight Tappan discovered that he had some broken bones.

.... 5. Before leaving the camp Tappan removed the tarpaulin from Jenet's back.

.... 6. Walking on the crust of the snow was as easy as walking on rocks and sand of the desert.

.... 7. Because Jenet broke through the crust so often, Tappan made the burro lie on the tarpaulin so he could drag her.

.... 8. When he was near the end of his stock of food, he reduced Jenet's share.

.... 9. Tappan and Jenet were rescued by a group of hunters.

.... 10. Tappan saved Jenet's life, but he lost his own.

C. Put a check mark (√) in front of the meaning (a, b, or c) which best fits the numbered word or phrase.

1. **leap:**   .... a. drag

                     .... b. jump

                     .... c. strike

2. **eventually:**   .... a. in the first place

                     .... b. harmlessly

                     .... c. at last

3. echo:
.... a. difficult situation
.... b. repetition of a sound
.... c. explanation

4. jerk:
.... a. lazy animal
.... b. bruised ankle
.... c. pull suddenly

5. stock of a rifle:
.... a. wooden part
.... b. barrel
.... c. strap

6. skull:
.... a. bony frame of the head
.... b. a kind of hat
.... c. pain in the back

7. crust on the snow:
.... a. snowflake
.... b. hard surface on the snow
.... c. snowshoe for animals

8. proceed:
.... a. tie
.... b. realize
.... c. advance

9. scream:
.... a. climb to the top
.... b. give a loud, sharp cry
.... c. give fresh hope

10. fist:
.... a. the hand when closed tightly
.... b. track made in the snow
.... c. endless task

This lesson is to be followed by Chapter 11 of Part II, p. 275: "Review: Meaning and Form."

SELECTION 12

A NEW ENGLAND SPINSTER[1]

Mary E. Wilkins Freeman

PART 1

Louisa Ellis had been sewing peacefully near the window all afternoon. Now she set her work carefully aside and put her needle and thread and scissors into her sewing basket. Louisa could not remember that she had ever misplaced any of these articles, which had become, from long and constant use, as necessary to her life as food and clothing and shelter.

Louisa tied a green apron[2] around her waist and put on a flat

---

[1] **spinster,** an unmarried woman
[2] **apron,** something worn over the front of a person to protect the clothes (see picture)

straw hat with a green ribbon. Then she went outside into the garden with a bowl to pick some berries for her tea. Afterwards she sat on the back doorstep and removed the stems from the berries, collecting the stems carefully in her apron and later taking them into the house. She looked at the grass beside the step to see if any had fallen there.

Louisa was slow in her movements. It took her a long time to prepare her tea, but when it was ready it was served with a certain ceremony— just as if she had guests. A little square table stood exactly in the center of the kitchen and was covered with a linen [3] tablecloth whose border had a

apron

beautiful pattern of flowers. Louisa put a linen napkin on her tea-tray, where she had neatly arranged some teaspoons, a silver cream pitcher,[4] a china [5] sugar bowl, and one pink china cup and saucer. Unlike her neighbors, Louisa used china every day. The neighbors talked about this among themselves. Their daily tables were set with ordinary dishes; their sets of best china stayed in the cupboard— and Louisa Ellis was no richer nor better than they. She ate a dish full of sugared berries and a plate of little cakes and pieces of bread. Also a leaf or two of lettuce,[6] which she cut into little pieces. Louisa was very fond of lettuce, which she raised in her garden. She seemed to enjoy eating,

pitcher

taking tiny bites, and it was surprising that any quantity of food should disappear.

After tea she filled a plate with thin corncakes and carried them into the back yard.

"Caesar!" she called. "Caesar! Caesar!"

There was a sudden rush, the rattle [7] of a chain, and a large

---

[3] **linen,** a kind of cloth
[4] **pitcher,** a vessel with a handle used to hold and pour liquids (see picture)
[5] **china,** dishes made from a fine, white clay
[6] **lettuce,** a garden plant with bright green leaves
[7] **rattle,** a series of short, sharp sounds

yellow and white dog appeared at the door of his tiny hut, which was half hidden among the tall grass and flowers. Louisa touched his head gently and gave him the corncakes. Then she returned to the house and washed the tea things, polishing the china carefully. It was darker now—almost night. Louisa took off her green apron; under this she was wearing a shorter apron of pink and white. She lighted the lamp and sat down to sew again.

In about half an hour Joe Dagget came. She heard his footsteps before he reached the house. She got up and took off her pink and white apron. Under it was still another apron—one of white linen. She wore this, without her sewing apron over it, only when she had a guest. She had just folded the pink and white apron and placed it in a table drawer when the door opened and Joe Dagget entered.

He seemed to fill the whole room. A little canary[8] that had been asleep in his green cage woke up and jumped about, beating his yellow wings against the wires of the cage. He always did this when Joe Dagget came into the room.

"Good evening," said Louisa. She extended her hand slowly and calmly.

"Good evening, Louisa," returned the man, in a loud voice.

She placed a chair for him, and they sat facing each other, with a table between them. He sat stiffly, with his heavy feet directly in front of him, looking around the room; his expression was one of good humor, but he seemed to be a little uncomfortable. Louisa sat straight with her hands folded in her lap.[9]

"It's been a pleasant day," remarked Dagget.

"Very pleasant," Louisa agreed, softly. "Have you been gathering hay?" she asked after a while.

"Yes, I've been working in the hayfield all day. It's pretty hot there."

"I'm sure it is."

---

[8] canary, a small yellow songbird
[9] lap, the front part of the body from the waist to the knees (when a person is sitting)

"Yes, the sun is pretty hot in the hayfield."

"How is your mother?"

"Mother's pretty well, thank you."

"I suppose Lily Dyer's with her now."

Dagget hesitated before answering. "Yes, she's with her."

He was not very young, but he had a big boyish-looking face. Louisa was not as old as he; her face was paler and smoother, and people thought she looked older.

"I suppose Lily helps your mother a good deal," she continued.

"I suppose she does; Mother needs someone, of course," said Dagget.

"Lily's a good worker. She's pretty, too."

"Yes, she's fairly pretty."

Presently Dagget began to tap the books on the table with his fingers. There was a square red photograph album [10] and a gift book which had belonged to Louisa's mother. He picked them up one after the other and opened them; then he put them down again, the album on the gift book.

Louisa kept watching them with mild discomfort. Finally she got up and changed the position of the books, putting the album underneath. That was the way they were arranged originally.

Dagget gave an awkward little laugh. "Now what difference does it make whether this book or that book is on top?" he asked.

Louisa's smile showed a certain disapproval. "I always keep the gift book on top," she answered.

"The things you do surprise me sometimes," said Dagget, trying to laugh again. His large face began to turn red.

He remained about an hour longer; then he got up to leave. Going out, his foot slipped on the edge of the rug, and he almost fell down; trying to regain his balance, he hit Louisa's sewing basket on the table and knocked it on the floor.

He looked at Louisa, then at the things on the floor—needles, pins, thread, scissors, and pieces of cloth. He started to pick them

---

10 **album,** a book with unprinted pages used to keep photographs, pictures, stamps, etc.

up, but she stopped him. "Never mind," she said; "I'll pick them up after you've gone."

She spoke with mild stiffness. She was either a little angry or his nervousness made her uncomfortable.

When Joe Dagget was outside he breathed easier, and he felt like an animal freed after a long period of time from his cage.

Louisa tied on her pink apron, then the green one, picked up all the scattered treasures and replaced them in her sewing basket. Then she set the lamp on the floor and began to examine the rug. She rubbed it with her fingers and looked at them.

"He's brought in a lot of dust," she said to herself. "I thought there was dust on his shoes."

Louisa took a dust pan and brush and swept Joe Dagget's track carefully.

He came twice a week to see Louisa, and every time, there in her spotless, well-arranged sitting room, he felt very uneasy.[11] He was afraid to move, because he might disturb the order of her things or break something. And Louisa always watched him, fearing that he might in some way change the appearance of the room.

Louisa and Joe Dagget were to be married in a month, after an engagement [12] which had lasted about fifteen years. For fourteen of the fifteen years the two had not seen each other, and they seldom exchanged letters. Joe had been all those years in Australia, where he had gone to make his fortune, and where he had stayed until he made it. If necessary he would have stayed fifty years. But in fourteen he made his fortune and had come home now to marry the woman who had been waiting for him patiently and without question all this time.

Shortly after they were engaged [13] he had told Louisa that he was going away and make a good deal of money before he would be ready for marriage. She had listened and agreed with her usual calmness, even when her lover started on that long and uncertain

---

[11] uneasy, uncomfortable; anxious
[12] engagement, an agreement or promise to marry
[13] engaged, promised to marry

journey. In spite of Joe's determination, he hesitated a little before going away, but Louisa kissed him with a mild blush [14] and said good-by.

"I'll come back soon," poor Joe had said; but he didn't return for fourteen years.

In that length of time many things had happened. Louisa's mother and brother had died, and she was all alone in the world. But most important of all, Louisa had changed and her way of life had changed. She had grown accustomed to living alone, and there was no room for anyone at her side.

Louisa's first thoughts when Joe Dagget came home (he did not inform her of his coming) were very confused. Fifteen years ago she had been in love with him—at least she believed so. Just at that time, following the usual tendencies of girlhood, she had seen marriage ahead as reasonable and probably desirable. She had listened to her mother's views on the subject. The mother had talked wisely to her daughter when Joe Dagget presented himself, and Louisa accepted with no hesitation. He was the first lover she had ever had.

She had been faithful all these years. She had never thought of the possibility of marrying anyone else. Her life, especially during the last seven years, had been full of peace and quiet and contentment. She had never felt unhappy nor impatient about her lover's absence; still she had always considered that he would return some day and they would be married. However, she had fallen into the habit of placing it so far in the future that it all seemed unreal somehow.

It was a shock when Joe came, although she had been expecting him and expecting to be married for fourteen years.

Joe's ideas also became confused, but at a later time. He admired Louisa the same as always. She had changed a little, but she still kept her nice manners and was just as attractive as ever. As for Joe, he was home now, his mind no longer occupied [15] with the fortune he was determined to make. He was interested

---

[14] blush, a reddening of the face
[15] occupied, busy

in love, a wife, a home, and a family. The center of his attention for so many years had been Louisa, but somehow his attention now seemed to wander elsewhere. Love for a man had never been a powerful force in Louisa's life. She realized it now more than ever, but she did not withdraw. She turned quietly away and went to work on her wedding [16] clothes.

EXERCISES

A. Put a check mark (√) in front of the item (a, b, or c) which best completes each unfinished sentence.

1. At the time of this story, Louisa Ellis lived—
.... a. with Lily Dyer.
.... b. alone.
.... c. with her husband.

2. She was—
.... a. married to a farmer.
.... b. married to a salesman.
.... c. unmarried.

3. Joe Dagget came to see Louisa—
.... a. twice a week.
.... b. every night.
.... c. occasionally.

4. When Louisa had a guest, she wore—
.... a. a long green apron with a white border.
.... b. a white linen apron, without her sewing apron over it.
.... c. an old black hat with feathers on it.

5. Her sewing apron was—
.... a. pink and white.
.... b. red and black.
.... c. yellow and green.

6. During Joe's visit they talked about—
.... a. life in Australia.
.... b. Joe's mother and Lily Dyer.
.... c. their wedding.

7. Joe and Louisa had been engaged—
.... a. for fifteen years.

---

[16] **wedding,** a marriage ceremony

.... b. only a few weeks.

.... c. for fifty years.

8. Sitting in Louisa's spotless, well-arranged sitting room, Joe always—

.... a. laughed at the canary.

.... b. felt uneasy.

.... c. fell asleep.

9. After Joe left, Louisa—

.... a. took off all her aprons.

.... b. looked for dust on the rug.

.... c. went to see Joe's mother.

10. Joe had gone to Australia—

.... a. to avoid marrying Louisa.

.... b. to find peace and quiet.

.... c. to make his fortune.

B. Write T for *True* in front of each sentence below which is true according to the story. Write F for *False* in front of the sentence if it is not true.

.... 1. Louisa Ellis did not use china every day.

.... 2. The dog that lived in Louisa's back yard was called Napoleon.

.... 3. Joe Dagget came to visit Louisa before she had her tea.

.... 4. Joe was older than Louisa.

.... 5. Louisa always kept the gift book on top of the photograph album.

.... 6. On leaving, Joe slipped and knocked Louisa's sewing basket on the floor.

.... 7. Louisa and Joe were to be married in a week.

.... 8. While Joe was in Australia, he and Louisa exchanged letters frequently.

.... 9. Joe stayed in Australia fifteen years.

.... 10. When Joe returned Louisa began to work on her wedding clothes.

C. Put a check mark (√) in front of the meaning (a, b, or c) which best fits the numbered word.

1. **pitcher:**   .... a. a kind of container

.... b. a kind of cloth

.... c. a kind of paper

2. **spinster:**   .... a. dry hayfield
.... b. mild discomfort
.... c. unmarried woman

3. **apron:**   .... a. something to eat
.... b. something to read
.... c. something to wear

4. **lap:**   .... a. part of a ship
.... b. part of a chain
.... c. part of the body

5. **occupied:**   .... a. neat
.... b. busy
.... c. surprised

6. **blush:**   .... a. gossip with the neighbors
.... b. comb and brush the hair
.... c. become red in the face

7. **uneasy:**   .... a. uncomfortable; anxious
.... b. difficult; hard
.... c. small; tiny

8. **album:**   .... a. a kind of bird
.... b. a kind of book
.... c. a kind of apron

9. **lettuce**   .... a. a doghouse
.... b. a dark night
.... c. a garden plant

10. **wedding:**   .... a. thin corncake
.... b. marriage ceremony
.... c. boyish-looking face

This lesson is to be followed by Chapter 12 of Part II, p. 281: "Adjectives and Nouns: Differences in Patterning."

A NEW ENGLAND

SPINSTER

PART 2

Joe had enlarged and rebuilt part of his house. It was a family home. The newly-married couple would live there; Joe could not leave his mother, and she refused to leave her old home. So Louisa must leave hers. Getting up every morning and going about her neatly-arranged possessions, she felt as one looking for the last time at the faces of dear friends. It was true that she could take them with her, but robbed of their old surroundings, they would never be quite the same. Then there were some habits and customs in her life which she would have to give up altogether. More important tasks than these familiar but half needless ones would probably descend upon her. There would be a large house to take care of; there would be guests to entertain; there would be Joe's elderly mother to wait on; and more than one servant in a single household would be unthinkable. Louisa loved to sew a linen seam,[1] not always for use, but for the mild pleasure it gave her. Many, many times she had removed the thread from a seam for the mere delight of sewing it together again. Sitting at her window during long afternoons, drawing her needle gently through the cloth, she spent the happiest hours of her life. But

---

[1] **seam**, a joining-line of two pieces of cloth

117

there was little chance of such foolish comforts in the future. Joe's mother, demanding and critical in her old age, and very likely Joe himself, with his honest, masculine [2] rudeness, would laugh and make fun of the ways she passed the time.

Louisa had the eye of an artist with regard to order and cleanliness. She had a feeling of real success at the sight of the windows which she had polished until they shone like jewels. She was proud of the orderly bureau [3] drawers, with their carefully folded contents scented with lavender. [4] Even this might not continue. She pictured coarse masculine belongings thrown about in confusion; she pictured dust and disorder arising necessarily from the presence of a man in the house.

bureau

She was disturbed too about Caesar. For the greater part of his life Caesar had lived in his lonely hut, away from the society of his kind and away from the many experiences which dogs seem to enjoy. He had never run after a rabbit or a squirrel; he had never known the delights of finding an old bone in a neighbor's back yard. Many years before, Caesar had behaved in a way which human society does not permit. Since that time he was never allowed to move about freely. Old Caesar seldom barked; he was fat and sleepy; and there were yellow rings like glasses around his old eyes. A neighbor still bore the marks of Caesar's white youthful teeth, and because of that he had lived at the end of a chain, all alone in a little hut, for fourteen years. The neighbor had demanded either Caesar's death or complete separation from the rest of the world. So Louisa's brother, to whom the dog had belonged, had built a little house for him and tied a chain to him. Fourteen years ago, in youthful play or perhaps anger, Caesar had bitten a man, and with the excep-

---

[2] masculine, male
[3] bureau, a chest of drawers for clothes (see picture)
[4] lavender, a plant with purple flowers that have an agreeable smell and are used in dried form to scent clothes

tion of short walks in the neighborhood, always at the end of a
chain, under the watchful eye of his master or Louisa, the old
dog had remained a prisoner. He was considered dangerous by
all the children in the village, and many adults.[5] Mothers warned
their children not to go near him. Villagers passing near Louisa's
yard sometimes inquired if the chain was strong. Without a
chain, wandering through the neighborhood, Caesar would probably not have been noticed; but chained, his reputation as a
fierce animal never disappeared. Joe Dagget regarded him as a
harmless old dog. In spite of Louisa's warning, Joe went to the
dog, patted [6] him on the head, and even tried to free him from
the chain. Louisa became so frightened that he left the chain
on the dog, but he expressed his opinion on the matter in no
uncertain words. "There's not a more peaceful dog in town,"
he said, "and it's cruel to keep him tied up there. Some day I'm
going to take him out."

Louisa was sure he would do it, when their interests and possessions were more completely joined together. She pictured
Caesar running through the quiet and unguarded village. She
thought of him attacking children and possibly adults. She was
very fond of the old dog, because he had belonged to her dead
brother, and he was always gentle with her; still she thought
he was dangerous. She always advised people not to go near him.
She fed him corncakes and other light foods, and never meat
or bones. Louisa looked at the old dog eating a simple meal; she
remembered her marriage in the near future and trembled. Still,
no expectation of disorder and confusion instead of peace and
orderliness, no worries about Caesar's being loose, and no wild
actions of her little canary, were enough to change her mind
about marrying Joe. Joe Dagget had been fond of her and had
worked hard all these years. It was not for her, whatever happened, to prove untrue and break his heart. She continued to
work on her wedding clothes, and the time passed until it was
only a week before her wedding day. It was Tuesday evening,

---

[5] adult, full-grown
[6] pat, tap or strike lightly with the open hand

and the wedding was to be on Wednesday of the following week.

There was a full moon that night. About nine o'clock Louisa took a walk down the road. There were harvest fields on both sides of the road, bordered by low stone walls. Big bushes grew beside the wall, and there were trees here and there. Presently Louisa sat down on the wall and looked around with a kind of sadness in her thoughts. Where she sat she was surrounded by tall bushes. On the opposite side of the road there was a spreading tree; the moon shone between the branches, and the moonlight reflected by the leaves looked like spots of silver. She sat there for some time. As she was about to get up and leave, she heard footsteps and low voices. She remained quiet. It was a lonely place, and she felt a little timid. She decided to stay in the shadows and let the persons, whoever they were, pass her.

But just before they reached her the voices stopped, and the footsteps too. She supposed that the persons had also found seats on the stone wall. She was wondering if she could leave quietly and unobserved when a voice broke the stillness. It was Joe Dagget's. She sat still and listened.

"Well, then," said Dagget, "you've made up your mind, I suppose."

"Yes," returned another voice; "I'm leaving the day after tomorrow."

"That's Lily Dyer," thought Louisa. In her mind there was the picture of a tall pretty girl with yellow hair. Lily Dyer was a favorite with the village folks; she had just the qualities which the local people admired. She was attractive and good and bright. Louisa had often heard praises of her good looks and her good work.

"Well," said Joe Dagget, "I'm not going to say anything."

"I don't know what you could say," returned Lily Dyer.

"Not a word," repeated Joe. Then there was a silence. "I'm not sorry," he began again, "that we told each other how we felt. Although we're in love with each other, we can't change anything. I'm going to be married next week. Louisa's been waiting for me for fourteen years. It would break her heart if we didn't get married."

"I don't expect you to change your plans," the girl said in a loud voice. "Of course you'll marry Louisa. It's the only right thing to do." Their voices sounded as if they were becoming angry. Louisa was listening eagerly.

"I'm sorry you feel that you must go away," said Joe, "but I suppose it's best."

"Of course it's best. You and I both know it's best."

Suddenly Joe's voice was softer. "Say, Lily," he said, "I know I'll be all right. But I hope—I hope you won't be unhappy a long time."

"You can be sure that I won't lose any sleep thinking about a married man."

"Well, I hope you won't—I hope you won't, Lily. Perhaps, before long, you'll find someone else."

"I imagine I will." Suddenly her voice changed. "No, Joe Dagget," she said, "I'll never marry any other man as long as I live. I have good sense, and I'm not going to be foolish; but I'm never going to be married. I could never feel this way again."

Louisa heard some movement beyond the bushes; she guessed they were now standing up; then Lily spoke again: "This must stop," she said. "We've stayed here long enough. I'm going home."

Louisa sat there motionless, listening to their steps as they walked away. After a while she got up and went home too.

The next day she did her housework as usual; that was almost as natural as breathing. But she did not work on her wedding clothes. She sat at her window and thought about what she had heard the night before. In the evening Joe came. Louisa never knew she had much skill in talking to people; that night she discovered she had a great deal of conversational skill and an ability to express her thoughts clearly. Even now she could hardly believe that Joe's interest had shifted [7] from her to Lily

---

[7] shift, change position

Dyer, and that she would do him no great injustice if the engagement was broken. They finally reached an understanding; it was difficult, however, because neither of them wanted the other to be unhappy.

She never mentioned Lily Dyer. She simply said that she had no reason to complain about him; but she had lived so long in a certain way, that she preferred not to make a change.

"Well, I never hesitated, Louisa," said Dagget. "I can say honestly that I think it's better if we don't get married; but if you'd wanted me, we'd have been married next week as planned. I hope you know that."

"Yes, I do," she said.

That night she and Joe parted with fewer worries and confused ideas.

"Well, I didn't think it was all going to end this way, Louisa," said Joe.

"Nor did I," responded Louisa shaking her head gently.

"Let me know if there's ever anything I can do for you," he said. "I'll never forget you, Louisa." Then he kissed her and left the house.

Louisa, all alone that night, cried a little; she didn't know why. But the next morning she felt like a queen who sees her position as chief of state firmly insured after it has been threatened for a long time.

Now the tall weeds and grass could grow around Caesar's little old hut; the snow could fall on its roof year in and year out. But he would never run loose through the unguarded village. Now the little canary could remain a peaceful yellow ball and have no need to wake up and beat his wings against the wires of the cage. Louisa could sew linen seams and dust and polish and lay her things away with bags of lavender as much as she liked. That afternoon she sat with her needlework at the window enjoying the wonderful peace of body and mind. Lily Dyer, tall and straight and attractive, went by; Louisa felt nothing but good will toward her.

Louisa looked ahead to future days like pearls on a string, all smooth and perfect, and her heart was filled with thankfulness.

EXERCISES

A. Put a check mark (√) in front of the item (a, b, or c) which best completes each unfinished sentence.

1. Louisa spent the happiest hours of her life—
.... a. working in the hayfield.
.... b. sewing by the window.
.... c. visiting Joe Dagget's mother.

2. The idea of moving to Joe Dagget's house after the wedding—
.... a. was not pleasant to Louisa.
.... b. made Louisa happy.
.... c. was objectionable to Caesar.

3. Caesar had been living at the end of a chain—
.... a. all his life.
.... b. since the Civil War.
.... c. for fourteen years.

4. The wedding was to be on—
.... a. Tuesday.
.... b. Wednesday.
.... c. Saturday.

5. One night Louisa overheard a conversation between—
.... a. Joe Dagget and his mother.
.... b. Joe Dagget and his father.
.... c. Joe Dagget and Lily Dyer.

6. Louisa discovered that—
.... a. Joe was going to Australia again.
.... b. Joe was in love with Lily Dyer.
.... c. Caesar was wandering through the neighborhood without a chain.

7. Lily was going to—
.... a. leave the village before the wedding.
.... b. continue working for Joe's mother.
.... c. marry a man from New York.

8. The next day Louisa—
.... a. worked on her wedding clothes as usual.

.... b. finished her wedding clothes.

.... c. did not work on her wedding clothes.

9. Joe and Louisa decided—

.... a. to get married as planned.

.... b. not to get married.

.... c. to invite Lily Dyer to the wedding.

10. Louisa especially liked to sew—

.... a. buttons on shirts.

.... b. baby clothes.

.... c. linen seams.

B. Write T for *True* in front of each word below which is true according to the story. Write F for *False* in front of the sentence if it is not true.

.... 1. Louisa believed that Caesar was harmless.

.... 2. She disliked disorder and confusion.

.... 3. Once Caesar bit a man.

.... 4. While taking a walk one night, Louisa sat down on a stone wall.

.... 5. She heard Joe and Lily singing.

.... 6. Joe said that Louisa was a stupid old spinster.

.... 7. Joe's interest had shifted from Louisa to Lily.

.... 8. Joe and Louisa broke their engagement.

.... 9. Afterwards, they were angry with each other.

.... 10. Joe gave Louisa some pearls as a wedding present.

C. Put a check mark (√) in front of the meaning (a, b, or c) which best fits the numbered word or phrase.

1. **linen:** .... a. a kind of bird

.... b. a kind of cloth

.... c. a kind of seam

2. **adult:** .... a. person under the age of eighteen

.... b. full-grown person

.... c. complaint

3. **pat:** .... a. tap lightly with the fist

.... b. tap lightly with the foot

.... c. tap lightly with the open hand

4. **seam:** .... a. joining-line of two pieces of cloth

.... b. conversational skill

.... c. shift of interest from one person to
another

5. **bureau:**   .... a. long period of time
.... b. sensible married person
.... c. chest of drawers

6. **shift:**   .... a. surround by bushes
.... b. change position
.... c. listen eagerly

7. **canary:**   .... a. songbird
.... b. bush
.... c. footstep

8. **china:**   .... a. wedding gift
.... b. dishes
.... c. side of the road

9. **engagement:**   .... a. female government
.... b. agreement to marry
.... c. contentment in one's old age

10. **masculine
rudeness:**   .... a. rudeness of men
.... b. rudeness of women
.... c. rudeness of both men and women

This lesson is to be followed by Chapter 13 of Part II, p. 286:
"Adjectives with Underlying Noun Forms."

SELECTION 14

THE MURDER OF
MR. HIGGINBOTHAM

Nathaniel Hawthorne

PART 1

A young fellow, a tobacco peddler [1] by trade, was on his way
from Morristown to Parker Falls one summer day in 1833. He
had a neat little cart, all green. There were pictures and signs
painted on the sides and back of the cart—to advertise the
products he had for sale. The peddler drove a nice-looking little
horse; he was a young man of excellent character, a very good

---

[1] **peddler**, a person who goes from place to place selling small articles

salesman, and well enough liked by the Yankees.[2] He was popular among the pretty girls along the Connecticut River, whom he brought presents of the best smoking tobacco in his stock; he knew that the country girls of New England were usually fond of smoking pipes. Also, as you will see later in this story, the peddler had an inquiring mind and enjoyed taking part in gossip, always anxious to hear news and anxious to tell it again.

After an early breakfast at Morristown, the tobacco peddler, whose name was Dominicus Pike, had traveled seven miles along a lonely road without speaking a word to anyone. It was nearly seven o'clock, and he was eager to talk with someone. After lighting a cigar he looked up and saw a man at some distance on the road ahead of him. The man was coming down a hill, at the foot of which the peddler had stopped his green cart. Dominicus watched him as he descended and noticed that he carried a bundle on his shoulder. He looked rather weary; the peddler guessed that the stranger had not started his journey in the freshness of the morning but had walked all night. He probably intended to do the same all day.

"Good morning, sir," said Dominicus, when the man was within hearing distance. "You're traveling pretty fast. What's the news at Parker Falls?"

The man lifted his gray hat a little in order to see better and answered rather suddenly that he had not come from Parker Falls. The peddler had mentioned Parker Falls because that town was his own destination.[3]

"Well, then," said Dominicus, "tell me the latest news from wherever you come."

The traveler appeared to hesitate a little, as if he was either searching his memory for news or trying to decide how to tell it. At last, stepping close to Dominicus' ear, he began to talk in a low voice.

"I do remember one little bit of news," he said. "Old Mr.

---

[2] **Yankees,** people living in the northern part of the United States, especially in the New England states

[3] **destination,** the place where a person is going

Higginbotham, of Kimballton, was murdered in his orchard [4] at eight o'clock last night—by an Irishman and a Negro. They hanged him on a big pear tree where nobody would find him till morning."

As soon as this terrible news was given, the stranger started walking on with more speed than ever, not even turning his head when Dominicus invited him to smoke a Spanish cigar and tell all the details. The peddler whistled to his horse and went up the hill, thinking of the fate of poor Mr. Higginbotham whom he had known slightly. He was rather astonished at the rapidity with which the news had spread. Kimballton was nearly sixty miles away; the murder had been committed [5] at eight o'clock the preceding night; yet Dominicus had heard about it at seven in the morning, when, in all probability, poor Mr. Higginbotham's own family had just discovered his corpse. [6] How could the stranger have traveled so fast?

"Bad news travels fast, they say," thought Dominicus Pike; "but this news has traveled faster than a railroad train. The Government should hire that fellow to carry messages for the President."

The difficulty was solved by supposing that the man had made a mistake of one day in the date of the event; so our friend did not hesitate to introduce the story at every tavern [7] and country store along the road, and pass a large bunch of Spanish cigars among at least twenty audiences. He discovered he was the first bearer of the news, and he was asked so many questions that he could not avoid filling up the outline, till it became an interesting story. One piece of information he found seemed to support the story. Mr. Higginbotham was a storekeeper; and a former clerk of his, who heard Dominicus' news, said that the old gentleman was in the habit of returning home through the orchard about nightfall, with money and valuable papers from

---

[4] **orchard,** a field of fruit trees
[5] **commit,** do something bad or wrong
[6] **corpse,** a dead body
[7] **tavern,** a place where liquor is sold and drunk

the store in his pocket. The clerk expressed little sorrow concerning Mr. Higginbotham's death, suggesting, what the peddler
had suspected, that he was not a generous old man but extremely
tight with his money. His property would descend to a pretty
niece who was now a schoolteacher in Kimballton.

Because he had been busy telling the news and selling tobacco
at the same time, Dominicus was so much delayed that he decided to stay overnight at a tavern, about five miles short of
Parker Falls. After supper, lighting one of his best cigars, he sat
down in the barroom and told the story of the murder again;
it had grown so fast that it now took half an hour to tell. There
were twenty people in the room, nineteen of whom received it
as the truth. The twentieth was an elderly farmer who had arrived on horseback a short time before, and was now seated in
a corner smoking his pipe. When the story ended, he got up,
brought his chair close to Dominicus, and sat down beside him.
He was smoking the worst kind of tobacco the peddler had
ever smelled.

"Will you swear," he demanded, "that old Mr. Higginbotham
of Kimballton was murdered in his orchard the night before
last and found hanging on his pear tree yesterday morning?"

"I've told the story as I heard it," answered Dominicus, dropping his half-burnt cigar; "I didn't see the murder. So I can't
swear that it happened exactly that way."

"But I can swear," said the farmer, "that Mr. Higginbotham
and I drank a glass of wine together this morning. If it wasn't
Mr. Higginbotham that I drank with, then it was his ghost.[8]
Being a neighbor of mine, he called me as I was riding by; we
had a drink and he asked me to deliver a message for him on the
road. He didn't tell me anything about a murder."

"Well, then, my story can't be true," said Dominicus.

"I suppose not," said the old farmer; and he moved his chair
back to the corner.

According to this information Mr. Higginbotham had not

---

[8] ghost, the spirit of a dead person which can be seen

died at all. The peddler felt a little foolish and did not want to take part in further conversation, so he went to bed. All night long he dreamed about Mr. Higginbotham hanging on a pear tree. To avoid the old farmer (whom he now despised, because he had questioned the truthfulness of the peddler's story), Dominicus got up early and drove on toward Parker Falls. The fresh morning breeze and the pleasant summer sunshine made him feel better; he was again ready to repeat the old story, but nobody was awake to hear it. He saw no living soul until he reached the Salmon River. There, just crossing the bridge, was a man with a bundle on his shoulder.

"Good morning, sir," said the peddler, stopping his horse. "If you come from Kimballton or that neighborhood, maybe you can tell me the real facts about old Mr. Higginbotham. Was the old fellow actually murdered two or three nights ago by an Irishman and a Negro?"

Dominicus had spoken too quickly to observe that the stranger himself had a dark skin and was probably a Negro. On hearing the sudden question the man, talking in a shaky voice, replied:

"No! No! There was no colored man.[9] It was an Irishman that hanged him last night, at eight o'clock. I left Kimballton at seven! I suppose his family hasn't found him in the orchard yet."

The man had scarcely spoken, when he turned and walked hastily on. Dominicus started after him greatly puzzled. If the murder had not been commited till Tuesday night, who was the fellow that predicted [10] it on Tuesday morning? If Mr. Higginbotham's corpse had not yet been discovered by his own family, how did the Negro, more than thirty miles away, know that he was hanging in the orchard—especially since he had left Kimballton before the unfortunate man was hanged? These questions, with the stranger's surprise and fear, made Dominicus think of following him and accusing him as one of the murderers. But he changed his mind.

"Let the poor fellow go," thought the peddler. "After all,

---

[9] **colored man**, Negro
[10] **predict**, say something will happen

punishing the Negro for the crime won't bring back Mr. Higginbotham. And if the Negro is not guilty, someone will prove that I am a liar again."

With these thoughts Dominicus Pike drove on to Parker Falls, which, as everybody knows, is a village with several cotton factories. The machinery was not in motion, and only a few stores had opened their doors for business. His first duty was to find some food for his horse, and his second duty, of course, was to tell the tavern-keeper of Mr. Higginbotham's unfortunate end. It seemed advisable, however, not to be absolutely certain of the date the murder occurred,[11] and also to be uncertain whether it was committed by an Irishman and a Negro or by an Irishman alone. He was careful to state that he had not witnessed the hanging himself; he mentioned it simply as a report which was spreading in that locality.

The story spread through the village like a fire among old dead trees. Soon everyone was talking about the murder and no one seemed to know where the story originated. Mr. Higginbotham was as well known at Parker Falls as any citizen of the place, since he was part owner of more than one of the cotton factories. The excitement was so great that the local newspaper printed the story with the heading TERRIBLE MURDER OF MR. HIGGINBOTHAM! Among other details the printed story described the mark of the cord around the dead man's neck and stated the amount of money (in thousands of dollars) which was stolen from him; a feeling of pity was expressed for the poor niece who had fainted several times since her uncle was found hanging on the pear tree with his pockets inside out. The councilmen of the village held a meeting and decided to distribute handbills offering a reward of five hundred dollars for capturing [12] his murderers and recovering [13] the stolen property.

---

[11] occur, happen
[12] capture, catch; make a prisoner of
[13] recover, get back

EXERCISES

A. Put a check mark (√) in front of the item (a, b, or c) which best completes each unfinished sentence.

1. Dominicus Pike was a—
.... a. storekeeper.
.... b. tobacco peddler.
.... c. factory worker.

2. The first traveler that Dominicus met said—
.... a. he had come from Parker Falls.
.... b. he had come from Morristown.
.... c. he had not come from Parker Falls.

3. According to the traveler's story, Mr. Higginbotham had been killed—
.... a. with a rifle.
.... b. by hanging.
.... c. two weeks ago.

4. Dominicus told the story of Mr. Higginbotham's murder—
.... a. only once.
.... b. many times.
.... c. to a ghost.

5. At the tavern where Dominicus spent the night, the truthfulness of his story about Mr. Higginbotham was questioned by—
.... a. an elderly farmer.
.... b. everybody.
.... c. nineteen people.

6. On the road the next day Dominicus met another stranger who was probably—
.... a. an Irishman.
.... b. a Negro.
.... c. a peddler.

7. What puzzled Dominicus especially was—
.... a. when the murder was committed.
.... b. where the murder was committed.
.... c. how the murder was committed.

8. At Parker Falls Dominicus told the story of the murder first to—
.... a. the councilmen.

.... b. Mr. Higginbotham's niece.

.... c. the tavern-keeper.

9. The newspaper story of Mr. Higginbotham's death mentioned—

.... a. that Dominicus Pike had witnessed the murder.

.... b. the amount of money that was stolen.

.... c. the day of the murder.

10. Mr. Higginbotham's niece was a—

.... a. schoolteacher.

.... b. boarding-house keeper.

.... c. factory girl.

B. Write T for *True* in front of each sentence below which is true according to the story. Write F for *False* in front of the sentence if it is not true.

.... 1. Dominicus Pike had a red cart and a burro.

.... 2. According to the story Dominicus heard, Mr. Higginbotham was murdered in bed.

.... 3. The peddler never smoked cigars.

.... 4. Mr. Higginbotham lived in Kimballton.

.... 5. The peddler was very much interested in gossip.

.... 6. Someone said that Mr. Higginbotham was in the habit of returning home about nightfall with money and valuable papers in his pockets.

.... 7. At Parker Falls Dominicus did not tell the story of the murder until he had found some food for his horse.

.... 8. Mr. Higginbotham was unknown in Parker Falls.

.... 9. The councilmen at Parker Falls offered a reward for the capture of the murderers and the recovery of the stolen property.

.... 10. According to a later story, Mr. Higginbotham was hanged on an apple tree.

C. Put a check mark (√) in front of the meaning (a, b, or c) which best fits the numbered word or phrase.

1. **Yankees:**   .... a. people living in New England

.... b. people living in the southern states

.... c. people living in Canada

2. **corpse:**   .... a. stolen property

.... b. schoolteacher

.... c. dead body

3. **ghost:**   .... a. outline of a story
                     .... b. spirit of a dead person
                     .... c. message of the President

4. **orchard:**   .... a. field of grain
                     .... b. field of fruit trees
                     .... c. field of hay

5. **destination:** .... a. place where a person is going
                     .... b. place a person came from
                     .... c. place where a person is

6. **peddler:**   .... a. person who sells small articles
                     .... b. person who speaks in a low voice
                     .... c. person who is tight with his money

7. **colored man:** .... a. American Indian
                     .... b. Negro
                     .... c. Eskimo

8. **tavern:**   .... a. place to get a haircut
                     .... b. place to get a drink
                     .... c. place to get a book of poetry

9. **predict:**   .... a. say something will happen
                     .... b. whisper
                     .... c. think of something evil

10. **recover:**   .... a. catch; make a prisoner of
                     .... b. get back; regain
                     .... c. express pity; feel sorry

This lesson is to be followed by Chapter 14 of Part II, p. 291: "Nouns with Underlying Adjective Forms; Contrasts in Stem Forms."

THE MURDER OF
MR. HIGGIN-
BOTHAM

PART 2

Later in the day, the whole population of Parker Falls—merchants, boarding-house keepers, factory girls, farmers, and schoolboys—were in the streets discussing the murder. The noise made by the crowd was much louder than the usual noise of the factories in operation. Our friend Dominicus, who had been careful at first about telling the origin and details of the story, announced that he had brought the news of the murder to Parker Falls. He immediately became the great man of the moment; he was just starting to retell the whole story when the stage [1] arrived in the village. It had traveled all night, and as usual it had stopped at Kimballton to change horses at 3 o'clock in the morning.

"Now we shall hear all the details," thought the people in the crowd.

The stage went as far as the tavern, followed by a thousand people. If any man had been minding his own business till then, he surely left it to hear the news. The peddler, one of the first to reach the stage, discovered two passengers—a lawyer and a

---

[1] stage, a public vehicle pulled by horses

135

young lady. As they stepped out, hundreds of questions were asked—all at the same time.

"Mr. Higginbotham! Mr. Higginbotham! Tell us about Mr. Higginbotham! Is Mr. Higginbotham's niece better?"

The stage driver did not say anything, except a few swear words, because nobody brought him a fresh team[2] of horses. After learning the cause of the excitement, the lawyer began to speak.

"Gentlemen—and ladies," said the lawyer, "there is surely some mistake. We passed through Kimballton at three o'clock in the morning. No one there mentioned a murder. And besides, I have some papers here which Mr. Higginbotham sent me last night. They are to be presented in court today. You will notice the place, date, and time that Mr. Higginbotham signed these papers—at Kimballton, last night, at ten o'clock."

The signature, with the place, date, and time, proved without a doubt that Dominicus' story was wrong again. The young lady, after listening to the lawyer, asked to be heard. She was a lovely girl, about twenty years old; at that moment Dominicus would have preferred a love story to a murder story.

"Good people," she said, "I am Mr. Higginbotham's niece."

Needless to say, the audience was very much surprised. After all, this was the girl—according to the newspaper—who had fainted again and again after she had heard of her uncle's murder.

"You see," continued Miss Higginbotham, with a smile, "that this story about me is quite untrue. I believe I can say that the story about my dear uncle is equally untrue. He has been kind enough to give me a place to live in his house, although I support myself largely—by teaching in school. I left Kimballton this morning to spend a few days with a friend, about five miles from Parker Falls. My generous uncle, when he heard me on the stairs, called me to his bedside. He gave me two dollars and fifty cents to pay my stage fare[3] and an extra dollar for my other expenses.

---

[2] team, group

[3] fare, money paid to ride on a vehicle when making a trip or journey

I am sure my uncle was alive when I left, and I expect to find him so when I return."

The young lady's speech was sensible and well worded. A stranger would have supposed that Mr. Higginbotham was a terrible enemy of the village; for instead of a general thanksgiving that no murder had been committed, the inhabitants became extremely angry on learning of their mistake. Dominicus Pike was suddenly in serious danger. Before any action began, however, Mr. Higginbotham's niece spoke again and asked that Dominicus be allowed to leave unharmed. Addressing a few words of thanks to the young lady, he jumped into the cart and left town, under a shower of stones and mudballs thrown by the schoolboys. As he turned his head for a final glance [4] at Miss Higginbotham, a big ball of mud hit him in the face.

Dominicus did not stop to clean his clothes, which were spotted with mud. However, the sun shone brightly on the poor peddler and the mud was easily brushed off when dry. Being by nature a good-humored fellow, he was soon cheerful again, and he had a good laugh every time he remembered the excitement and disturbance his story had caused. The handbills distributed by the councilmen would probably cause the arrest of wanderers throughout the state. The story in the local newspaper would be reprinted in other newspapers from Maine to Florida, and misers [5] everywhere would tremble on reading about the fate of Mr. Higginbotham. The peddler thought a good deal about the charms of the young schoolteacher, and he remembered what a wonderful thing she had done: she had defended him against the angry population of Parker Falls.

Dominicus was now on the road to Kimballton. He had expected to visit that place after he left Parker Falls, but he had not expected to leave the latter village so suddenly. As he came nearer the scene of the supposed murder, he continued to wonder about the events of the past two days. The whole situation seemed

---

[4] **glance,** a quick look
[5] **miser,** one who saves and loves money

very strange: there was the first traveler's story, partly supported by Mr. Higginbotham's former clerk; then there was the Negro who was familiar with either the report or the fact, and he was surprised and nervous when Dominicus had questioned him. After all, there was general agreement concerning Mr. Higginbotham's character and habits of life; he had an orchard and he always passed near a big pear tree at nightfall. The evidence [6] was so strong that Dominicus felt sure there was some truth in the story. Making careful inquiries along the road, the peddler further learned that an Irishman of doubtful character was employed by Mr. Higginbotham. He had hired the Irishman without a recommendation.

"I won't believe that Mr. Higginbotham wasn't hanged," thought Dominicus, "until I see him alive with my own eyes."

It was growing dark when he reached Kimballton. A man on horseback was a few yards ahead of him on the road; Dominicus hardly noticed him. The peddler stopped at the edge of the village to talk with a friend whom he always visited whenever business took him to Kimballton. The friend had just come home from his work and was about to go into the house when Dominicus arrived. After an exchange of greetings, the peddler immediately began to inquire about the reported murder.

"I suppose," he said, "that you haven't seen old Mr. Higginbotham lately."

"Why yes," answered the friend, "he passed by just before you arrived. He's been to Woodfield this afternoon; he's thinking of buying some property there. Ordinarily he stops to talk a while when he sees me, but this evening he only nodded and went on. Wherever he goes, he must always be at home by eight o'clock."

"So they tell me," said Dominicus.

The peddler promised to return later, and he began to follow the horseman, who was now several hundred yards ahead of him. He seemed to recognize the rear [7] of Mr. Higginbotham, but

---

[6] evidence, anything that shows or proves something
[7] rear, the back part of anything

through the evening shadows and the dust from the horse's feet, the figure appeared gray and unclear.

He drove on and stayed about the same distance behind the shadowy figure until it reached a bend in the road. There the figure disappeared. On reaching this point the peddler no longer saw the man on horseback; he found himself near the center of the village, not far from a number of stores and two taverns and a church. There was a stone wall and a gate on his left which marked the edge of Mr. Higginbotham's property. Beyond a bunch of trees just inside the wall lay an orchard, and farther still, a house. Dominicus knew the place; and his little horse stopped at the gate without any signal from the driver; he seemed to understand that the peddler did not want to pass the gate until he went to see whether Mr. Higginbotham was hanging on the pear tree.

He jumped from the cart and ran along a green path toward the orchard. Just then the village clock began to strike eight, and with each stroke Dominicus went faster until he reached the middle of the orchard. There he saw the pear tree. One big branch stretched from the old trunk across the path and threw a dark shadow on that one spot. There was some kind of struggle beneath the branch!

The peddler had never pretended to have more courage than an ordinary man with a peaceable occupation, and he could not account for his bravery in this awful emergency.[8] It is certain, however, that he rushed forward and knocked a sturdy [9] Irishman to the ground. He did not find anyone hanging on the pear tree, but trembling beneath it, with a rope around his neck, he found old Mr. Higginbotham!

"Mr. Higginbotham," said Dominicus. "You're an honest man, and I'll believe what you tell me. Have you been hanged or not?"

If the reader has not already guessed what had happened, a few words will clarify [10] the whole story. Three men had planned

---

8 **emergency,** a sudden unexpected event that requires quick action
9 **sturdy,** strong; strongly built
10 **clarify,** make clear

to rob and murder Mr. Higginbotham; two of them, one after the other, lost courage and left—the first traveler that Dominicus met and the Negro. When the first man left, the crime was delayed by one night. Then when the second man left it was delayed by another night. The third man was actually committing the crime when a rescuing hero appeared in the person of Dominicus Pike.

It only remains to say that Mr. Higginbotham was extremely grateful to the peddler, who later married the old gentleman's charming niece. In due time the old fellow died—in bed—and Dominicus' children inherited all the Higginbotham money and property. After that Dominicus Pike and his family moved from Kimballton and made their home in my native village.

EXERCISES

A. Put a check mark (√) in front of the item (a, b, or c) which best completes each unfinished sentence.

1. The crowd in the streets at Parker Falls expected to hear details of the murder—
.... a. when the train arrived.
.... b. when the stage arrived.
.... c. when Mr. Higginbotham arrived.

2. The lawyer who arrived carried some papers—
.... a. for Dominicus Pike.
.... b. signed by Mr. Higginbotham.
.... c. which had been signed during the morning.

3. The young lady with the lawyer was—
.... a. Mr. Higginbotham's daughter.
.... b. Mr. Higginbotham's niece.
.... c. Mr. Higginbotham's granddaughter.

4. What the young lady said proved that Dominicus' story was—
.... a. incorrect.
.... b. true.
.... c. sensible.

5. When the inhabitants of the village learned of their mistake,—
.... a. they were angry.
.... b. they were happy.
.... c. they were sad.

6. On reaching Kimballton, Dominicus stopped to see—
.... a. Mr. Kimball.
.... b. a friend.
.... c. the tavern-keeper.

7. Dominicus decided to visit—
.... a. Mr. Higginbotham's house.
.... b. Mr. Higginbotham's store.
.... c. Mr. Higginbotham's orchard.

8. When Dominicus left his cart at the gate of Mr. Higginbotham's property,—
.... a. he heard a shout.
.... b. the clock began to strike.
.... c. he sat down to rest.

9. Dominicus found Mr. Higginbotham—
.... a. trembling beneath the pear tree.
.... b. hanging on the pear tree.
.... c. with his niece.

10. On his death, Mr. Higginbotham's money and property were inherited by—
.... a. Dominicus' wife.
.... b. Dominicus.
.... c. Dominicus' children.

B. Write T for *True* in front of each sentence below which is true according to the story. Write F for *False* in front of the sentence if it is not true.

.... 1. Two people arrived in Parker Falls on the stage: a lawyer and Mr. Higginbotham's niece.

.... 2. Dominicus announced that he had brought the news of the murder to Parker Falls.

.... 3. Mr. Higginbotham's niece said her uncle was dead when she left him.

.... 4. Miss Higginbotham said she had fainted many times.

.... 5. Dominicus left Parker Falls under a shower of stones and mudballs.

.... 6. The peddler was a good-humored fellow by nature.

.... 7. Mr. Higginbotham's former clerk defended Dominicus against the angry population of Parker Falls.

.... 8. On leaving Parker Falls Dominicus went to Woodfield.

.... 9. When Dominicus finally saw Mr. Higginbotham he was not dead.

.... 10. Dominicus prevented Mr. Higginbotham's murder.

C. Put a check mark (√) in front of the meaning (a, b, or c) which best fits the numbered word.

1. glance:
.... a. lost courage
.... b. a quick look
.... c. pretense

2. rear:
.... a. front part
.... b. middle part
.... c. back part

3. team:
.... a. group
.... b. occupation
.... c. guess

4. stage:
.... a. a kind of tobacco
.... b. a kind of vehicle
.... c. a kind of store

5. sturdy:
.... a. strongly built
.... b. peaceful
.... c. honest

6. clarify:
.... a. classify
.... b. make clear
.... c. lengthen

7. capture:
.... a. hate
.... b. appear suddenly
.... c. catch

8. commit:
.... a. do something wrong
.... b. do something fast
.... c. do something noticeable

9. miser:
.... a. one who spends money foolishly
.... b. one who saves money and spends little
.... c. one who never has any money

10. fare:
.... a. money paid for a trip
.... b. money paid for a peddler's articles
.... c. money paid for stolen property

This lesson is to be followed by Chapter 15 of Part II, p. 296: "Adjectives and Verbs: Differences in Patterning."

SELECTION 16

THE EGG

Sherwood Anderson

PART 1

My father was intended by nature, I am sure, to be a kind and cheerful man. Until he was thirty-four years old he worked as a farmhand [1] for a man named Thomas Butterworth, whose farm was near the town of Bidwell, Ohio. At that time he had a horse of his own, and on Saturday evenings he rode to town to spend a few hours in the companionship of other farmhands. In town he drank several glasses of beer [2] and stood about in Ben Head's

---

[1] **farmhand,** a man hired to work on a farm
[2] **beer,** a bitter drink made from grain

143

saloon [3]—crowded on Saturday evenings with visiting farm-hands. They sang songs, told jokes and stories, and everyone had a good time. At ten o'clock father rode home along a lonely country road, made his horse comfortable for the night, and went to bed, quite satisfied with his position in life.

It was in the spring of his thirty-fifth year that father married my mother, then a country schoolteacher, and in the following spring I came into the world. Something happened to the two people. They became ambitious. The American urge to get ahead [4] took possession of them.

Maybe mother was responsible. Being a schoolteacher she had no doubt read many books. She had, I suppose, read how Garfield, Lincoln, and other Americans had risen from poverty to fame and greatness, and as I lay beside her—only a few days old—she probably dreamed that some day I would be a ruler of men and cities. Anyhow she persuaded father to leave his work as a farmhand, sell his horse, and start an independent business of his own. She was a tall silent woman with a long nose and troubled gray eyes. For herself she wanted nothing, but for father and myself she was extremely ambitious.

Their first attempt in the world of business was a failure. They rented some land on Grigg's Road, eight miles from Bidwell, and started a chicken farm. I grew into boyhood on this farm and got my first impressions [5] of life there. From the beginning they were impressions of defeat, and if I am one of those people who see only the darker side of life, the reason is that I spent my early childhood on a chicken farm.

One unfamiliar with such matters can have no idea of the many things that can happen to a chicken. It is born from an egg and looks for a few weeks like a tiny ball of yellow cotton such as you see on Easter cards; [6] then it becomes ugly and naked, eats quantities of corn, and gets diseases called pip, cholera, and

---

[3] **saloon,** a place where liquor is sold and drunk
[4] **get ahead,** improve one's position in life
[5] **impression,** an effect produced on the mind
[6] **Easter cards,** cards sent to friends and relatives at Eastertime

other names; it stands looking with stupid eyes at the sun, becomes sick and dies. A few hens and an occasional rooster,[7] intended to serve God's mysterious purposes, struggle to adulthood. The hens lay eggs from which other chickens are born, and the same problems begin again. It is all difficult to understand. One hopes for so much from a chicken and is so often disappointed. Small chickens, just starting the journey of life, look so bright and clever, but they are really very stupid. They are so much like people, they confuse one's expectations. If disease

rooster

does not kill them, your expectations will grow, and then they walk under the wheels of a wagon—to be crushed and return to their maker. Tiny insects attack the young ones and costly medicines are necessary to get rid of them. In later life I have seen literature on the subject of chicken-raising and how one can make a fortune in the chicken business. It is a hopeful literature and declares that much can be done by simple ambitious people who own a few hens. Do not believe it. It was not written for you. Go look for gold in the frozen hills of Alaska, put your faith in the honesty of a politician, believe if you wish that the world is daily growing better and that good will conquer evil in the end, but do not believe the literature that is written concerning the hen. It was not written for you.

My story is not primarily concerned with the hen. If correctly told the center of attention is the egg. For ten years my father and mother struggled to make our chicken farm successful; finally they decided it was hopeless. They moved to the town of Bidwell, Ohio, and started a restaurant business. After ten years of worry about eggs that did not hatch,[8] and about tiny balls of yellow cotton that passed on into semi-naked pullethood[9] and from that into dead henhood, we threw everything

---

[7] **rooster,** a male chicken (see picture)
[8] **hatch,** produce young (chickens) from eggs
[9] **pullet,** a young hen

aside; we loaded our belongings on a wagon and went along Grigg's Road toward Bidwell—a tiny group of hopeful characters looking for a new place from which to start on our upward journey through life.

I imagine we were a sad-looking group, not unlike refugees [10] trying to escape from a battleground. Mother and I walked in the road. The wagon that contained our possessions had been borrowed for the day from Mr. Albert Grigg, a neighbor. The legs of cheap chairs hung over the sides, and at the back of a pile of beds, tables, and other household furnishings there was a box containing live chickens; on top of that there was a baby carriage in which I was pushed about before I learned to walk. Why we kept the baby carriage I don't know. My parents would probably have no more children, and the wheels were broken. People who have few possessions hold tightly to those they have. That is one of the facts which makes life so discouraging.

Father rode on top of the wagon. He was then a bald-headed [11] man of forty-five, a little fat, and from long association with mother and the chickens he had become habitually silent and discouraged. All during our ten years on the chicken farm he had worked as a laborer [12] on neighboring farms, and most of the money he had earned was spent for remedies to cure chicken diseases—Wilmer's White Wonder Cholera Cure, or Professor Bidlow's Egg Producer, or other preparations that mother found advertised in newspapers for farmers. There were two little bunches of hair on father's head just above his ears. As a child I used to sit looking at him when he had gone to sleep in a chair on Sunday afternoons. At that time I had already begun to read books and have ideas of my own; the bald path on the top of his head was, I imagined, similar to a broad road—such a road as Caesar had made to lead his soldiers from Rome into an unknown world. The little bunches of hair that grew above father's ears, I thought, were like forests.

---

[10] refugee, a person forced to leave a place because of danger
[11] bald, with little or no hair
[12] laborer, one who works with his hands

Walking alongside the wagon I was half asleep most of the time, dreaming I was going to a beautiful place far away where there were no chicken farms and where life was a happy eggless affair.

One could write a book concerning our flight from the chicken farm into town. Mother and I walked the entire eight miles. Her duty was to pick up anything that fell from the wagon. On the seat of the wagon beside father was his greatest treasure. I will tell you about that.

On a chicken farm, where hundreds and even thousands of chickens come out of eggs, surprising things sometimes happen. Strange little beings are born from eggs as from people. The accident does not occur often—perhaps once in a thousand births. A chicken is born that has four legs, two pairs of wings, two heads, or in some other way that is unnatural. The fact that the poor little things could not live was one of the greatest disappointments of father's life. He had some idea that if he could bring a five-legged hen or a two-headed rooster into henhood or roosterhood he could make a fortune. He believed that many people would pay money to see such a wonder.

Anyhow, he saved all these strange little creatures that were born on our chicken farm. They were preserved in alcohol and each one put into its own glass bottle. Father had put these carefully into a box, and on our journey into town he carried them on the wagon seat beside him. He drove the horses with one hand and kept his other hand on the box. At the end of our journey he took the box down and removed the bottles as carefully as possible. All during our days as keepers of a restaurant in Bidwell, Ohio, these bottles sat on a shelf behind the counter.[13] Mother sometimes objected, but father was determined to keep them there. These little creatures, he declared, were valuable. He said that people like to look at strange and wonderful things.

Did I say we started a restaurant business in the town of Bidwell? This is not quite correct. The town itself lay at the

---

[13] **counter,** a long table where customers are served

foot of a low hill and on the shore of a small river. The railroad did not run through the town; the station was a mile north of the town at a place called Pickleville. In the morning and in the evening busses came to the station from the hotel in Bidwell. It was mother's idea that we open a restaurant at this location. She talked about it for a year, and then one day she went off and rented an empty store building opposite the railroad station. It was her idea that the restaurant would be profitable. She said there would always be traveling men waiting to take outgoing trains and townspeople would come to the station to wait for incoming trains. They would come to the restaurant for a sandwich or coffee or something else. Now that I am older I know that she had another reason for moving. She was ambitious for me. She wanted me to rise in the world, to attend a school in town and become a man of the towns.

At Pickleville father and mother worked hard, as they had always done. First it was necessary to rebuild the place inside—so it could become a restaurant. That took a month. Father built shelves and a counter and painted everything. He painted a sign with his name in large letters. Under his name was the sharp command—EAT HERE—that was seldom obeyed. They bought a showcase and filled it with cigars and tobacco. Mother scrubbed [14] the floor and walls of the room. I went to school in town and was glad to be away from the presence of sad-looking chickens. Still I was not overjoyed. In the evening I walked home from school and remembered the children I had seen playing in the schoolyard. A group of little girls had been hopping [15] and singing. I tried that. Along the frozen road I went hopping solemnly on one leg. "Hippity Hop to the Barber Shop," I sang. Then I stopped and looked around doubtfully. I thought that no one should see me as a gay young fellow. It seemed somehow that it was wrong to do things like that—at least it was wrong for me, since I was a native of a chicken farm where death was a daily visitor.

---

[14] **scrub**, clean thoroughly with a brush
[15] **hop**, move in short jumps

Mother decided that our restaurant should remain open at night. At ten in the evening a passenger train went north and it was followed by a local freight train.[16] The crew on the freight train had work to do in Pickleville, and when the work was finished they came to our restaurant for hot coffee and food. Sometimes one of them ordered a fried egg. In the morning at four some of the crew visited us again. Our restaurant trade began to grow a little. Mother slept at night and during the day managed the restaurant and fed our customers while father slept. He slept in the same bed that mother occupied during the night, and I went off to the town of Bidwell and to school. During the long nights, while mother and I slept, father cooked meats and made sandwiches for the lunch baskets of our customers. Then an idea for getting ahead in the world came to him. He also became ambitious.

EXERCISES

A. Put a check mark (√) in front of the item (a, b, or c) which best completes each unfinished sentence.

1. The author of this story was born in the state of—
   .... a. Michigan.
   .... b. Ohio.
   .... c. Texas.

2. His father was a—
   .... a. farmhand.
   .... b. schoolteacher.
   .... c. railroad man.

3. What a person writes about his own life we call an *auto-biography*. And what a person writes about someone else's life we call a *biography*. This story is—
   .... a. neither a biography nor an autobiography.
   .... b. a biography.
   .... c. an autobiography.

4. The chicken farm which the author's parents started—
   .... a. was successful.

---

[16] **freight train,** train that carries goods, not people

.... b. was a failure.

.... c. was located near Lincoln, Nebraska.

5. According to the author, his story is not primarily concerned with the hen. If correctly told the center of attention is—

.... a. the rooster.

.... b. the restaurant.

.... c. the egg.

6. Most of the chickens which were hatched on the chicken farm—

.... a. did not reach henhood or roosterhood.

.... b. were frozen in the hills of Alaska.

.... c. had four legs, two pairs of wings, and two heads.

7. After ten years the author's parents left the chicken farm. They decided to start a—

.... a. furniture business.

.... b. advertising business.

.... c. restaurant business.

8. They moved their household furnishings—

.... a. by train.

.... b. in a wagon.

.... c. in a bus.

9. The idea of opening a restaurant originated with—

.... a. the author's father.

.... b. the author.

.... c. the author's mother.

10. The author at this time went to school in—

.... a. Pickleville.

.... b. Bidwell.

.... c. Garfield.

B. Write T for *True* in front of each sentence below which is true according to the story. Write F for *False* in front of the sentence if it is not true.

.... 1. The author's father owned a farm near Bidwell, Ohio.

.... 2. In the spring of his thirty-fifth year the author got married.

.... 3. The author spent his early childhood on a chicken farm.

.... 4. After ten years on the chicken farm, the family moved to Pickleville.

.... 5. The entire family rode on the wagon with the household furnishings.

.... 6. The restaurant they opened was opposite a hotel.

.... 7. A freight train crew came to the restaurant at night.

.... 8. The author worked in the restaurant all night with his father.

.... 9. No coffee was served in the restaurant.

.... 10. The author's father built a counter for the restaurant.

C. Put a check mark (√) in front of the meaning (a, b, or c) which best fits the numbered word or phrase.

1. **beer:**
.... a. something to read
.... b. something to eat
.... c. something to drink

2. **get ahead:**
.... a. improve one's position in life
.... b. see only the darker side of life
.... c. confuse one's expectations

3. **rooster:**
.... a. wagon wheel
.... b. male chicken
.... c. hopeful literature

4. **hatch:**
.... a. cure chicken diseases
.... b. produce young (chickens) from eggs
.... c. hold tightly to one's possessions

5. **bald:**
.... a. broad
.... b. determined
.... c. with little or no hair

6. **farmhand:**
.... a. man hired to work on a farm
.... b. owner of more than one farm
.... c. person who sells farm machinery

7. **scrub:**
.... a. preserve in alcohol
.... b. clean with a brush
.... c. obey a command

8. **impression:**
.... a. native of a chicken farm
.... b. person with a lot of ambition
.... c. effect produced on the mind

9. **pullet:**
.... a. customer
.... b. young hen
.... c. sign

10. **pip:** .... a. a kind of corn
.... b. a kind of insect
.... c. a kind of disease

This lesson is to be followed by Chapter 16 of Part II, p. 301: "Adjectives with Underlying Verb Forms and Verbs with Underlying Adjective Forms."

THE EGG

During the long nights when there was little to do, father had time to think. He decided that he had been an unsuccessful man in the past because he had not been cheerful; in the future he was going to adopt a more cheerful outlook[1] on life. Early one morning he came upstairs and talked with mother. From my bed in the corner I listened.

It was father's idea that he and mother should try to entertain the people who came to eat at our restaurant. I cannot now remember his words, but he gave the impression that he was about to become a public entertainer of some kind. When people, especially young people from Bidwell, came into our restaurant (as on rare occasions they did), mother and father were to make bright entertaining conversation. Mother was probably doubtful from the first, but she said nothing to discourage him. It was father's idea that a great desire to be in the company of himself and mother would arise among the younger people of the town. In the evening bright happy groups would come singing down the road. They would enter our restaurant shouting with joy

---

[1] **outlook**, point of view

and laughter. There would be songs and gaiety. I do not mean to say that father spoke of the matter exactly in this way. My own imagination has supplied part of this information. But father was convinced [2] that the younger people wanted a place to go, and that he and mother could provide an attractive place for them.

For two or three weeks this idea of father's continued to grow. We did not talk much, but in our daily lives we tried hard to make smiles take the place of sad looks. Mother smiled at the customers, and I smiled at my school companions. Father became a little feverish in his anxiety to please. No doubt he was beginning to feel somewhat like a showman [3] in need of an audience. He did not waste his showmanship on the railroad men he served at night; he seemed to be waiting for a young man or woman from Bidwell to come in. On the counter in the restaurant there was a wire basket kept always filled with eggs; he was probably looking at this basket when the idea of entertainment was born in his brain. Eggs were connected in some way with the development of his idea. Anyhow, an egg ruined his new outlook on life. Late one night I was awakened by a roar of anger coming from father's throat. Both mother and I sat up in our beds. With nervous hands she lighted a lamp that stood on a table by her head. Downstairs the front door of our restaurant closed with a bang, [4] and a few minutes later father came up the stairs. He held an egg in his hand and the hand was trembling. His eyes looked like those of a wild man. As he stood there looking at us I thought he was going to throw the egg at one of us. Then he set it gently on the table beside the lamp and dropped on his knees beside mother's bed. He began to cry like a boy, and I, being frightened, began to cry too. The two of us filled the upstairs room with our tearful voices. It was ridiculous [5] really; when I think of that scene, I can only remember that mother's hand continually patted the bald path that ran across the top of

---

[2] convince, persuade
[3] showman, an entertainer in a show or theater
[4] bang, a loud, sudden noise
[5] ridiculous, foolish; unreasonable

his head. I have forgotten what mother said to him and how she persuaded him to tell her what had happened downstairs.

On that evening young Joe Kane, son of a storekeeper in Bidwell, came to Pickleville to meet his father. He expected his father on the ten-o'clock train from the South. The train was three hours late, and Joe came into the restaurant to wait for its arrival. The local freight train arrived and father fed the freight crew as usual. Afterwards, he and Joe were alone.

Father's actions probably puzzled Joe Kane. He noticed that the restaurant-keeper seemed to be disturbed by his presence and he thought of leaving. However, it was raining, and he did not want to walk back to town and then have to return later. He bought a cigar and ordered a cup of coffee. He had a newspaper in his pocket; he took it out and began to read. "I'm waiting for the evening train," he said. "It's late tonight."

For a long time father, whom Joe Kane had never seen before, remained silently staring at his visitor. He no doubt was suffering from an attack of stage fright.[6] This was the opportunity father had been waiting for, but he did not know how to begin.

For one thing, he did not know what to do with his hands. He extended one of them nervously over the counter and shook hands with Joe Kane. "How do you do?" he said. Joe put his newspaper down and looked at him. Father's eyes fell on the basket of eggs that always remained on the counter and he began to talk. "Well," he began hesitatingly, "well, you've heard of Christopher Columbus, of course. Well," he continued, "Christopher Columbus was a cheat. He talked of making an egg stand on its end. He talked, and then he broke the end of the egg."

Father's words came as no little surprise to Joe Kane. He declared it was wrong to teach children that Christopher Columbus was a great man when, after all, he had cheated: Columbus had been unable to make an egg stand on its end without breaking the end first. Then father took an egg from the basket on the counter. He rolled the egg between the palms [7] of his hands.

---

[6] stage fright, fear felt by an actor or speaker before facing an audience
[7] palm, the inner surface of the hand

He smiled and then began to talk about the effect produced on an egg by electricity from the human body. He declared that, without breaking its shell and by rolling it back and forth in his hands, he could stand the egg on its end. He explained that the warmth of his hands and the gentle rolling movement gave the egg new balancing possibilities; Joe Kane was mildly interested. "I've handled thousands of eggs," father said. "No one knows more about eggs than I do."

He stood the egg on the counter and it fell on its side. He tried the trick again and again, each time rolling the egg between the palms of his hands and saying the words regarding the wonders of electricity and balance. When, after a half-hour's effort he did succeed in making the egg stand for a moment, he discovered that his visitor was no longer watching. By the time he called Joe Kane's attention to the success of his effort, the egg had again rolled over and lay on its side.

Anxious to entertain and at the same time disappointed by the failure of his first effort, father now took the bottles containing the abnormal [8] baby chickens and began to show them to his visitor. "How would you like to have seven legs and two heads like this one?" he asked, pointing to the most remarkable of his treasures. He smiled cheerfully, and reached over the counter and tried to give Joe Kane a friendly tap on the shoulder. His visitor was made slightly ill by the sight of the tiny chicken's body floating in alcohol and he got up to go. Coming from behind the counter, father took hold of the young man's arm and led him back to his seat. He became a little angry and for a moment he had to turn his face away and force himself to smile. Then he put the bottles back on the shelf. He urged Joe Kane to have a fresh cup of coffee and another cigar. Then he took a pan and filling it with vinegar,[9] he declared he was going to do another trick. "I'll heat this egg in this pan of vinegar," he said. "Then I'll put it through the neck of a bottle without breaking the shell. When the egg is inside the bottle it will

---

[8] **abnormal**, different from the usual
[9] **vinegar**, a sour liquid used for flavoring food

return to its normal shape and the shell will become hard again. Then I'll give you the bottle with the egg in it. You can take it with you wherever you go. People will want to know how you put the egg inside the bottle. Don't tell them. That's the way to have fun with this trick."

Father smiled at his visitor. Joe Kane decided that the man in front of him was mildly insane [10] but harmless. He drank the cup of coffee and began to read his newspaper again. When the egg had been heated in vinegar, father carried it on a spoon to the counter and he brought a bottle from a back room. He was angry because his visitor did not watch him as he began to do his trick, but nevertheless he continued and tried to smile. For a long time he struggled, trying to put the egg through the neck of the bottle. He put the pan of vinegar back on the stove, intending to reheat the egg; then when he picked it up he burned his fingers. After a second bath in the hot vinegar, the shell of the egg was softer, but not soft enough for his purpose. He worked and worked. When he thought at last he was about to complete the trick, the delayed train arrived at the station and Joe Kane started toward the door. Father made a final attempt to do the trick and thus gain the reputation as one who knew how to entertain guests who came into his restaurant. He swore softly and sweat began to roll down his face. Then the egg broke under his hand, and some of the contents fell on his clothes. Joe Kane, who had stopped at the door, turned and laughed.

A roar of anger rose from my father's throat. He shouted a string of words which no one could understand. Taking another egg from the basket on the counter, he threw it, just missing the head of the young man as he went through the door.

Father came upstairs to mother and me with an egg in his hand. I do not know what he intended to do. I imagine he had some idea of destroying it, of destroying all eggs, and he wanted mother and me to see him begin. However, something happened which changed his mind. He put the egg gently on

---

[10] **insane,** mad; crazy

the table and began to cry as I have already explained. He later decided to close the restaurant for the night; then he came upstairs and went to bed. When he did so, he blew out the light and after much conversation in a low voice he and mother went to sleep. I suppose I went to sleep also, but my sleep was troubled. I woke up at daybreak and for a long time looked at the egg on the table. I wondered why eggs exist and why from the egg comes the hen who again lays eggs. The question remains unanswered in my mind. I am sure that no one in my family will ever try again to conquer the egg. It brings nothing but defeat.

EXERCISES

A. Put a check mark (√) in front of the item (a, b, or c) which best completes each unfinished sentence.

1. The author's father decided he had been an unsuccessful man in the past—
   .... a. because he had been too rich.
   .... b. because he had been happy.
   .... c. because he had not been cheerful.

2. He now believed that people who came into the restaurant—
   .... a. should cook their own food.
   .... b. should be entertained.
   .... c. should eat nothing but eggs.

3. On the counter in the restaurant there was a wire basket full of—
   .... a. sandwiches.
   .... b. eggs.
   .... c. lunch baskets.

4. The author's father did not waste his showmanship on the railroad men. He was waiting for a—
   .... a. young man or woman from Bidwell.
   .... b. salesman from out of town.
   .... c. man with a bald head.

5. He attempted to entertain—
   .... a. Christopher Columbus.
   .... b. Joe Kane.
   .... c. Ben Head.

6. One of his tricks was—

.... a. to balance an egg on his nose.

.... b. to stand on an egg without breaking the shell.

.... c. to put an egg inside a bottle without breaking the shell.

7. Joe Kane was in Pickleville to meet the 10-o'clock train from the South. That night the train was—

.... a. on time.

.... b. three hours late.

.... c. an hour early.

8. Joe decided that the author's father was—

.... a. mildly insane but harmless.

.... b. a great showman.

.... c. a successful businessman.

9. When Joe saw the abnormal baby chickens,—

.... a. he laughed.

.... b. he became slightly ill.

.... c. he became angry.

10. The author's name—

.... a. appears in the story several times.

.... b. was Thomas Butterworth.

.... c. was not mentioned in the story.

B. Write T for *True* in front of each sentence below which is true according to the story. Write F for *False* in front of the sentence if it is not true.

.... 1. The restaurant was located in the railroad station.

.... 2. The author's father had no hair on his head.

.... 3. Joe Kane was the son of a Bidwell storekeeper.

.... 4. The author's father said that Christopher Columbus was a cheat.

.... 5. Joe Kane did not buy anything in the restaurant.

.... 6. The abnormal chickens were kept in bottles.

.... 7. The author's father said he had handled thousands of eggs.

.... 8. When the delayed train arrived at the station, Joe left the restaurant.

.... 9. In the evening bright happy groups came into the restaurant shouting with joy and laughter.

.... 10. The family had a bedroom upstairs.

C. Put a check mark (√) in front of the meaning (a, b, or c) which best fits the numbered word.

1. **laborer:**
   .... a. one who writes newspaper stories
   .... b. one who swims in deep water
   .... c. one who works with his hands

2. **palm:**
   .... a. healthy point of view
   .... b. inner surface of the hand
   .... c. rare occasion

3. **bang:**
   .... a. daily visitor
   .... b. entertainment
   .... c. loud, sudden noise

4. **abnormal:**
   .... a. different from the usual
   .... b. ambitious
   .... c. feverish

5. **vinegar:**
   .... a. storekeeper
   .... b. sour liquid
   .... c. tearful voice

6. **insane:**
   .... a. nervous
   .... b. puzzled
   .... c. mad

7. **showman:**
   .... a. treasure
   .... b. entertainer
   .... c. counter

8. **outlook:**
   .... a. point of view
   .... b. successful effort
   .... c. warmth of the hands

9. **saloon:**
   .... a. place where liquor is sold
   .... b. place where fish are sold
   .... c. place where furniture is sold

10. **ridiculous:**
   .... a. foolish; unreasonable
   .... b. angry; disturbed
   .... c. mysterious; puzzling

This lesson is to be followed by Chapter 17 of Part II, p. 306: "Adjectives with Prefixes; Prefixes in Derivation."

MAP OF
MAYSVILLE

New York Standard

STATEMENT
INDEPENDENT GAS CO.

SELECTION 18

THE MAYSVILLE "POET"

Ring W. Lardner

PART 1

A story is told about a man who lived in Maysville during the first quarter of this century. It is hard to believe that a man could be so dull and foolish, but this is the way they tell it.

Maysville was a town of five thousand inhabitants and its gas company served eight hundred homes, offices, and stores.

The company's office staff consisted of two men—Ed Hunter, repairman and reader of meters,[1] and Stephen Gale, whose title was bookkeeper, but his work was much harder than the title suggests.

[1] **meter**, an instrument that measures (the amount of gas used)

161

From the first to the tenth of the month, Stephen stayed in the office; he received checks and money from the customers who were ready to pay their gas bills; he argued with many customers who thought their gas bills were too high; and he tried to sell new stoves to customers who were always complaining about defects [2] in the stoves they had bought fifteen or twenty years before.

After the tenth, he kept the front door locked and went to see people who owed money to the gas company; some had not paid their gas bills for several months and probably had no intention of paying them. This tiring, useless task usually lasted until the twenty-seventh, when Hunter started reading meters and Stephen prepared the monthly bills.

When old Mr. Townsend, who owned the company and five other gas companies in larger towns, came to visit Maysville every two months, he scolded Stephen for not collecting all the money due the company and for allowing Hunter to drink too much liquor.

Stephen earned $22.50 per week—the same salary he had received when he first began to work for the gas company eight years before. He was now thirty-one. At twelve, he had stopped going to school and had gone to work as a messenger boy for the telegraph company. His father had died when he was very young and his mother—a dressmaker—needed the few dollars Stephen could earn as a messenger boy. Later he had held jobs [3] as a delivery boy for a food store, as a clerk in a drug store, and as assistant to the freight manager at the Lackawanna Railroad station. The $22.50 offer from the gas company came as a welcome surprise; it was $7.50 higher than any previous salary he had received.

After Stephen's mother died, he married Stella Nichols, to whom lack of money was nothing new. But they had a couple of children and soon found themselves in debt. This made Stephen less efficient than ever as a collector of the company's unpaid bills. He could not blame other people for not paying

[2] **defect**, fault; something wrong
[3] **job**, employment; work

their gas bills when he owed a good deal of money himself. All
he could do was hope that old Mr. Townsend would increase
his salary, but he realized that such an action was very unlikely.

The Gales were too poor to go to the movies;[4] besides, there
was no one to stay with the children. So Stephen and Stella
stayed at home in the evenings and read books from the town
library. The books Stephen read were books of poetry. And
often, after Stella had gone to bed, he wrote poetry of his own.

He wrote a poem for Stella and gave it to her on one of her
birthdays; she thought it was wonderful and said he ought to
stop working for the gas company and write poetry for a living.
Stephen laughed and said that as a poet he could probably not
earn any money at all. He did not show Stella his other poems—
poems about nature, flowers, the Lackawanna Railroad, the
beauties of Maysville, etc.—but kept them locked in a drawer
of his desk at the gas company.

A man named Charley Roberts, who was a traveling salesman
for a water heater company in New York, came to Maysville
from time to time. For years he had been trying to interest old
Mr. Townsend in some of the heaters manufactured by his company, but old Mr. Townsend said the heaters used too much gas
and the customers would complain about them. They complained enough already. Roberts was a determined young man,
however, and he kept trying to convince Mr. Townsend that
the heaters he sold were the finest in the country.

Roberts was a humorous New Yorker who was fond of jokes
and wisecracks.[5] When at home (in New York), he lunched
where his heroes lunched, just to be near them, look at them,
and overhear some of their wisecracks which he could repeat to
others while traveling. These heroes were writers for newspapers, writers of plays, and cartoonists.[6]

His favorite newspaper column[7] was the one written by
George Balch in the *New York Standard*. When he was in a

---

[4] movies, moving pictures
[5] wisecrack, a funny remark
[6] cartoonist, an artist who draws funny pictures for the newspapers
[7] column, a narrow section of a newspaper page

small town, he frequently cut funny stories and articles from the local newspapers and sent them to Balch, who sometimes reprinted them in his column.

Someone in a neighboring town told Charley that old Mr. Townsend would be in Maysville on a certain day, so he made arrangements to visit Maysville on that day. When Charley reached the gas company, Stephen had just returned to the office from an unsuccessful collection tour and was telling Ed Hunter that Mrs. Harper was having trouble with her stove. While waiting for the conversation to end, Roberts looked idly at Stephen's desk and saw a book. It was a volume of poems by Amy Lowell. A moment later Hunter left, and they were alone.

"Hello, Gale. How are you?" said Roberts.

"O. K. How are you, Mr. Roberts?" replied Stephen.

"Fine. I heard Mr. Townsend was here," said Roberts.

"You've missed him," said Stephen. "He was here yesterday afternoon, but he left for Haines City last night."

"Will he be here tomorrow?"

"I don't know."

"Well, I expect to be in Haines City tomorrow. Maybe I'll see him there. I notice you read poetry."

"Oh, that's a book from the library."

"How do you like it?"

"I don't care much for [8] poetry that doesn't rhyme," [9] said Stephen.

"Maybe it's easier to write," suggested Roberts.

"I don't believe so. It isn't hard to make the lines rhyme. I imagine Edgar Guest writes poetry easily."

"Why do you think that?"

"I've tried it," said Stephen.

"Oh, so you're a poet?" asked Roberts.

"Well, not exactly. I've written a few verses, and it was more like fun than work. Other people would think the verses are

---

[8] **care for,** like
[9] **rhyme,** the ends of the words have the same or similar sounds

not very good, but writing them gives me a good deal of pleasure."

"I'd like to read them, Gale," said Roberts eagerly.

"I don't know if I've saved any. I wrote a poem for my wife on her birthday three years ago. She thought it was pretty good. You can read that one, if I can find a copy of it."

"See if you can find it," urged Roberts.

Stephen looked in two or three drawers before he unlocked the one that contained his poems.

"It's just a little thing I wrote for my wife on her birthday. You'll probably think it's pretty bad. It's called 'To Stella.' Stella's my wife's first name."

Charley Roberts read the poem:

> Stella, you today are twenty-three years old,
> And yet your hair is still pure gold.
> Stella, they tell me your name in Latin means a star,
> And to me that is what you are;
> With your eyes and your hair so yellow,
> I rate [10] myself a lucky fellow, Stella.
> You know I cannot afford [11] a costly gift.
> As you know, it costs us all I make to live.
> And as you know, we are already in debt.
> But if you will stay well and healthy
> Until I am rich and wealthy,
> Maybe I will be more able then to give you a present,
> Better than I can at present.
> So now, Stella, good-by for the present,
> And I hope next year I can make things more pleasant.
> May you live to be old and ripe and mellow [12]
> Is my kind birthday wish for you, Stella.

"Do you mean," asked Roberts, "that poetry like this is easy to write?"

"It took me less than half an hour," said Stephen.

---

[10] rate, consider

[11] afford, have enough money for

[12] mellow, sympathetic and wise because of age or experience

"Let me take it with me," said Roberts.

"Why do you want it?"

"I can have it printed."

"Where?"

"In the *New York Standard*. I have a friend, George Balch, who would put it in his column. He doesn't pay anything, but if he put it in his column with your name as the author, it might attract the attention of people who do pay for poetry. Then you could make a lot of money."

"How much do they pay?"

"Well, some magazines [13] pay as much as a dollar a line."

"How many lines are in that one?"

Roberts counted them.

"Seventeen," he said. "Seventeen dollars. I'd guess that old Mr. Townsend doesn't pay you much more than seventeen dollars per week."

"And it took me less than half an hour to write that," said Stephen.

"Can I send it to Balch?"

"I don't know if I have another copy."

"Your wife has one, doesn't she?"

"I suppose she has."

"I'll mail this to Balch tonight, with a note. If he puts it in his column, I'll send you a copy of the newspaper."

"I have another poem longer than that one," said Stephen.

"Well, let me see it."

"No. I'll keep it—since your friend doesn't pay for poetry."

"You're absolutely right. A man shouldn't work for nothing. Keep your other poems until this one appears in the newspaper and you hear from some magazine editors.[14] Then you can sell what you've already written and write more. Eventually you'll have so much money you'll be able to buy the Maysville Gas Company from old Mr. Townsend."

---

[13] **magazine**, a weekly or monthly publication containing articles and stories
[14] **editor**, one who prepares material (written by other people) for printing

"I don't want a gas company. I'd like to leave this one. I only want to write."

"Why don't you leave now?"

"I have to earn a living."

"Living! If you can earn seventeen dollars in half an hour, you can earn thirty-four dollars an hour. How many hours do you work here every day?"

"Ten."

"Ten hours of writing poetry would bring you three hundred and forty dollars a day! Is that enough for a living?"

"I couldn't spend ten hours a day writing poetry. Sometimes I don't feel like writing."

"A dollar a line would make most people want to write all the time. But if you didn't feel like writing sometimes, you could hire someone to write for you."

"That would be dishonest. People would know the difference anyway. It's hard to imitate another man's style.[15] I tried once to write like Edgar Guest, but nobody familiar with his poetry believed that Guest had written my poem."

"Nobody can write like Guest. And you don't need to. Your own style is just as good as his and maybe better. And speaking of Guest, do you think he's starving? He gives away money all the time."

This argument convinced Stephen that fame and fortune might soon be his. After Roberts left, he pictured in his mind poem after poem written by his own hand and printed in places of honor in all the best magazines of the day.

EXERCISES

A. Put a check mark (√) in front of the item (a, b, or c) which best completes each unfinished sentence.

    1. The office staff of the Maysville Gas Company consisted of—

    .... a. two men.

    .... b. a dozen employees.

    .... c. Charley Roberts and Mr. Townsend.

---

[15] style, a way of writing

2. From the tenth to the twenty-seventh of the month, Stephen attempted to—
.... a. read meters and repair stoves.
.... b. sell new stoves to old customers.
.... c. collect money from people with unpaid bills.

3. Mr. Townsend came to Maysville—
.... a. every day.
.... b. every two months.
.... c. monthly.

4. At twelve, Stephen had quit school and gone to work as a—
.... a. dressmaker.
.... b. messenger boy for the telegraph company.
.... c. clerk in a drug store.

5. Stella and Stephen spent their evenings—
.... a. at the movies.
.... b. reading library books.
.... c. with Mr. Townsend.

6. Once Stephen wrote a poem for Stella and gave it to her—
.... a. on her birthday.
.... b. on the Fourth of July.
.... c. on New Year's Day.

7. When Charley Roberts came to Maysville,—
.... a. Stephen bought some water heaters.
.... b. he brought George Balch with him.
.... c. Mr. Townsend was not there.

8. Roberts wanted to take Stephen's poem and—
.... a. send it to George Balch.
.... b. send it to Edgar Guest.
.... c. send it to Amy Lowell.

9. According to Roberts, some magazines paid—
.... a. seventeen dollars a line for poetry.
.... b. a dollar a line for poetry.
.... c. thirty-four dollars a line for poetry.

10. Stephen said he worked—
.... a. eight hours a day at the gas company.
.... b. twelve hours a day at the gas company.
.... c. ten hours a day at the gas company.

B. Write T for *True* in front of each sentence below which is true according to the story. Write F for *False* in front of the sentence if it is not true.

.... 1. Mr. Townsend owned six gas companies.

.... 2. Ed Hunter was assistant to the freight manager at the Lackawanna Railroad station.

.... 3. Sometimes Stephen wrote verses at night after Stella had gone to bed.

.... 4. The customers of the gas company never complained.

.... 5. Stephen kept his poems locked in a desk drawer.

.... 6. Charley Roberts was fond of jokes and wisecracks.

.... 7. When Roberts came to Maysville he was hoping to see Mr. Townsend.

.... 8. Stephen said Amy Lowell's poems were wonderful.

.... 9. Roberts read one of Stephen's poems and said it should be printed in the local newspaper.

.... 10. Stephen said he wrote the poem in less than half an hour.

C. Put a check mark (√) in front of the meaning (a, b, or c) which best fits the numbered word or phrase.

1. **afford:**
.... a. receive checks and money
.... b. have enough money for
.... c. argue about gas bills

2. **rhyme:**
.... a. the ends of the words have the same or similar sounds
.... b. the beginnings of the words have the same or similar sounds
.... c. the ends of the words have completely different sounds.

3. **wisecrack:**
.... a. messenger boy
.... b. funny remark
.... c. locked door

4. **job:**
.... a. employment; work
.... b. heater; stove
.... c. author; writer

5. **meter:**
.... a. an instrument that heats
.... b. an instrument that measures
.... c. an instrument that cuts

6. **defect:**
.... a. fault
.... b. end
.... c. article

7. **style:**
.... a. occupation
.... b. way of writing
.... c. a good deal of pleasure

8. **mellow:**
.... a. difficult and strange
.... b. safe and sure
.... c. sympathetic and wise

9. **column:**
.... a. section of a newspaper page
.... b. a line of poetry
.... c. newspaper editor

10. **care for:**
.... a. be late
.... b. like
.... c. call

This lesson is to be followed by Chapter 18 of Part II, p. 310: "How We Recognize Adjectives."

THE MAYSVILLE
"POET"

PART 2

Stephen was anxious to tell Stella what had happened, but he was afraid that George Balch might not like the poem. If Balch didn't put it in his column Stella would be disappointed. Stephen decided to wait until he saw it actually printed, if ever, and then show it to her.

He didn't have to wait long. In less than a week he received a copy of the *Standard* by mail from New York, and there in George Balch's column he saw his verse with his name under it. The verse had a heading: "To Stella—A Maysville Man Writes a Poem in Honor of His Wife's Birthday."

For the first time in his career [1] as a gas company employee, Stephen quit [2] his work five minutes early and almost ran home. He and Stella were both excited.

Stephen told her the rest of the story—how Roberts had predicted that the poem would attract the attention of magazine editors and there would be a demand for his verses at a dollar a line. And he confessed that he had other poems all ready to sell. He had brought two of them home from the office, and he read them aloud for her approval:

---

[1] career, an occupation or profession; a way of earning a living
[2] quit, stop

"1. The Lackawanna Railroad.
"The Lackawanna Railroad where does it go?
It goes from Jersey City to Buffalo.
Some of the trains stop at Maysville but they are few;
Most of them go right through,
Except the 8:22
Going west. But the 10:12 bound for [3] Jersey City—
That is the train we like the best,
As it takes you to Jersey City
Where you can take a ferry [4] or tube [5] to New York City.
The Lackawanna runs many freights.
Sometimes they run late;
But that does not make so much difference with a freight,
Except to people who have to wait for their freight.
Maysville people ride the Interurban,[6] especially the farmers,
So the Interurban cuts into the business of the Lackawanna.
But if you are going to New York City or Buffalo,
The Lackawanna is the way to go.
Will say in conclusion [7] that we consider it an honor
That the City of Maysville is on the Lackawanna.

"2. The Gas Business.
"The Maysville Gas Co. has eight hundred meters.
The biggest consumer [8] in town is Mrs. Arnold Peters,
Who owns the big house on Taylor Hill,
And is always giving parties come who will.
Our collections amount to about $2600.00 per month,
Five per cent discount [9] if paid before the tenth of the month.
Mr. Townsend, the owner, considers people a fool,
Who do not at least use gas for fuel.[10]
As for lighting he claims it beats electricity,
As electric storms often cut off the electricity;

---

[3] bound for, going to
[4] ferry, a boat that carries cars and people across a river
[5] tube, an underground railroad; subway
[6] interurban, an electric railroad running between cities and towns
[7] conclusion, the end
[8] consumer, user
[9] discount, an amount subtracted from the bill if paid by a certain date
[10] fuel, anything burned to produce heat

And when you have no light at night,
And have to burn candles all night.
This is hardly right,
Especially if you have company,
Who will ask you what is the matter with the electricity.
So patronize [11] the Gas Company which storms do not affect,
And your friends will have no reason to object."

Stella thought they were both good, but she had a practical suggestion to make.

"You are cheating yourself, dear," she said. "The poem about the railroad—the way you wrote it—is nineteen lines, or nineteen dollars if they really pay a dollar a line. But it would almost double the amount if you arranged the lines differently."

"How do you mean?"

Stella took a pencil and showed him:

> The Lackawanna Railroad,
> Where does it go?
> It goes from Jersey City
> To Buffalo.

"See?" she said. "You can cut most of the lines in half and make thirty-eight dollars instead of nineteen."

But Stephen, thinking of additional money and also of art, could only increase the lines of "The Lackawanna Railroad" from nineteen to thirty and those of "The Gas Business" from seventeen to twenty-one.

Three days later a special-delivery letter came for Stephen. It said:

Dear Mr. Gale:

On September second there was a poem entitled "To Stella" in the *New York Standard*. The poem was signed by you. I liked it very much, and if you have written others as good or will write others as good, our magazine will be glad to buy them, paying you one dollar a line.

---

[11] **patronize,** do business with

We shall hope to hear from you in the near future, and please send us any poems you have already completed.

Sincerely,

WALLACE JAMES

Editor, *James' Weekly*

New York City

Stephen had never heard of *James' Weekly*. He did not notice either that the letter was mailed in Philadelphia and written on the stationery [12] of a Philadelphia hotel.

He rushed home, addressed and mailed the railroad and gas verses, and after talking briefly with Stella, he decided to resign his job.

Old Mr. Townsend, visiting Maysville the following morning, heard about the decision and was very displeased. He knew that he could never find anyone else to do Stephen's work at Stephen's salary.

"I'll raise your salary to twenty-four dollars a week," he said.

"I'm not asking for a raise. I have to quit so I can spend all my time writing poetry."

"Poetry!"

"Yes, sir."

"You'll starve to death."

"Edgar Guest is still alive."

"I don't care if he's alive or not," said Mr. Townsend, "To-day's the twelfth of the month; Hunter can do his work and yours for about two weeks. If you want to return at the end of that time, I'll pay you twenty-three dollars a week."

It was Stephen's intention to finish some older poems which he had started and write a few fresh ones. He wanted to have several ready for the *James' Weekly* as the demand for his verses increased. But he found it almost impossible to write while the fate of the railroad and gas verses was still uncertain. He decided to finish the older ones later and began a new one:

---

[12] **stationery,** writing paper and envelopes

The Delaware River

Not a great many miles from Maysville is the Delaware River,
But there is no fish in this part of the River.
The upper part of the River is narrow and shallow,
But they claim it is much wider near Philadelphia.

On the twentieth the envelope containing "The Lackawanna Railroad" and "The Gas Business" was returned from New York. Several notices were stamped on it, such as "Addressee Unknown" and "Return to Sender."

Then Stephen realized that the whole matter had been a big joke. Charley Roberts no doubt thought Stephen's verses were funny. There was no *James' Weekly;* the letter Stephen received was probably written by Roberts himself.

While Stella was crying, Stephen tore up all his poems except "To Stella," which he could not find because she had hidden it somewhere.

"Mr. Townsend arrived on the interurban at eight-thirty," he said. "I'll have to see him."

"All right," said old Mr. Townsend when Stephen walked into the office. "I'll hire you again at your old salary, but I don't want any more foolishness. Now go and try to collect some money from old Mrs. Harper. She hasn't paid her gas bill for eight months."

"I wanted to speak to you about those water heaters that Mr. Roberts sells," said Stephen.

"What about them?"

"I was going to advise you not to buy them. They use too much gas."

"Thanks for your advice, but I ordered some of those heaters from Roberts in Haines City. I told him to send six here," said old Mr. Townsend.

"Will he be here to show us how they operate?" asked Stephen.

"He said he would come."

"Good. I think I'd like to see him again."

Even as he spoke, however, Stephen realized there was nothing he could do to Charley Roberts. Once more he had been a failure. He had been made a fool of, he had refused a raise, and he had lost eight days' pay. And to make his feeling of despair complete, the man who had caused his troubles had finally succeeded in selling his heaters to Stephen's employer. Surely Stephen was a man born without understanding or luck, a man who would always finish last in any contest or be defeated by any rival. And never again would poetry cheer his soul.

EXERCISES

A. Put a check mark (√) in front of the item (a, b, or c) which best completes each unfinished sentence.

1. Stephen's poem "To Stella" was printed in the—
.... a. *Maysville Standard.*
.... b. *New York Standard.*
.... c. *New York Times.*

2. Another one of Stephen's poems was called—
.... a. "The Pennsylvania Railroad."
.... b. "The Jersey City Railroad."
.... c. "The Lackawanna Railroad."

3. Stella said he could lengthen his poems by—
.... a. cutting some of the lines in half.
.... b. writing more lines.
.... c. putting more words on each line.

4. The letter Stephen received came from—
.... a. Philadelphia.
.... b. New York.
.... c. Buffalo.

5. After the letter was received, Stephen decided to—
.... a. go to New York.
.... b. resign his job.
.... c. work in Haines City.

6. Stephen increased the lines of "The Gas Business"—
.... a. from nineteen to thirty.

.... b. from seventeen to forty.

.... c. from seventeen to twenty-one.

7. When old Mr. Townsend heard that Stephen had decided to resign,—

.... a. he congratulated Stephen.

.... b. he was very displeased.

.... c. he wrote a poem.

8. Stephen started a new poem with the title of—

.... a. "The Delaware River."

.... b. "The Beauties of Maysville."

.... c. "Nature and Wild Flowers."

9. In his poem about the gas business—

.... a. freight trains were mentioned.

.... b. electric storms were mentioned.

.... c. ferries were mentioned.

10. The envelope containing two of Stephen's poems—

.... a. was delivered to the *James' Weekly*.

.... b. was lost in the mail.

.... c. was returned from New York.

B. Write T for *True* in front of each sentence below which is true according to the story. Write F for *False* in front of the sentence if it is not true.

.... 1. The biggest consumer of gas in Maysville was Mrs. Arnold Peters.

.... 2. After his poem "To Stella" was printed, Stephen expected to sell some of his poetry.

.... 3. One of Stephen's poems was called "The Interurban."

.... 4. Edgar Guest was one of Stephen's friends.

.... 5. The special-delivery letter for Stephen was signed by Charley Roberts.

.... 6. Stephen mailed six poems to the *James' Weekly*.

.... 7. Mr. Townsend said he would raise Stephen's salary if Stephen would not resign.

.... 8. After Stephen resigned he wrote two more poems.

.... 9. Stephen said that Mr. Townsend should order some water heaters from Charley Roberts.

.... 10. Mr. Townsend hired Stephen again at his old salary.

C. Put a check mark (√) in front of the meaning (a, b, or c) which best fits the numbered word or phrase.

1. **quit:**
.... a. predict
.... b. disappoint
.... c. stop

2. **bound for:**
.... a. going to
.... b. prefer
.... c. run late

3. **ferry:**
.... a. a kind of train
.... b. a kind of car
.... c. a kind of boat

4. **conclusion:**
.... a. the beginning
.... b. the least
.... c. the end

5. **consumer:**
.... a. user
.... b. seller
.... c. deliverer

6. **fuel:**
.... a. something to read
.... b. something to burn
.... c. something to wear

7. **stationery:**
.... a. double the usual amount
.... b. additional money
.... c. writing paper and envelopes

8. **patronize:**
.... a. do business with
.... b. spend one's time on
.... c. write fresh poetry

9. **career:**
.... a. occupation; profession
.... b. alive; living
.... c. starve; go hungry

10. **interurban:**
.... a. a kind of boat
.... b. a kind of bus
.... c. a kind of railroad

This lesson is to be followed by Chapter 19 of Part II, p. 315: "Review: Latin, Greek, and English."

SELECTION 20

A PIECE OF RED CALICO

Frank R. Stockton

While getting ready to go into town one morning last week, my wife handed me a little piece of red calico [1] and asked if I would have time during the day to buy her two yards of calico like that. I told her I would be glad to do it. And putting the piece of calico into my pocket I took the train for town.

At lunch-time I went to a department store to buy the cloth that my wife wanted. I saw a well-dressed man walking between

---

[1] calico, a kind of cotton cloth used for dresses, bed sheets, and covering furniture

the counters where long lines of salespeople were waiting on much longer lines of customers; I asked him where I could see some red calico.

"This way, sir," and he led me to a counter near the back of the store. "Miss Stone," he said to a young lady, "show this gentleman some red calico."

"What shade do you want?" asked Miss Stone.

I showed her the little piece of calico that my wife had given me. Then she took down a huge [2] roll of red calico and spread it on the counter.

"That isn't the right shade!" I said.

"No, not exactly," she answered, "but it's much prettier than your sample."

"Yes, I agree with you," I said, "but I want to match this piece of cloth."

The girl made no answer; she took down another roll.

"That's the shade," she said.

"Yes," I replied, "but it's striped."

"Striped calico is worn more than any other kind of calico," she said.

"Maybe so; but this is not for a dress. It's for furniture. Anyway, I want some perfectly plain cloth which will match this piece."

"Well, I don't think you will find it perfectly plain, unless you get Turkey red." [3]

"What's Turkey red?" I asked.

"Turkey red is perfectly plain," she answered.

"Well, show me some Turkey red."

"We don't have any. But I can show you some plain calico in other colors."

"I don't want any other color. I want some calico to match this."

"It's hard to match cheap calico like that," she said. So I left her.

---

2 huge, very large
3 Turkey red, a bright red color

NEXT I went to a store farther down the street. When I entered I handed my sample to the first salesman in sight and asked:

"Do you have any calico like this?"

"Yes, sir," he replied. "Third counter to your right."

I went to the third counter and showed my sample to the salesman there. He looked at it on both sides. Then he said:

"We don't have this kind of calico. You'll have to get it from an upholsterer." [4]

I went across the street to an upholsterer's shop.

"Do you have any cloth like this?" I asked a salesman.

"No, we don't," he said. "Is it for furniture?"

"Yes," I replied.

"Then Turkey red is what you want."

"Is Turkey red just like this?" I asked.

"No," he said, "but it's much better."

"I don't care if it *is* better. I want some calico just like this."

"But they don't use that kind for furniture."

"Can't people use whatever they want for furniture?"

"They can, but they don't. They don't use red like that. They use Turkey red."

I said no more; I left. The next place I visited was the largest department store in town. I asked the first salesman I saw if the store had any red calico like my sample.

"You'll find that on the second floor," he said.

I went upstairs and asked a man there:

"Where will I find some red calico?"

"In that far room on your left. Over that way." And he pointed to a distant doorway.

I walked through the crowd of shoppers [5] and salespeople and around the counters and tables covered with merchandise [6] to the far room on the left. I asked for red calico.

---

[4] **upholsterer,** one who provides padding, springs, cushions, coverings, etc. for furniture, especially for chairs and sofas

[5] **shoppers,** customers

[6] **merchandise,** articles for sale

"The second counter down this side," I was told.

I went there and produced my sample.

"Calicoes are downstairs," said the salesman.

"They told me downstairs that calicoes were on this floor," I said.

"Not the plain ones. You'll find that kind downstairs at the back of the store."

I went downstairs to the back of the store.

"Where will I find red calico like this?" I asked.

"At the next counter," said the man I had spoken to and he walked with me in the direction of the next counter.

"Mr. Dunn," he said, "show this gentleman some red calico."

Mr. Dunn took my sample and looked at it.

"We don't have this shade in the same quality of goods,"[7] he said.

"Well, do you have the same shade in any quality of calico?" I asked.

"I think we have it in heavier goods."

He took down a piece of calico and unrolled a couple of[8] yards of it on the counter.

"That's not the right shade," I said.

"No," he replied, "the cloth is thicker and the color's better."

"But I want some calico to match this," I said.

"Oh, I didn't understand. I thought you were interested in a better quality of calico. If you want that quality of goods, you ought to get Turkey red."

I did not think it was necessary to answer this remark; I said:

"Then you have nothing to match this?"

"No, sir. But perhaps they will have it in the upholstery department on the sixth floor."

So I took the elevator[9] and went to the sixth floor.

"Do you have any red stuff like this?" I asked a young man.

"Red stuff? Upholstery department—straight ahead."

---

[7] goods, cloth

[8] couple of, two

[9] elevator, a machine that carries people up and down to different floors in a building

I walked ahead to the upholstery department.

"I want some red calico," I said to a salesman.

"Furniture goods?" he asked.

"Yes," I said.

"Fourth counter on the left."

I went to the fourth counter and showed my sample to a salesman. He looked at it and said:

"You can get this down on the first floor—calico department."

I turned, went down on the elevator, and out to the street. I was thoroughly sick of [10] red calico. I decided to try once more. My wife had bought her red calico not long before; surely it was possible to buy some more somewhere. I should have asked her where she bought it, but I had thought it would be a simple matter to buy the same kind of calico almost anywhere.

I went to another department store and presented my sample to a young salesman with the usual question.

"Back room—counter just inside the door."

I went there.

"Do you have any red calico like this?" I asked the woman behind the counter.

"No, sir," she answered, "but we have Turkey red."

Turkey red again!

"All right," I said, "give me some Turkey red."

"How much, sir?" she asked.

"I don't know. About five yards, I suppose."

The woman looked at me rather strangely, but she measured five yards of Turkey red calico and cut it. She wrote the number of yards, the name of the goods, her own number, the price, the amount of money I handed her, and some other matters on a piece of paper. Then she copied all this information in a little book she had with her. She said:

"Wait here. I'll bring your change."

After a very long time the woman returned bringing my change and the package of Turkey red calico.

Very little time remained for anything else that afternoon.

---

[10] **sick of,** tired of thinking about

When I reached home, I handed the package of calico to my wife. She unrolled it and said in protest: [11]

"This doesn't match the piece I gave you."

"Match it!" I replied. "You didn't want me to match that piece. You were mistaken. What you wanted was Turkey red—third counter to the left. Turkey red is what everybody uses now."

My wife looked at me in amazement,[12] and then I told her all about my difficulties.

"Well," she said, "this Turkey red is much prettier than the calico I had; since you bought so much of this, I don't need to use the other at all. I wish I had thought of Turkey red in the first place."

"I certainly wish you had," I replied.

EXERCISES

A. Put a check mark (√) in front of the item (a, b, or c) which best completes each unfinished sentence.

1. Before the author left for town, his wife handed him—
.... a. an umbrella.
.... b. a piece of cloth.
.... c. a letter.

2. The calico she wanted was for—
.... a. furniture.
.... b. a dress.
.... c. curtains.

3. In town, the author went to—
.... a. one store.
.... b. two stores.
.... c. more than two stores.

4. The salespeople he talked with were—
.... a. all women.
.... b. both men and women.
.... c. all men.

---

[11] **protest,** disapproval; objection
[12] **amazement,** astonishment; surprise

5. The sample he wanted to match was—
.... a. striped.
.... b. Turkey red.
.... c. plain.

6. Two salespeople in this story were called—
.... a. Mr. Smith and Miss Jones.
.... b. Mr. Dunn and Miss Stone.
.... c. Miss Dunn and Mr. Stone.

7. The author's wife had bought her calico—
.... a. only a short time before.
.... b. ten years before.
.... c. twenty years before.

8. Since the author was unable to find any calico to match his
sample, he decided to buy—
.... a. another color.
.... b. Turkey red.
.... c. white.

9. He brought home—
.... a. ten yards of calico.
.... b. two yards of calico.
.... c. five yards of calico.

10. When his wife saw the goods he had bought, she said:
.... a. "This calico is beautiful."
.... b. "This matches the sample exactly."
.... c. "This doesn't match the piece I gave you."

B. Write T for *True* in front of each sentence below which is
true according to the story. Write F for *False* in front of the sentence if it is not true.

.... 1. The author went into town by train.

.... 2. He never showed anyone the piece of calico that he carried
in his pocket.

.... 3. According to one saleswoman, Turkey red calico is perfectly plain.

.... 4. A salesman at the upholsterer's shop said that people only
use Turkey red calico for furniture.

.... 5. The author finally found some red calico to match his
sample.

.... 6. One saleswoman said the sample he had was cheap calico.

.... 7. When the author went to the sixth floor of a department store, he took the elevator.

.... 8. Once he referred to his sample as *red stuff*.

.... 9. The author's occupation was mentioned in this story.

.... 10. When the author bought the calico, the saleswoman made no record of the sale.

C. Put a check mark (√) in front of the meaning (a, b, or c) which best fits the numbered word or phrase.

1. **Turkey red:**
    .... a. the color of a white turkey
    .... b. a shade of red
    .... c. the color of all calico

2. **calico:**
    .... a. cotton cloth
    .... b. woolen cloth
    .... c. linen cloth

3. **huge:**
    .... a. very large
    .... b. perfectly plain
    .... c. cheap

4. **goods:**
    .... a. cloth
    .... b. counters
    .... c. departments

5. **shoppers:**
    .... a. furniture
    .... b. customers
    .... c. rolls

6. **couple of:**
    .... a. one
    .... b. two
    .... c. a hundred

7. **amazement:**
    .... a. dissatisfaction
    .... b. encouragement
    .... c. astonishment

8. **protest:**
    .... a. disapproval; objection
    .... b. difficulty; trouble
    .... c. strangeness; peculiarity

9. **sick of:**
    .... a. very happy about
    .... b. thicker than calico
    .... c. tired of thinking about

10. **merchandise:**   .... a. articles for sale
                        .... b. a small stairway
                        .... c. salespeople

This lesson is to be followed by Chapter 20 of Part II, p. 322: "Adverbs and Adjectives: Differences in Patterning."

SELECTION 21

THE HEADLESS HORSEMAN

Washington Irving

PART 1

On the eastern shore of the Hudson River there is a small market town which by some is called Greenburg. It is more generally known, however, as Tarry Town. This name was given to it in former days by the good housewives of the neighboring country, because their husbands liked to tarry [1] about the village inn on market days. Not far from this village, perhaps two miles, there is a little valley among high hills, which is one of the quietest

---

[1] **tarry**, pass the time

places in the whole world. A small stream passes through it almost noiselessly, and an occasional whistle from a bird is almost the only sound that is heard in the entire valley.

I remember that, as a young fellow, my first attempt at squirrel-shooting was in a group of tall trees that shades one side of the valley. I had wandered there one day about noontime, when all nature is peculiarly quiet, and was surprised by the roar of my own gun as it broke the stillness around. If I ever want a quiet resting-place to escape from the world and its problems, I know of none more promising than this little valley. Because of the peacefulness of the place and the peculiar character of its people who are descendants of the original Dutch settlers, this valley has long been known as SLEEPY HOLLOW, and its young men are called the Sleepy Hollow Boys throughout all the surrounding countryside. A kind of dreamy influence seems to hang over the land. Some say that the place was bewitched [2] by a German doctor during the early days of the settlement. Others say that an old Indian [3] chief bewitched the valley before the country was discovered by Hendrick Hudson. Some witching power [4] still has an effect on the minds of the inhabitants there. They have all kinds of mysterious beliefs, they see strange sights and hear music and voices in the air, and they tell of haunted places [5] throughout the valley.

Indian

The main spirit, however, that haunts the valley is a figure with no head, riding a horse. It is said to be the ghost of a Hessian soldier, whose head was shot off in some nameless battle during the Revolutionary War,[6] and who is now and then seen by the local people hurrying along in the night, moving as fast as the wind.

2 **bewitch**, use an evil power over a person or place
3 **Indian**, a native inhabitant of America (see picture)
4 **witching power**, mysterious evil power over people
5 **haunted places**, places visited or inhabited by spirits
6 **Revolutionary War**, the War of Independence

His appearance is not limited to the valley, but extends at times to other roads of the countryside, and especially to the neighborhood of the church. Certain historians of those parts, who have been careful in collecting floating facts concerning this spirit, say the body of the soldier was buried in the churchyard,[7] and the ghost rides forth nightly to the scene of battle looking for his head. They say the reason for the speed with which he sometimes passes along the Hollow is that he is late and in a hurry to return to the churchyard before daylight.

This belief has supplied material for many wild stories in that valley of shadows, and the ghost is known by the name of the Headless Horseman of Sleepy Hollow.

The effect of the witching power is not limited to the natives of the valley; everyone who lives there for a time is subject to this same strange power. Although they may have been wide awake before they entered Sleepy Hollow, they are sure, in a little time, to feel the witching influence in the air, and to begin to imagine things and to see things.

I mention this peaceful spot with all possible praise; for it is in such little valleys found here and there in the great state of New York that population, manners, and customs remain unchanged. The movements of masses of people and improvements, which make continuous changes in other parts of this restless country, pass by them unobserved. These valleys are like little bodies of still water at the edge of a rapid stream, undisturbed by the passing current. It was long ago that I walked through Sleepy Hollow, but I suppose that nothing in that valley has changed—the same trees and the same families are there as always.

At some time in the past history of America, there lived in this valley a worthy man by the name of Ichabod Crane, who taught the children of that neighborhood. He was a native of Connecticut, a state which at that time supplied the country

---

[7] It was the custom of the time to bury the dead near the church. The churchyard in this story was probably the burial ground for the surrounding country.

with pioneers [8] and schoolmasters. The name of Crane [9] applied to some extent to his appearance. He was tall and thin, with narrow shoulders, long arms and legs, and large flat feet. His head was small, and flat on top, with big ears, large green eyes, and a long nose like the beak of a bird.

crane

His schoolhouse was a low building made of logs, having only one room. It stood in a rather lonely but pleasant location, just at the foot of a wooded hill, with a stream running close by. From there the sound of pupils' voices could be heard while learning their lessons on a lazy summer's day, interrupted now and then by the voice of the master, in a tone of threat and command. He thoroughly believed in that famous rule expressed in a few words, "Spare the rod and spoil the child." [10] Ichabod Crane's pupils certainly were not spoiled.

You should not imagine, however, that he was one of those cruel masters who take pleasure in punishing their pupils. He carefully distinguished between right and wrong. He considered discipline [11] as "doing his duty," and he never punished a pupil without telling him that "he would remember it and someday thank him for it."

When school hours were over, he was even the companion and playmate of the larger boys. On holiday afternoons he would take some of the smaller ones to their homes—those that happened to have pretty sisters or mothers noted for the good food they prepared. It was important for him to be friends with all his pupils. The pay he received as schoolmaster was small and would hardly have been enough to supply him with food, for he was a big eater. According to custom in those parts, teachers lived and

8 **pioneers**, the first settlers of the West (in the United States)
9 **crane**, a large bird with long legs, neck, and beak (see picture)
10 Spare the rod and spoil the child. If a child is not punished when he misbehaves, he will not learn to behave properly.
11 **discipline**, punishment for misbehavior

were provided meals in the houses of the farmers whose children they taught. He stayed for a week at a time with one family; then he would move to the house of another family, carrying his possessions tied up in a cotton handkerchief.

He helped the farmers occasionally in the lighter work of their farms; he took the horses to water, repaired fences, and cut wood for the winter fire. The mothers all liked him, for he showed special kindness to the children, particularly the youngest; he would sit with a child on one knee and rock a cradle [12] with his foot, sometimes for hours.

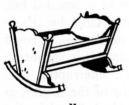

cradle

In addition to other things, he was the singing master of the neighborhood and earned some money by teaching church music to the young people. Every Sunday he proudly stood in front of a group of chosen singers in church and led them in their songs. His own voice sounded far above all the rest, and it is said that echoes of his thin shaky notes could be heard as far as the old mill, half a mile away.

And so in these ways Ichabod Crane managed to live well enough and was thought, by all who understood nothing of "headwork," to have a very easy life.

The schoolmaster was generally a man of some importance among the women of a country neighborhood. He was considered a kind of idle gentleman having much finer tastes and skills than the rough country fellows and second in learning only to the minister of the church. His appearance, therefore, usually caused some little excitement at the tea table of a farmhouse, and extra dishes of cake and a silver teapot were often set out. Our Ichabod, therefore, delighted in the smiles of the country ladies. On Sundays he was often seen standing among them in the churchyard, gathering flowers for them, reading for their amusement all the words written on the gravestones, or walking with

---

[12] **cradle,** a bed with rockers for a small baby (see picture)

a number of them along the banks of a nearby stream, while the country men stood to one side envying his fine manners and speech.

Because he traveled around a good deal he was also a kind of newspaper, carrying local gossip from house to house, so that people were always glad to see him. The women considered him a man of great learning, for he had read several books on the history of witchcraft,[13] in which, by the way, he firmly believed.

He was, in fact, a strange mixture of small wisdom and a simple willingness to believe. His powers of discovering and remembering unusual facts about witchcraft were extraordinary, and they were probably increased by living in this bewitched neighborhood. No story was too impossible or too foolish for him to believe. One of his frequent pleasures, after school was dismissed in the afternoon, was to stretch out on the thick grass near the little stream that ran by the side of his schoolhouse. As he lay there, he read and thought about all the strange and fearful stories in his books about witchcraft, until the darkness of evening made the pages fade before his eyes. Then, as he walked over the muddy ground, along streams, and through the stillness of the woods to the farmhouse where he happened to be staying, every sound of nature at that hour excited his imagination—the calls and cries of birds from the trees and their sudden movements in the bushes as he passed. Shining insects frightened him as they flew before his eyes, and if, by chance, a large fly brushed against him, the poor man was certain that a witch [14] had struck him. At such times, either to hide his thoughts or to drive away evil spirits, he always sang church songs. And so the good people of Sleepy Hollow, as they sat by their doors in the evening, could hear his trembling voice floating from the distant hill or along the dark road.

Another of his fearful pleasures was to pass long winter evenings with the old Dutch wives as they sat spinning by the fire. He listened to their strange stories of ghosts, and haunted fields,

---

[13] witchcraft, the art or practice of using evil spirits
[14] witch, a woman with power to control and make use of evil spirits

and haunted streams, and haunted bridges, and haunted houses, and particularly of the headless horseman. He delighted them equally with his stories of witchcraft and the terrible sights and sounds in the air which had been observed by early inhabitants of the state of Connecticut. He frightened them with the unbelievable fact that the earth made a complete turn every day and that half the time all the people were upside down.

Although the schoolmaster enjoyed sitting safely in a comfortable corner of the room lighted by a shining wood fire where, of course, no ghost dared to show its face, his walk home later was no pleasure for him at all. Fearful shapes and shadows appeared near his path in the darkness of a snowy night. With an envious eye he looked across the empty fields at every light from some distant window. Often he trembled at the sight of a bush covered with snow; its appearance was so ghostlike. Often too the sound of his own steps on the frozen surface of the snow made him fear that some strange being was following close behind him. And sometimes the sound of the wind painted a picture in his mind of the headless horseman on one of his nightly rides.

All these, of course, were only night time fears, mysterious creatures of the mind that walk in darkness; daytime always put an end to such evils. In spite of the devil and all his works, Ichabod was a reasonably happy soul and expected to remain so, but a woman crossed his path—a being that causes more trouble than all kinds of ghosts and witches in the world.

EXERCISES

A. Put a check mark (√) in front of the item (a, b, or c) which best completes each unfinished sentence.

    1. Sleepy Hollow is a valley in the state of—
       .... a. Connecticut.
       .... b. New York.
       .... c. Pennsylvania.

    2. The Headless Horseman, according to the story,—
       .... a. is an Indian chief.
       .... b. is a Dutch settler.
       .... c. is a ghost.

3. Ichabod Crane's schoolhouse had—
.... a. one room.
.... b. two rooms.
.... c. several rooms.

4. According to custom, the schoolteacher lived—
.... a. with the families of the neighborhood.
.... b. in the Tarry Town inn.
.... c. with the pioneers of the West.

5. The women in Sleepy Hollow considered Ichabod—
.... a. a rough country fellow.
.... b. a useless member of society.
.... c. a kind of idle gentleman.

6. The country men envied Ichabod's—
.... a. great wealth.
.... b. fine manners and speech.
.... c. singing voice.

7. Ichabod had read several books on—
.... a. witchcraft.
.... b. the history of New York.
.... c. the Revolutionary War.

8. Walking home from his schoolhouse in the evening, Ichabod often—
.... a. whistled popular tunes.
.... b. pretended to be a witch.
.... c. sang church songs.

9. One of the schoolmaster's pleasures was listening to stories of—
.... a. Hendrick Hudson.
.... b. ghosts and haunted places.
.... c. market towns.

10. When Ichabod moved from one house to another he carried his possessions in a—
.... a. handkerchief.
.... b. suitcase.
.... c. bag.

B. Write T for *True* in front of each sentence below which is true according to the story. Write F for *False* in front of the sentence if it is not true.

.... 1. According to the inhabitants of Sleepy Hollow there are many haunted places in the valley.

.... 2. Sleepy Hollow is not far from Tarry Town.

.... 3. Ichabod Crane was the minister of the church.

.... 4. The teacher never went home with his pupils.

.... 5. Besides being a schoolmaster, Ichabod was also the singing master of the neighborhood.

.... 6. Ichabod knew nothing about local gossip.

.... 7. The schoolmaster was popular with the country ladies.

.... 8. The people of Sleepy Hollow were not interested in Ichabod's stories of witchcraft.

.... 9. The author of this story praises Sleepy Hollow.

.... 10. The author probably does not believe in evil spirits.

C. Put a check mark (√) in front of the meaning (a, b, or c) which best fits the numbered word or phrase.

1. **cradle:**
    .... a. spirit
    .... b. pupil
    .... c. bed

2. **Indian:**
    .... a. Dutch settler in the Catskills
    .... b. native inhabitant of America
    .... c. shining insect of the forest

3. **discipline:**
    .... a. evil thought
    .... b. punishment for misbehavior
    .... c. bank of a stream

4. **tarry:**
    .... a. pass the time
    .... b. remember unusual facts
    .... c. carry local gossip

5. **echoes:**
    .... a. extra dishes of cake
    .... b. busy neighbors
    .... c. repetitions of sounds

6. **crane:**
    .... a. a kind of bird
    .... b. a kind of farm animal
    .... c. a kind of plant

7. **bewitch:**
    .... a. amuse by funny stories
    .... b. use an evil power
    .... c. change by the movement of people

8. **pioneers:**   .... a. valleys and mountains
                       .... b. people living on the Atlantic coast
                       .... c. first settlers of the West

9. **witchcraft:**   .... a. art and practice of using evil spirits
                       .... b. place where evil spirits live
                       .... c. one who controls evil spirits

10. **Revolutionary
    War:**   .... a. War between the states
                       .... b. War of Independence
                       .... c. World War II

This lesson is to be followed by Chapter 21 of Part II, p. 327: "Adverbs with Underlying Adjective and Noun Forms."

THE HEADLESS
HORSEMAN

PART 2

Among the young people who came together one evening a
week to receive music lessons from the schoolmaster was Katrina
Van Tassel, the daughter and only child of a wealthy Dutch
farmer. She was an attractive girl of eighteen and well known
not only for her beauty but also for her great expectations. She
enjoyed the attention and admiration of the young men of the
neighborhood. She wore a tempting mixture of ancient and modern fashions—gold ornaments brought from Holland by members of her family many years before and skirts short enough to
show the prettiest foot in the whole countryside.

Ichabod Crane had a soft and foolish heart toward women,
and it is no wonder that a young lady with many charms attracted him as well as the others, especially after he had visited
her at her father's fine home. Old Baltus Van Tassel was a
successful, contented, and generous farmer. He seldom thought
about matters beyond the boundaries of his own farm, but within
those boundaries everything was comfortable, happy, and in
good order. He was satisfied with his wealth, but not proud of
it; he cared more about having plenty of everything than the
manner in which he lived. His land stretched along the banks of

the Hudson River, in one of those rich, green, sheltered valleys where the Dutch farmers settled in the early days. Big old trees spread their branches over it, and there was a spring with the coolest and best-tasting water you can find anywhere. The barn,[1] not far from the farmhouse, was filled and overflowing with the treasures of the farm. Rows of pigeons, some with their heads under their wings, and others swelling and bowing, sat on the roof enjoying the sunshine. Fat awkward pigs made low contented noises as they ate their plentiful supply of food and rested in the shade; snowy geese[2] and ducks swam in a nearby pool; chickens and turkeys[3] happily dined on the good things which they found in the farmyard.

The schoolmaster looked with hungry eyes at this fine promise of food for the winter. As he rolled his green eyes over the land, the rich fields, and the orchards heavy with ripe fruit, which surrounded the Van Tassel home, his heart longed for the young lady who would some day own them.

The Van Tassels had one of those large farmhouses with a high roof that sloped at the sides almost to the ground; the roof at the front covered a wide porch[4] which was open in the summer and closed in the winter. Here farm tools and fishing nets were kept. Seats were built along the sides, and a large spinning wheel[5] at one end and a churn[6] at the other end showed the many uses of this important porch. The hall, which formed the center of the big house, was the place where the family usually gathered. Here rows of shining cups and bowls stood on a long shelf. In one corner there was a large bag of wool

spinning wheel

---

1 barn, a building used for storing things on a farm, especially grain and other food for farm animals
2 goose, plural geese, a large water-bird
3 turkey, a large domesticated bird
4 porch, a raised floor built outside the front or back door of a house
5 spinning wheel, a household machine for spinning thread (see picture)
6 churn, a vessel used for making butter (see picture)

ready for the spinning wheel; in another a bundle of
cloth already woven; ears of corn and strings of dried
apples hung along the walls. Through an open door
it was possible to see the best room of the house, with
its beautiful chairs and tables of fine dark wood. The
tools at the fireplace were brightly polished, and shells
and flowers ornamented the mantel.[7] A corner cupboard, purposely left open, showed immense treasures
of old silver and well-preserved china.

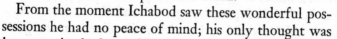

churn

From the moment Ichabod saw these wonderful possessions he had no peace of mind; his only thought was
how to win the love of Van Tassel's daughter. In this, however,
he had more real difficulties than the daring young man of old,

fireplace and
mantel

who usually had only to overcome giants [8]
and all kinds of fierce animals and crash
through gates of iron and over thick walls
into the castle where his ladylove was
held prisoner. Then, of course, the lady
gladly became his wife. Ichabod, on the
other hand, had to win the heart of a gay
country beauty who had many desires
and ideas, which kept presenting new
difficulties. Also, he had to meet a great number of rivals, the
country youths who always surrounded her, watching each
other, and ready to join battle against a new person showing
interest in the fair Katrina.

The rival offering the most competition was a big, happy
fellow with a loud voice named Abraham (shortened by the
Dutch people to "Brom") Van Brunt, a kind of hero of the
neighboring country because of his unusual strength and skill
in races and fights. He had broad shoulders, short curly black
hair, and a rough but pleasant face. The people of the neighborhood had given him the nickname [9] "Brom Bones" because

---

[7] **mantel**, a shelf above the fireplace (see picture)
[8] **giants**, very large, powerful people
[9] **nickname**, a name used instead of a person's real name

he had such a large frame and powerful arms and legs, as hard as bones. His knowledge and skill in horsemanship was well known to everyone, and he was always out in front at every race. Bodily strength gave Brom a great deal of importance in local affairs. He was the judge in all quarrels, and his decision allowed no disagreement or further discussion. He was always ready for either a fight or a good time, but fun and laughter interested him most, in spite of his roughness. He had three or four companions who regarded him as their model. As their leader he traveled around looking for whatever trouble or gaiety he could find. In cold weather he was distinguished by a fur cap with the bushy tail of an animal on top. When the people at a gathering saw this well-known head ornament at a distance, floating around among a group of riders, they always expected excitement. Sometimes he and his companions would rush along past the farmhouses at midnight with loud shouts and cries, and old ladies, waked from their sleep, would listen for a moment until all the noise had passed and then declare, "There goes Brom Bones and his followers!" The neighbors looked upon him with a mixture of respect, admiration, and friendliness; and when any tricks or disturbances took place, they always shook their heads and decided that Brom Bones was the cause of them.

This noisy fellow had chosen Katrina to receive his attention; although his attention was something like the gentle touch of a bear,[10] the neighbors believed that she did not altogether dislike him. It is certain that his interest in her was a signal for his rivals to retire; they, of course, had no desire to interfere with the loves of a lion.[11] So when his horse was tied to Van Tassel's gate on a Sunday night, a sure sign that Brom Bones was there to see Katrina, all other young men passed by without stopping.

bear

---

[10] **bear,** a large, heavy animal with rough hair (see picture)
[11] **lion,** a large, strong, flesh-eating animal (see picture)

Such was Ichabod's main rival. Braver men than Ichabod refused to compete; and wiser men dared not interfere. Ichabod, however, was not one to give up easily; he was yielding, but tough; though he bent, he never broke; and though he bowed beneath the slightest pressure, yet, the moment the pressure was lifted, he was straight again, and carried his head as high as ever.

lion

He was not foolish enough to battle openly with his rival, for real danger threatened anyone who opposed Brom Bones. Ichabod, therefore, showed his interest in a quiet and gentle manner. Under cover of his duty as singing teacher he made frequent visits to the farmhouse. Fortunately he did not have to worry about interfering parents, which sometimes block the path of young lovers. Balt Van Tassel was an easy-going [12] soul; he loved his daughter better even than his pipe, and, like a reasonable man and an excellent father, he always let her have her way. His good little wife, too, had enough to do attending to her housekeeping and managing the farmyard; as she wisely remarked, ducks and geese are foolish things and we must take care of them, but girls can take care of themselves. So while the busy woman was working around the house or using the spinning wheel at one end of the porch, Balt sat smoking his evening pipe at the other. In the meantime, Ichabod walked with Katrina by the spring under the trees, or the two of them wandered through the fields as the sun set—that time of day so favorable to lovers.

I do not claim to know how women's hearts are won. To me they have always been matters of mystery and admiration. Some seem to have only one weak point or door to their hearts; while others have a thousand avenues and may be captured in a thousand different ways. It takes great skill to gain the first, but still

---

[12] **easy-going soul,** a person who worries very little

greater skill to keep possession of the second, for the man must fight for his conquest at every door and window. He who wins a thousand ordinary hearts naturally becomes well known; but he who keeps complete mastery over the heart of a beautiful and popular girl is indeed a famous man. This was certainly not the case with Brom Bones; and from the moment Ichabod Crane came on the scene, Brom's chances seemed to change for the worse. His horse was no longer seen at Van Tassel's on Sunday nights, and a terrible rivalry gradually arose between Brom and the teacher of Sleepy Hollow.

Brom, who had a clear sense of fair play, would have preferred to carry on open warfare with his rival and settle their claims in the manner of the brave men of old times—by a man-to-man fight. Ichabod, however, knew the greater strength of his rival very well and dared not go into battle against him. He had heard that Brom Bones was going to "bend the schoolmaster double and lay him on a shelf in his own schoolhouse;" and he was too cautious to give Brom an opportunity. There was something extremely annoying in Ichabod's peaceful system; it left Brom no choice but to employ the tricks of his rough nature and play practical jokes on his rival. Brom and his companions continued to annoy Ichabod at every possible opportunity. They made trouble for him in all the usually peaceful places where he lived and worked. They smoked out his singing school by dropping things in the chimney; they went into the schoolhouse at night, in spite of the strong locks on the windows and door, and turned everything upside down; so that the poor schoolmaster began to think that all the witches in the country held their meetings there. But what was still more annoying, at every opportunity Brom made fun of him in the presence of Katrina, and he had taught a dog to howl [13] the moment her singing lessons began.

The rivalry continued in this way for some time without any noticeable change. Certainly there was no weakening on the part of either rival.

---

[13] **howl,** make a long, sad cry

EXERCISES

A. Put a check mark (√) in front of the item (a, b, or c) which best completes each unfinished sentence.

1. Katrina Van Tassel was the daughter of—
.... a. the schoolmaster.
.... b. Brom Bones.
.... c. a wealthy Dutch farmer.

2. The "treasures of the farm" in the barn probably means—
.... a. gold ornaments brought from Holland.
.... b. food for the family and the farm animals.
.... c. old silver and well-preserved china.

3. At the Van Tassel home, fishing nets were kept—
.... a. in a corner cupboard.
.... b. on the mantel.
.... c. on the porch

4. Brom Bones was well known for his unusual skill in—
.... a. racing and fighting.
.... b. singing and dancing.
.... c. using the spinning wheel.

5. Ichabod visited the Van Tassel farmhouse—
.... a. frequently.
.... b. rarely.
.... c. only once.

6. Katrina's mother said that—
.... a. girls should not interfere with their parents' wishes.
.... b. girls are like geese and ducks.
.... c. girls can take care of themselves.

7. Ichabod believed that Brom Bones—
.... a. was not as strong as Ichabod.
.... b. was stronger than Ichabod.
.... c. had about the same strength as Ichabod.

8. When Ichabod came on the scene, Brom's chances—
.... a. seemed to improve.
.... b. stayed about the same.
.... c. seemed to change for the worse.

9. In Katrina's presence, Brom often—
.... a. made fun of Ichabod.

.... b. fought with Ichabod.

.... c. threw things at Ichabod.

10. Brom said that he was going to—

.... a. kill the schoolmaster.

.... b. bend the schoolmaster double.

.... c. stop annoying the schoolmaster.

B. Write T for *True* in front of each sentence below which is true according to the story. Write F for *False* in front of the sentence if it is not true.

.... 1. Baltus Van Tassel was Katrina's uncle.

.... 2. Katrina was admired by the young men in the neighborhood.

.... 3. There were no turkeys on the Van Tassel farm.

.... 4. Ichabod wanted to win Katrina's love.

.... 5. The schoolmaster's main rival was Abraham Van Brunt.

.... 6. Ichabod battled openly with his rival.

.... 7. Katrina's mother and father were interfering parents.

.... 8. Brom and his companions annoyed Ichabod at every possible opportunity.

.... 9. When Ichabod went to visit Katrina, they stayed in the farmhouse.

.... 10. Ichabod was Brom's best friend.

C. Put a check mark (√) in front of the meaning (a, b, or c) which best fits the numbered word or phrase.

1. **orchards:**   .... a. fields of corn

.... b. fields of fruit trees

.... c. fields of grass

2. **barn:**   .... a. a kind of building

.... b. a kind of tree

.... c. a kind of wild animal

3. **giants:**   .... a. very large powerful people

.... b. ancient and modern fashions

.... c. fierce animals

4. **mantel:**   .... a. shelf in the cupboard

.... b. shelf above the bed

.... c. shelf above the fireplace

5. **nickname:**   .... a. name of Ichabod's singing school

.... b. name of something that blocks the path of young lovers

        .... c. name used instead of a person's real
        name

6. china:
    .... a. fur caps
    .... b. dishes
    .... c. signals

7. easy-going soul:
    .... a. person who worries about his family
    .... b. person who worries about money
    .... c. person who worries very little

8. bear:
    .... a. an animal
    .... b. a bird
    .... c. a building

9. captured:
    .... a. taken
    .... b. visited
    .... c. admired

10. porch:
    .... a. a raised floor outside the house
    .... b. a raised floor in the barn
    .... c. a raised floor inside the house

This lesson is to be followed by Chapter 22 of Part II, p. 332:
"How We Recognize Adverbs."

THE HEADLESS
HORSEMAN

PART 3

One fine autumn afternoon, the schoolmaster was sitting on a high seat where he could keep an eye on all parts of his busy little educational kingdom. The flat stick he held in his hand was the sign of complete power; a larger stick on the wall, resting on three nails, was the symbol [1] of justice—a threat to all evil-doers. A group of forbidden articles taken from the pupils lay on the desk in front of him—toy guns, pet animals in tiny cages, and a large number of paper birds. The pupils were busy with their books, and there was an unusual stillness all through the schoolroom. Suddenly this stillness was interrupted by the appearance of a Negro servant boy who arrived at the schoolhouse door bringing the schoolmaster an invitation to a party that evening at the Van Tassel farm. With a great feeling of importance and an effort at fine language he delivered the message; then he hurried away.

Now the quietness of the schoolroom changed to noise and speed. The master hurried the pupils through their lessons, without stopping to correct small mistakes. Those who were quick omitted half of their work without punishment, and those who

---

[1] symbol, a sign

were slow received a blow from the stick of justice to hurry
them on. No one took the trouble to put the schoolbooks away,
nor leave the schoolroom in neat order. The whole school was
dismissed an hour before the usual time, and the crowd of young
devils burst out of the room shouting and running about in their
joy over their early freedom.

Ichabod now spent at least an extra half hour getting dressed,
brushing his best and only suit of rusty black, and making his
appearance a little more respectable by looking at himself in a
piece of broken mirror that hung in the schoolhouse. He borrowed a horse from the farmer he was living with—a lively old
Dutchman named Hans Van Ripper; his arrival on horseback,
he felt, would be more fitting on this occasion. The noble animal
he was riding, however, was a worn-out workhorse noted for
nothing but his bad temper. He had a thin body, a short fat
neck, and a head like a hammer. The hair on his neck and tail
was dusty and full of knots. When younger he was probably a
high-spirited animal, for he had the name of Gunpowder. He
had once been Van Ripper's favorite horse; being a hard rider,
Van Ripper doubtless passed some of his own spirit on to the
animal, for that creature was more devilish than any other horse
in the country.

Ichabod was well suited to such an animal. He rode with his
knees high—nearly up to the top of the saddle. His arms stuck

grasshopper

out like the legs of a grasshopper,[2] and
as the horse moved his arms waved like
a pair of wings. A small woolen hat
rested on the top of his nose, and the
tails of his black coat floated in the air
and stretched almost to the horse's tail.
Such was the appearance of Ichabod and his horse as they hurried
toward the Van Tassel farm; it was a sight seldom met with in
the light of day.

It was, as I have said, a fine day in autumn; the sky was clear

---

[2] grasshopper, an insect with long back legs (see picture)

and peaceful, and nature wore the rich and golden colors which always remind me of harvest-time. The forests had put on their dark brown and yellow, while some of the younger trees already touched by the cold had turned to bright shades of orange, purple, and red. Groups of wild ducks began to appear high in the air; there were squirrels jumping about in the trees and birds in the neighboring fields enjoying their last feast before flying south for the winter.

As Ichabod rode slowly on his way, his eyes, always open to all signs of plentiful food, moved with delight over the treasures of joyful autumn. Everywhere he saw great quantities of apples; some still hanging on the trees; some gathered into baskets and barrels for the market; others heaped up in piles for the cider-press.[3] Then he passed fields full of yellow corn and pumpkins.[4]

Feeding his mind with many sweet thoughts he made his journey along the sides of the hills which look out upon the most beautiful scenery of the Hudson Valley. The sun was setting in the west, and the river waters lay still and shining, reflecting the long blue shadows of the distant mountains. A few orange clouds floated in the sky, without a breath of air to move them. The golden horizon was changing slowly to light green and from that to the deep blue of the sky. A boat in the distance moved slowly down the river with the tide, her sail hanging useless; and as the reflection of the sky shone on the still water, it seemed as if the boat was hanging in the air.

It was nearly evening when Ichabod reached the Van Tassel home, which was found filled with the best people of the surrounding countryside. Old farmers were dressed in home-made coats and trousers, blue stockings, big shoes—all the country fashions of that time. Their busy little wives wore close-fitting caps and dresses with long waists. Big strong girls seemed almost as old-fashioned as their mothers, but here and there a straw hat, a fine ribbon, or a white dress showed some influence from the city. The sons wore short square coats with large brass but-

---

[3] **cider-press,** an instrument or machine that presses the juice from apples
[4] **pumpkin,** a large yellow fruit which grows on the ground

tons and long thin hair pulled to the back of the head and tied like a tail.

Brom Bones was a hero of the scene. He had come to the party on his favorite horse, Daredevil, a creature, who, like himself, was full of daring and tricks. Brom said he preferred horses that were difficult to manage, for only a high-spirited horse was suited to a high-spirited rider.

Here I wish to describe the wonderful world that met the delighted eyes of the schoolmaster as he entered Van Tassel's great house. The many charms of the pretty young girls attracted him much less than the plentiful charms of a real Dutch country tea table, particularly during the harvest season. Plates were heaped high with cakes of every kind, many known only to the experienced Dutch housewives—sweet cakes, plain cakes, sticky cakes, fancy cakes—the whole family of cakes. And there was apple pie and pumpkin pie and peach [5] pie; slices of ham [6] and smoked beef; [7] dishes of preserved plums [8] and peaches and pears; boiled fish and roasted chicken. In the midst of all this, a motherly teapot sent up its clouds of steam.

Ichabod was a kind and thankful person. His heart became warmer as his stomach got fuller. Eating had the same effect on him as drinking has on many men. As his eyes circled the room, he thought again about the possibility of someday being lord of all this wealth. Then, he thought, he would leave his schoolhouse forever and laugh in the face of all the old Dutch farmers who provided him with the barest means of existence.

Old Baltus Van Tassel moved about among his guests in his usual good humor, his face as round and jolly [9] as the harvest moon. His greetings were short but sincere. He shook hands with a word of welcome to everyone and invited them to "make themselves at home."

---

[5] **peach,** a soft fruit with a rough stone
[6] **ham,** meat from the leg of a pig
[7] **beef,** meat from a cow
[8] **plum,** a fruit
[9] **jolly,** happy; merry

And now the sound of music from the hall urged everyone to dance. The musician was an old gray-haired Negro who had been a one-man music-maker of the neighborhood for more than half a century. His instrument was as old and worn as himself. Most of the time he scraped a bow [10] over two or three strings of the violin,[11] moving his head with every movement of the bow; and the regular beat of his foot on the floor helped make the music suitable for dancing.

violin

Ichabod was as proud of his dancing ability as his singing ability. Not a single part of his body was idle; and his loose frame in motion was a sight well worth watching. He was the admiration of all the Negroes, who stood at every door and window, gazing with delight at the dancing couples. The schoolmaster was overjoyed; the lady of his heart was his partner in the dance, smiling as they moved back and forth across the room. Brom Bones, filled with jealous envy, sat alone in one corner with an unhappy look on his face.

When the dancing stopped, Ichabod was attracted to a group of wise old fellows, who, with Van Tassel, sat smoking at one end of the porch. Their conversation was largely gossip about old times, and they took turns telling long stories about the war. At one time during the war the British and American line of battle had been near this neighborhood. So the older inhabitants were not unfamiliar with some of the main events and the names of great men in the war. Just enough time had passed that each person could dress up his story with extra details and make himself a hero. Most of those present felt that their own actions had been largely responsible for bringing the war to a happy end.

Then followed the stories of ghosts and witches. The people

---

[10] **bow**, a piece of wood with hairs stretched from one end to the other, used for playing the violin (see picture)
[11] **violin**, a musical instrument with four strings, played with a bow (see picture)

from Sleepy Hollow at the Van Tassel party had new information about the headless horseman who, according to them, tied his horse every night among the graves in the churchyard.

The situation of this churchyard seems to have made it a favorite meeting-place for all troubled spirits. It stood on a little hill almost hidden by trees and bushes. On one side of the church the land was heavily wooded and a stream wound in and out among broken rocks and the trunks of fallen trees. Someone had built a wooden bridge over the deep part of the stream, not far from the church; the road that led to the bridge, and the bridge itself, were thickly shaded by overhanging trees. In the fearful darkness of night at this lonely place the headless horseman often appeared, so they said. Old Brouwer told of meeting the horseman and riding behind him over hills and swamps until they reached the bridge; there the horseman turned into a skeleton,[12] threw old Brouwer into the stream, and rode away into the night.

Brom Bones' adventure with the headless horseman equaled Brouwer's. Returning one night from the neighboring village of Sing Sing, he was overtaken by this midnight wanderer; Brom offered to race him, and the horseman agreed. But as they came to the bridge, the horseman disappeared. Brom was disappointed for he was sure of winning the race; Daredevil was far ahead when both horse and rider disappeared.

All these stories sank deep into Ichabod's mind. He also told of frightening events that had taken place in his native state of Connecticut and listed the fearful things he had seen on his nightly walks in Sleepy Hollow.

EXERCISES

A. Put a check mark (√) in front of the item (a, b, or c) which best completes each unfinished sentence.

1. The schoolmaster received an invitation to a party at—
.... a. Hendrick Hudson's house.
.... b. the village inn.
.... c. the Van Tassel farm.

---

[12] **skeleton,** the bony frame of the body

2. The symbol of justice was—
.... a. the quietness of the schoolroom.
.... b. a stick.
.... c. a noble animal.

3. At this time the schoolmaster was living at the home of—
.... a. Hans Van Ripper.
.... b. Rip Van Winkle.
.... c. Abraham Van Brunt.

4. *Gunpowder* was the name of a—
.... a. grasshopper.
.... b. horse.
.... c. valley.

5. Ichabod wore a—
.... a. green suit and a big hat.
.... b. rusty brown suit and a small straw hat.
.... c. black suit and a small woolen hat.

6. When Ichabod reached the Van Tassel home, it was—
.... a. late in the evening.
.... b. early in the evening.
.... c. almost evening.

7. What attracted the schoolmaster most was—
.... a. the food.
.... b. the pretty girls.
.... c. the clothes the people wore.

8. The music for dancing was played by—
.... a. Daredevil.
.... b. an old gray-haired Negro.
.... c. Baltus Van Tassel.

9. When the dancing stopped, Ichabod joined—
.... a. the ladies in the kitchen.
.... b. a group of men at one end of the porch.
.... c. Katrina.

10. Two people told stories of the headless horseman:—
.... a. old Brouwer and Brom Bones.
.... b. old Brouwer and Van Tassel.
.... c. old Brouwer and Van Ripper.

B. Write T for *True* in front of each sentence below which is true according to the story. Write F for *False* in front of the sentence if it is not true.

.... 1. An invitation was delivered to the schoolmaster by Brom Bones.

.... 2. After the invitation was delivered, the school was dismissed an hour early.

.... 3. Ichabod used a piece of broken mirror to make his appearance a little more respectable.

.... 4. The horse Ichabod rode to the party was young and high-spirited.

.... 5. There was not much to eat at the party.

.... 6. Ichabod was proud of his dancing ability.

.... 7. While Ichabod was dancing, Brom Bones sat with Katrina in a corner.

.... 8. The musician at the party played the piano.

.... 9. Brom Bones said he had raced the headless horseman.

.... 10. The churchyard was situated on a little hill, almost hidden by trees and bushes.

C. Put a check mark (√) in front of the meaning (a, b, or c) which best fits the numbered word or phrase.

1. **peach:**
.... a. a kind of insect
.... b. a kind of fruit
.... c. a kind of meat

2. **jolly:**
.... a. worthy
.... b. happy
.... c. proud

3. **symbol:**
.... a. a place
.... b. a situation
.... c. a sign

4. **skeleton:**
.... a. charm of a Dutch tea table
.... b. square coat
.... c. bony frame of the body

5. **violin:**
.... a. something to make music with
.... b. something to shake hands with
.... c. something to cook with

6. **gazing:**
.... a. telling stories
.... b. eating grass
.... c. looking

7. **trousers:**
.... a. something to ride
.... b. something to wear
.... c. something to harvest

8. **ham:**
.... a. meat from a pig
.... b. meat from a cow
.... c. meat from a goat

9. **cider-press:**
.... a. instrument for pressing juice from pumpkins
.... b. instrument for pressing juice from apples
.... c. instrument for pressing juice from corn

10. **pumpkin:**
.... a. fruit which grows on trees
.... b. fruit which grows on the ground
.... c. fruit which grows on bushes

This lesson is to be followed by Chapter 23 of Part II, p. 336: "Other Word Groups."

THE HEADLESS
HORSEMAN

PART 4

The party came to an end. The old farmers gathered their families together and said good night. Some left in wagons and others on horseback. Ichabod stayed behind, according to the custom of country lovers, to spend a few minutes with Katrina. He was certain now that he was on the road to success. What happened while the two of them were together I do not know. Something certainly went wrong, for the schoolmaster left the house in a fit of anger. Oh, these women! These women! his expression seemed to say. Without looking to the right or left to notice the scene of great wealth he had thought about so often, he went to find his horse who was sleeping soundly, dreaming of mountains of corn and whole valleys of green grass.

It was about midnight when the unhappy Ichabod started his travel homeward, along the sides of the sloping hills which rise above Tarry Town. In the stillness of the night he could hear the barking of a watchdog from the opposite shore of the Hudson River. There were no signs of life near him, except the occasional noise of a cricket.[1]

---

[1] cricket, a small, brown insect that makes a noise by rubbing its wings together (see picture)

All the stories of ghosts he had heard during the evening came crowding into his mind. The night grew darker and darker; the stars sank deeper and deeper into the sky, and big clouds occasionally hid them from his sight. He had never felt so lonely before, and he knew that a haunted tree and a haunted stream were directly ahead of him. As he came near the tree he began to whistle; he thought for a moment that he heard an answer to his whistle but decided it was only the wind blowing against the tree and producing a whistling sound. Then he thought he saw something white hanging in the tree, but with a closer look

cricket

he discovered a place where lightning had struck the tree and had left the white wood bare. Then he thought he heard a groan; however, it was only the rubbing of one branch on another as the wind pushed them back and forth. He passed the tree safely, but new worries lay before him.

About two hundred yards from the tree a small stream crossed the road. A few logs, laid side by side, served as a bridge over the stream. Beyond the stream the road was overgrown with bushes and trees. To pass this bridge at night was a real test of bravery, because the road beyond it was the scene of many of the neighborhood ghost stories.

As he came near the stream, his heart beat quicker. He gave his horse several kicks in the ribs [2] hoping to pass quickly over the bridge; but instead of going forward, the horse went sideways and ran into a fence. Ichabod, whose fears increased with the delay, pulled and kicked. The horse started at last, but only to jump to the other side of the road. Now the schoolmaster began to use his whip and sank his toes into the horse's ribs. Old Gunpowder speedily went forward but before he reached the bridge he stopped suddenly and almost sent his rider over his head. Just at this moment Ichabod heard a noise in the bushes

---

[2] **ribs,** the curved bones along a horse's sides

near the bridge. In the shadow of the trees at the edge of the stream, he saw something big, tall, shapeless, black, and motionless.

The frightened schoolmaster's hair stood up straight. What was he going to do? It was too late to turn and run; and besides, if it was a ghost, how could he escape from it? He knew very well that ghosts can travel faster than human beings. Deciding to show some courage, he demanded—"Who are you?" He received no reply. He repeated the question in a louder voice. Still there was no answer. Once more he kicked Gunpowder's sides, and shutting his eyes, he began to sing a church song. Just then the shadowy object he feared started moving and was soon standing in the middle of the road. The night was dark, but now the object seemed to take on a distinguishable shape. It appeared to be an extra-large man riding an extra-large horse. The horseman stayed on one side of the road and said nothing; he just rode along in the same direction that Gunpowder was traveling.

Ichabod had no desire to become more familiar with this strange midnight companion. He thought again about Brom Bones' experience with the headless horseman. He decided to make Gunpowder go faster and perhaps leave the man behind, but as he did so, the stranger also made his horse speed up. Ichabod then slowed his horse to a walk,—the other did the same. As the two riders came to a hill, they started upward; this brought the figure of his fellow-traveler in relief against the sky. The hair on Ichabod's head stood up straight a second time as he saw that the figure was headless! He also observed that the head, instead of being on its shoulders, was carried at the front of the saddle. Ichabod showered Gunpowder with kicks and blows, hoping, by a sudden movement, to escape from his companion, but the figure stayed with him. They raced down the road with Gunpowder's feet moving at top speed.

Soon they reached the road which entered Sleepy Hollow. Gunpowder, instead of following the road, made an opposite turn and went downhill to the left, in the direction of the churchyard.

Because Gunpowder, as well as Ichabod, was terribly frightened, his speed had put them several yards ahead of the black figure; but with so much activity, the saddle was now becoming loose. In spite of his efforts to keep it on the horse, Ichabod suddenly felt it slip from under him. Ichabod managed to save himself from a fall, however, by holding on to the horse's neck. Being an unskilled rider and having lost his saddle, he slid from one side of the horse to the other and many times he almost fell.

An opening in the trees now cheered him with hopes that the church-bridge was not far away. He remembered that the bridge was where Brom Bones' ghostly companion had disappeared. "If I can only reach that bridge," Ichabod thought, "I'll be safe." Just then he could hear the breath of the black horse blowing close behind him; he even imagined he felt hot breath on his back. Another kick in the ribs and old Gunpowder jumped upon the bridge and quickly reached the other side. Then Ichabod looked back to see if the black figure was gone. As he turned, he saw the horseman in the act of throwing his head at Ichabod. He tried to move out of the way—but too late. It struck his own head with a crash,—he fell face forward into the dust.

The next morning Van Ripper found the horse without his saddle near the front gate to the house. Ichabod did not appear for breakfast;—dinner-time came, but no Ichabod. The boys were at the schoolhouse as usual, but no schoolmaster. Van Ripper now began to worry about Ichabod. The neighbors joined Van Ripper and made a search for the schoolmaster. In one part of the road leading to the church they found a saddle in the dirt. Deep horse tracks in the road were followed to the bridge. On the bank of the stream beyond the bridge they found poor Ichabod's hat and beside it a pumpkin broken to pieces. They searched the stream, but they did not discover the schoolmaster's body.

The mysterious event caused a good deal of talk at the church the following Sunday. Little groups gathered in the churchyard, at the bridge, and at the spot where the hat and pumpkin had been found. The stories of Brouwer, Brom Bones, and a whole list of others were called to mind; and when they had considered everything they decided the headless horseman had carried Ichabod away. Since he was not married and had no unpaid debts, nobody worried about where the unfortunate man had gone. The school was moved to a different part of Sleepy Hollow, and another schoolmaster came to replace Ichabod.

One old farmer, who had been down to New York on a visit several years later, brought back the news that Ichabod Crane was still alive. He reported that Ichabod had left the neighborhood partly on account of his fear of the headless horseman and partly on account of his disappointment in love; that he had moved to a distant part of the country, had been a schoolmaster again and studied law at the same time, had become a lawyer and politician, and later was made a court judge. Brom Bones, shortly after his rival's disappearance, married Katrina Van Tassel. He always looked very wise whenever someone told the story of Ichabod Crane, and he always laughed loud and long at the mention of the pumpkin. Some people suspected that Brom knew more about the matter than he chose to tell.

The old country wives, who are the best judges of these matters, believe that Ichabod was carried away by the headless horseman; and it is a favorite story often told in the neighborhood around the winter evening fire. The schoolhouse, being deserted, soon fell to decay and was reported to be haunted by the schoolmaster's ghost. Many a passerby on a summer evening has believed he could hear the voice of the schoolmaster singing a sad church song in the peaceful darkness of Sleepy Hollow.

EXERCISES

A. Put a check mark (√) in front of the item (a, b, or c) which best completes each unfinished sentence.

1. When the party was over, the people left in—
.... a. busses and cars.
.... b. wagons and on horseback.
.... c. wagons and on foot.

2. Ichabod started home about—
.... a. midnight.
.... b. two A. M.
.... c. 10 o'clock.

3. On his way home the schoolmaster had to pass a—
.... a. haunted house and a haunted field.
.... b. haunted barn and a haunted mountain.
.... c. haunted tree and a haunted stream.

4. At a small stream Ichabod was joined by—
.... a. Gunpowder and Daredevil.
.... b. Hans Van Ripper and old Brouwer.
.... c. someone riding a black horse.

5. Ichabod's midnight companion carried his head—
.... a. at the front of his saddle.
.... b. on his shoulders.
.... c. in a box.

6. After Ichabod crossed the bridge, the black horseman—
.... a. threw rocks at Ichabod.
.... b. threw his horse at Ichabod.
.... c. threw his head at Ichabod.

7. The next morning Ichabod—
.... a. went to the schoolhouse.
.... b. went to see Katrina.
.... c. did not appear.

8. Someone said the schoolmaster had become—
.... a. a court judge.
.... b. another headless horseman.
.... c. a doctor.

9. The old country wives believed that Ichabod—
.... a. was carried away by the headless horseman.
.... b. went elsewhere to conduct a singing school.
.... c. left because of his disappointment in love.

10. The person who threw the pumpkin at Ichabod was probably—

.... a. Hans Van Ripper.

.... b. Brom Bones.

.... c. Baltus Van Tassel.

B. Write T for *True* in front of each sentence below which is true according to the story. Write F for *False* in front of the sentence if it is not true.

.... 1. Something went wrong while Katrina and Ichabod were together.

.... 2. Ichabod was angry when he left the house.

.... 3. As Ichabod came near the haunted tree he began to whistle.

.... 4. The black figure that began to accompany Ichabod was headless.

.... 5. The black figure finally spoke to Ichabod.

.... 6. Ichabod thought he could escape from the black figure at the bridge.

.... 7. The next morning the schoolmaster appeared for breakfast as usual.

.... 8. Van Ripper and the neighbors went to look for Ichabod.

.... 9. Everybody worried about where the schoolmaster had gone.

.... 10. Another schoolmaster came to replace Ichabod.

C. Put a check mark (√) in front of the meaning (a, b, or c) which best fits the numbered word.

1. **cricket:**   .... a. a fruit

                      .... b. an insect

                      .... c. a valley

2. **wagon:**   .... a. a high-spirited horse

                      .... b. a cake

                      .... c. a vehicle

3. **ribs:**   .... a. curved bones

                      .... b. midnight companions

                      .... c. winter fires

4. **groan:**   .... a. make a deep sound

                      .... b. speak in a whisper

                      .... c. ride in the same direction

5. **beef:**   .... a. meat from a pig
                    .... b. meat from a deer
                    .... c. meat from a cow
6. **plum:**   .... a. a berry
                    .... b. a fruit
                    .... c. a teapot
7. **haunted:**   .... a. inhabited by spirits
                    .... b. limited in size
                    .... c. threatened with cruelty
8. **witch:**   .... a. woman who teaches church music
                    .... b. woman who controls evil spirits
                    .... c. woman who tarries at the village inn
9. **crane:**   .... a. a Dutch settler
                    .... b. a large bird
                    .... c. a pioneer
10. **lion:**   .... a. an animal
                    .... b. a wire
                    .... c. a building

This lesson is to be followed by Chapter 24 of Part II, p. 343: "Review and Conclusion."

Word Study

Subjects

Nouns
Verbs
Adjectives
Adverbs
Structure Words

PART II

Word Study

Nouns
Verbs
Adjectives
Adverbs
Structure Words

CHAPTER 1

Nouns and Verbs: Differences in Patterning

We can set up four large classes of words (or parts of speech) on the basis of their positions of occurrence in English sentence patterns: nouns, verbs, adjectives, and adverbs. A very high percentage of English words—possibly as high as 90 per cent—fall into one or more of these classes. Let us examine first some occurrences of nouns and verbs and see how the words of these two classes pattern in sentences.

Nouns

Nouns occur in patterns like

I saw a(n) _____.
He doesn't have any _____.
The _____ is interesting.
The _____(e)s are interesting.

Any word that will fit in one of these blanks is a noun. Words like **bench, animal, dish, water,** and **neighbors** occur as nouns because they fit in at least one of the blanks. The following are normal English sentences:

I saw a **bench.**
I saw an **animal.**
He doesn't have any **water.**
He doesn't have any **neighbors.**
The **bench** is interesting.
The **animals** are interesting.
The **dishes** are interesting.

On the other hand, words like **sit, happy,** and **usually** will not fit these patterns. These are not English sentences:

* I saw a **sit.**[1]

---

[1] Examples that are not English are marked with an asterisk (*). This means they would not be accepted as English by native speakers of the language.

* He doesn't have any **happy.**

* The **usually** is interesting.

Using these patterns alone, we could find thousands of English words which belong to the noun class. If we wanted to list all the nouns in the language, however, we would need additional patterns.

Take *proper nouns,* for example. Many proper nouns will fit the pattern "The _____ is/are interesting": [2]

The **Mississippi** is interesting.

The **Philippines** are interesting.

For certain other proper nouns, however, we would need a pattern like "_____ is/are interesting" (without **the**):

Arthur is interesting.

Californians are interesting.

This pattern, "_____ is/are interesting," will also give us many *pronouns,* which we shall consider a special sub-class of nouns (since they pattern very much like nouns) rather than a separate word class:

He is interesting.

They are interesting.

One important difference between pronouns and proper nouns is that we do not ordinarily begin conversations with pronouns but we often do with proper nouns. A conversation may occasionally begin with **I** or **you,** but any other pronoun in this position would be extremely rare. Actually, proper nouns and pronouns are only of minor interest to us here; we shall have more to say about them later. Right now we are concerned with the noun class as a whole rather than special groups of words within the class.

Our purpose, of course, is not to list all the nouns in English; this would be impossible. Rather, we are interested in being able to recognize nouns in English sentences, and we want to see some of the formal differences between nouns and other classes of words.

Verbs

Verbs occur in other patterns. We find one kind of verb in patterns like

---

[2] The diagonal line(/) means that one word or the other is appropriate, but not both words.

Let's _____.
Don't _____.

We find another kind of verb in patterns like

Let's _____ it.
Don't _____ it.

Many verbs fit both sets of patterns. Any word that will fit in one or more of these blanks is a verb. Words like **go, carry,** and **stop** occur as verbs. The following examples are normal English sentences:

Let's **go.**   Don't **go.**
Let's **carry** it.   Don't **carry** it.
Let's **stop.**   Don't **stop.**
Let's **stop** it.   Don't **stop** it.

Words like **newspaper, happy,** and **usually** will not fit these patterns. These are not English sentences:

* Don't **newspaper.**   * Don't **happy.**
* Let's **happy** it.   * Let's **usually** it.

Using these patterns alone, we could find hundreds of English words which belong to the verb class. However, in order to make a list of all verbs in the English language we would need some additional patterns.

For example, we would need patterns like "Rip _____ tired" and "They _____ good" for a small, but important, group of words called *linking verbs:*

Rip **is** tired.   They **taste** good.
Rip **became** tired.   They **smell** good.
Rip **looks** tired.   They **sounded** good.

The most common linking verbs are the forms of **be** (**am, is, are, was, were**), **become, seem, appear, look, sound, feel, taste, smell, grow,** and **remain.** We shall have more to say about linking verbs in later chapters.

We are not interested here in listing all the verbs in English any more than we are interested in listing all the nouns in English. But we do want to be able to recognize verbs, and we want to examine some of the formal differences between verbs and other classes of words.

Words Which Are Both Nouns and Verbs

Many words will fit both noun patterns and verb patterns. When they occur in noun positions they are nouns, and when they occur in verb positions they are verbs. Here are some examples:

He finished his **work** early.   (noun)

What hours do you **work?**   (verb)

Let's get a cold **drink.**   (noun)

Drink your coffee before you leave.   (verb)

EXERCISES

A. In each of the groups of words below, there are four nouns and one verb or four verbs and one noun. See if you can pick out the word which does not belong with the others. Remember that nouns will fit a pattern like "His _____ surprised us" or "They wanted some _____." Verbs will fit a pattern like "Let's _____" or "Let's _____ it."

1. disappear, colonists, settle, bring, receive.
2. government, neighbors, wife, difficulties, argue.
3. playthings, sit, games, dogs, country.
4. follow, obey, stillness, go, wear.
5. clothes, habit, rob, idleness, ears.
6. bread, men, business, birds, agree.
7. attention, enter, animal, courage, beard.
8. hear, see, continue, vessel, suggest.
9. descend, chief, discussion, newspaper, opinion.
10. tell, neighborhood, companion, noise, children.
11. listen, doors, read, encourage, avoid.
12. food, think, trees, expression, friends.

B. In the numbered sentences below, the words in heavy type pattern as nouns. See if you can make a sentence in which each of these words will pattern as a verb.

Example: His **work** was well done.

On the farm we **worked** from sunrise till dark.

1. Rip Van Winkle lived on a **farm.**
2. Thank you very much for your **help.**
3. The **rain** started a few minutes ago.

4. Let's sit down in the **shade.**
5. Did they have **fish** for dinner last night?
6. What you need is a good **drink.**
7. I like the **taste** of that coffee.
8. Rip's **visit** was a long one.
9. Nobody heard the **whistle.**
10. I'm not going to listen to his **demand.**

C. In the numbered sentences below, the words in heavy type pattern as verbs. See if you can make a sentence in which each of these words will pattern as a noun.

Example: You'll **fall** if you're not careful.
        Last night Rip had a bad **fall.**

1. I have to **sign** this check.
2. Let's **walk** to the hotel.
3. We shall **return** tomorrow afternoon.
4. You don't need to **hurry** now.
5. They **dress** as soon as they get up.
6. **Turn** right at the next corner.
7. Nicholas Vedder wanted to sit here and **smoke.**
8. Can you **stop** this bus?
9. Rip's actions were **controlled** by his wife.
10. He decided to **climb** the mountain.

CHAPTER 2

Words Which Pattern as Both Nouns and Verbs

Here are some lists of words which occur both as nouns and verbs. Look over these lists carefully, and be sure you know the meanings of all the words given. If necessary, consult a good dictionary. Also, be sure you can spell them all.

List 1

The words in this list pattern as nouns more frequently than as verbs. All of them can occur in the pattern "He remembered the _____." Try each word in this pattern and see if the meaning is clear to you. If any of the sentences formed are not clear, ask your teacher for an explanation of the meaning.

arrest	doubt	heat	ornament
attack	dream	honor	outline
bottle	dust	influence	place
brush	end	iron	plan
button	exchange	joke	plant
chain	experience	judge	plow
color	experiment	land	point
control	face	light	quarrel
copy	fan	load	question
cost	favor	map	race
crack	feast	milk	rain
crash	fence	mine	reason
crowd	fish	mistake	request
curve	flavor	nail	rest
damage	flood	notice	review
date	form	number	reward
delay	group	nurse	risk
demand	hammer	oil	rule
desire	hand	order	saddle

sample	slope	supply	trouble
search	snow	tax	water
shade	speed	test	work
ship	stamp	tip	
signal	step	trick	

List 2

The words in this list pattern as verbs more frequently than as nouns. Some of the words can occur in the pattern "Please don't _____," making normal English sentences:

> Please don't **answer.**
> Please don't **boast.**
> Please don't **call.**

The other words in the list can occur after "Please don't" but additional words are needed to make normal English sentences:

> Please don't **address the letter.**
> Please don't **blame us.**
> Please don't **lock the door.**

Try each word in the pattern "Please don't _____." If it does not fit, see if it will fit when you add some more words.

address	fall	paint	struggle
answer	finish	pause	surprise
bend	fold	play	swim
blame	guess	polish	talk
boast	help	pull	touch
burn	hurry	push	travel
call	increase	return	turn
cheer	jump	ride	twist
climb	kick	roll	visit
cover	kiss	rush	wait
cry	knock	scratch	walk
curl	laugh	shout	whisper
cut	lie	sound	whistle
dress	lock	stain	worry
drink	look	start	
drop	mark	stay	
escape	neglect	stop	

List 3

The words in this list pattern with about equal frequency as nouns and verbs. All the words can occur in these two patterns: "The _____ was unnoticed" and "The captain _____(e)d. . . ."
Examples are:

The **guard** was unnoticed.

The captain **guarded** the men.

Try each word in the first pattern, and see if the meaning of each sentence formed is clear to you. If not, ask your teacher for an explanation of the meaning. What do we call the words we use in this pattern? Then try each word in the second pattern. Here you notice that you must complete the sentence yourself. If you have any difficulty, ask your teacher to help you. Be sure you understand the meaning of each sentence after it has been completed correctly. What do we call the words we use in this pattern?

aim	dance	note	share
attempt	defeat	pile	sign
cause	exercise	pin	smile
change	fear	promise	smoke
comb	flash	pump	support
command	guard	regret	witness
cook	guide	reply	wound
cure	hope	report	wreck
curse	limit	roar	

EXERCISES

A. Some of the words in the list below occur both as nouns and verbs; for example, the word **face** in "His **face** is dirty" and "The speaker has to **face** the audience." Other words in the list occur only as nouns or only as verbs. Decide which ones occur as nouns only, as verbs only, or as both.

accept	forbid	caution	wish
face	decay	nature	village
accident	bite	puzzle	period
fight	lesson	rescue	bark
street	heart	hour	opinion
wave	recommend	satisfy	

B. Look at List 1 again. Select one of the words from the list and make a sentence in which it patterns as a verb. Then see if you can find ten other words on the list which you can substitute for the one you selected. Take **arrest**, for example. You can make a sentence like "They didn't **arrest** him." And for **arrest**, you can substitute various words from the list:

> They didn't arrest him.
>> attack
>> delay
>> face
>> honor
>> notice
>> question
>> reward
>> signal
>> test
>> trouble

C. Now look at List 2 again. Select one word from the list and make a sentence in which it patterns as a noun. Then see if you can substitute ten other words from the list for the one selected. Take **cover**, for example:

> He didn't see the cover.
>> cut.
>> dress.
>> drink.
>> escape.
>> kick.
>> lock.
>> paint.
>> roll.
>> scratch.
>> struggle.

CHAPTER 3

Noun and Verb Suffixes

Derivational Suffixes

If we compare words that occur in noun positions with those that occur in verb positions, we can find differences of word form in most instances. In the two lists below we see that the nouns and verbs are similar, the main difference being one of length.

VERBS	NOUNS
govern	government
agree	agreement
argue	argument
settle	settler
settle	settlement
attend	attention
express	expression
discuss	discussion

The nouns seem to consist of the verb form with something extra at the end. We call this "something extra" a *suffix*. The suffixes in the noun list above are **-ment, -er,** and **-ion.** Suffixes such as these, which mark a difference in word class, are called *derivational suffixes.* (They mark the difference here between noun and verb.) Not all derivational suffixes separate word classes in this way, but most of them do. The term *derivational* suffix suggests *derivation:* that we *derive* some words from others by means of a suffix. We derive the nouns **government** and **argument,** for example, by adding the suffix **-ment** to the verbs **govern** and **argue** respectively. Because of such formal differences between word classes, a study of derivation is an important part of English word study. We shall have more to say about derivation in later chapters.

Inflectional Suffixes

The words in the verb list above can occur with certain *inflectional suffixes* which you have probably studied already. To refresh your memory these inflectional suffixes are shown below—in heavy type.

SIMPLE (OR DICTIONARY) FORM:	govern	discuss	agree
3RD PERSON PRESENT TENSE:	governs	discusses	agrees
PAST TENSE:	governed	discussed	agreed
PRESENT PARTICIPLE:	governing	discussing	agreeing
PAST PARTICIPLE:	governed	discussed	agreed

Some of the words in the noun list above can occur with other inflectional suffixes which you probably know:

DICTIONARY FORM:	government	settler
PLURAL:	governments	settlers
POSSESSIVE, SINGULAR:	government's	settler's
POSSESSIVE, PLURAL:	governments'	settlers'

Inflectional suffixes never mark a difference in word classes; for example, **govern** and **governed** are both verbs, and **government** and **governments** are both nouns. Inflectional suffixes receive little attention in this book. We shall be mainly concerned with word elements which precede inflectional suffixes—derivational suffixes, stems, and prefixes. (Stems and prefixes will be discussed in Chapters 7 and 8.)

Underlying Forms

In the discussion above we used the term *suffix* as a label for certain word endings like -ment, -er, -ion, -s, -es, -ed, -ing, etc. We shall call the other part of the word the *underlying form*. In the word **government**, for example, we have a suffix -ment and an underlying form **govern-**. We say that **govern** underlies **government**, and that **govern** also underlies **governs**, **governed**, and **governing**. But **government** underlies **governments**. The underlying form in the words we have mentioned so far, then, is that part before the final suffix.

Verb and Noun Lists

In the next two chapters several groups of nouns are listed along with corresponding verb forms. The difference between nouns and verbs is clearly marked by a derivational suffix; each word in the noun lists has a suffix which the verb form does not have. Let us examine some of the pairs listed. In the following, the words in the verb list and the underlying forms in the noun list are identical (for purposes of the present discussion):

VERBS	NOUNS	VERBS	NOUNS
employ	employment	resist	resistance
punish	punishment	invent	inventor
differ	difference	row	rower

In many of the pairs listed we can note certain other differences between verb forms and the underlying forms of the nouns—differences of spelling and/or pronunciation; for example:

VERBS	NOUNS	VERBS	NOUNS
educate	education	pronounce	pronunciation
explode	explosion	type	typist
compose	composition	run	runner

Meanings of Derivational Suffixes

It is not always easy to find "meaning" in derivational suffixes. Those spelled -or, -er, -ar, -ist, -ant, -ent have a meaning something like "performer of an action" or "instrument for performing an action." These are called *agent nouns*.

VERBS	NOUNS	VERBS	NOUNS
collect	collector	fasten	fastener
hear	hearer	roll	roller
examine	examiner	stop	stopper

In a few instances the traditional contrast of "action" (verb) and "person, place, or thing" (noun) appears to be evident:

VERBS	NOUNS	
manage	manager	(a person)
settle	settlement	(a place)
refresh	refreshment	(something to eat or drink)
apply	application	(a form or letter)
receive	receiver	(an instrument—part of a telephone)

In other instances the meaning seems to be nothing more than "noun marker"; that is, the suffix simply marks the form of the word it must have in order to fit the noun position of a sentence. The meaning of the noun suffixes in the following words, for example, is very vague; but only the words in the noun lists can occur in noun positions.

VERBS	NOUNS	VERBS	NOUNS
encourage	encourage**ment**	discuss	discuss**ion**
develop	develop**ment**	explore	explor**ation**
attract	attrac**tion**	annoy	annoy**ance**

EXERCISES

A. In the sentences below, the suffixes are shown in heavy type. Examine each one and tell whether it is a derivational suffix or an inflectional suffix. Remember that most of the time, but not always, derivational suffixes mark a difference in word classes. The suffix **-ion,** for example, marks a difference between the noun **discussion** and the verb **discuss.** Inflectional suffixes never mark such a difference: **discuss** and **discussed** are both verbs; **discussion** and **discussions** are both nouns.

1. There was nothing to see but the edg**es** of the wav**es** which look**ed** like the point**s** of sharp rocks.
2. Since Rip was a favor**ite** among all the good wiv**es** of the village, they took his part in all family argument**s.**
3. His wife complain**ed** of his idle**ness** and the ruin he was bring**ing** on the family.
4. From all appear**ances** they were travel**ing** in no single di-rec**tion.**
5. It was real punish**ment;** it was nothing but misery to a per-son's arms and back.
6. The old man soon attract**ed** the crowd's atten**tion.**
7. The settlers' hous**es** were still stand**ing.**
8. The discover**er** of the river and the country visit**ed** the moun-tains every twenty year**s.**

B. If we use any of the words below in the pattern "He wants us to _____ them," we will find that it does not fit. But if we use only the part of the word in heavy type, we will find that it does fit the pattern. Take the word **movements,** for example. This is not an English sentence:

* He wants us to **movements** them.

But this one is a perfectly normal English sentence:

He wants us to **move** them.

Try each word in the pattern; then try only the part in heavy type.

Explain why the "complete" words do not fit the pattern; explain
why the parts in heavy type do fit.

government	discussions	quietly	election
directly	punishment	distrustful	comfortable
favorite	slowly	attractive	cheerful
tasteless	movements	discoverer	completely

C. The words below will not fit the pattern "We need more
_____(s)." But if we change the endings of each word in some
way, we can produce words which will fit the pattern. For example,
we cannot use **friendly** and **discuss** in this pattern:

* We need more **friendly.**

* We need more **discuss.**

But we can use **friend** and **discussion:**

We need more **friends.**

We need more **discussion.**

Try each word in the pattern; then see if you can change the ending in some way so that the word will fit the pattern. What class of
words can we use in this pattern?

sleepy	courageous	noisy	encourage
settle	populate	silent	wooden
profitable	lucky	quieting	loyal
invent	comfortable	powerful	

CHAPTER 4

Nouns With Underlying Verb Forms

Here are some lists of nouns with underlying verb forms. Look over these lists carefully, and be sure you know the meanings of all the words given. If necessary, consult your dictionary. All the words in the noun lists can occur in the pattern "We were surprised by the _____." Try the nouns in this pattern and make sure the meaning of each sentence formed is clear to you. Also, be sure you can spell all the words listed. You will notice that spelling changes sometimes accompany derivation.

Group 1. Suffix -ment

VERBS	NOUNS	VERBS	NOUNS
advertise	advertisement	judge	judg(e)ment
agree	agreement	manage	management
appoint	appointment	measure	measurement(s)
argue	argument	move	movement
arrange	arrangement(s)	pay	payment
astonish	astonishment	punish	punishment
develop	development	refresh	refreshment(s)
employ	employment	retire	retirement
encourage	encouragement	settle	settlement
entertain	entertainment	ship	shipment
excite	excitement	state	statement
govern	government	treat	treatment
improve	improvement		

Group 2. Suffixes -ion, -tion

VERBS	NOUNS	VERBS	NOUNS
act	action	associate	association
admit	admission	attend	attention
adopt	adoption	attract	attraction

VERBS	NOUNS	VERBS	NOUNS
collect	collection	invent	invention
confuse	confusion [3]	object	objection
congratulate	congratulation(s)	omit	omission
connect	connection	operate	operation
correct	correction	permit	permission
decide	decision	persuade	persuasion
describe	description	populate	population
destroy	destruction	possess	possession(s)
direct	direction	produce	production
discuss	discussion	protect	protection
divide	division	recognize	recognition
educate	education	reduce	reduction
elect	election	reflect	reflection
except	exception	reproduce	reproduction
explode	explosion	separate	separation
express	expression	situate	situation
extend	extension	solve	solution
imitate	imitation	suggest	suggestion
intend	intention	suspect	suspicion
interrupt	interruption	translate	translation

Group 3. Suffixes -ation, -ition, -cation

VERBS	NOUNS	VERBS	NOUNS
admire	admiration	explore	exploration
apply	application [4]	imagine	imagination
classify	classification	inform	information
combine	combination	invite	invitation
compete	competition	multiply	multiplication
compose	composition	observe	observation
converse	conversation	organize	organization
examine	examination	prepare	preparation(s)
expect	expectation	pronounce	pronunciation

---

[3] Spelling Rule No. 1: If a word ends in a silent e, we usually drop the e before a suffix beginning with a vowel; for example: confuse—confusion, admire—admiration, enclose—enclosure.

[4] Spelling Rule No. 2: If a word ends in y, preceded by a consonant, we usually change the y to i before a suffix; for example: apply—application, supply—supplier, bury—burial, marry—marriage.

Verbs	Nouns	Verbs	Nouns
qualify	qualification(s)	repeat	repetition
recommend	recommendation	resign	resignation

Group 4. Suffixes -ance, -ence

Verbs	Nouns	Verbs	Nouns
admit	admittance [5]	excel	excellence
allow	allowance	hinder	hindrance
appear	appearance	interfere	interference
attend	attendance	obey	obedience
confide	confidence	perform	performance
differ	difference	prefer	preference
disturb	disturbance	refer	reference
insure	insurance	resist	resistance
enter	entrance		

Group 5. Suffix -t

Verbs	Nouns	Verbs	Nouns
complain	complaint	join	joint
contain	content(s)	produce	product
deceive	deceit	receive	receipt
descend	descent	see	sight
fly	flight	think	thought
give	gift	weigh	weight

EXERCISES

A. Underline the suffix in each of the following words:

government	punishment	hindrance
attention	entrance	existence
suspicion	repetition	classification
complaint	disturbance	arrangement
population	joint	description
independence	combination	appearance
gift	possession	product

---

[5] Spelling Rule No. 3: If a word ends in a single consonant preceded by a single vowel and the accent falls on the last syllable, we usually double the final consonant before a suffix beginning with a vowel; for example: admit—admittance, run—runner, bag—baggage.

B. Give a noun related to each of the verbs below; use one of the following suffixes in each case: **-ment, -ion, -tion, -ation, -ition, -cation, -ance, -ence,** or **-t.**

examine	fly	receive
employ	organize	translate
invent	entertain	weigh
receive	educate	move
apply	multiply	inform
solve		

C. Each verb below is given with a suffix. Put the verb and suffix together and spell the resulting word correctly.

Example: decide -ion — **decision**

imagine -ation	destroy -tion
explode -ion	extend -ion
admit -ance	interfere -ence
omit -ion	introduce -tion
obey -ence	deceive -t

D. Fill each blank in the answer with a noun related to the verb in the question.

Example: Did they **discuss** the problem?
    Yes, they did; and their **discussion** was very interesting.

1. Did they **advertise** the book?

    Yes, they did; and their .... was very interesting.
2. Did they **explain** the problem?

    Yes, they did; and their .... was very interesting.
3. Did they **examine** Mary?

    Yes, they did; and their .... was very interesting.
4. Did they **entertain** the guests?

    Yes, they did; and their .... was very interesting.
5. Did they **combine** the colors?

    Yes, they did; and their .... was very interesting.
6. Did they **classify** the pictures?

    Yes, they did; and their .... was very interesting.

7. Did they **suggest** a program?

Yes, they did; and their .... was very interesting.
8. Did they **treat** the patient?

Yes, they did; and their .... was very interesting.
9. Did they **translate** the sentence?

Yes, they did; and their .... was very interesting.
10. Did they **resist** the change?

Yes, they did; and their .... was very interesting.

CHAPTER **5**

More Nouns With Underlying Verb Forms

Here are some additional lists of nouns with underlying verb forms. Examine these lists carefully, and be sure you know the meanings of all the words given. Use your dictionary if necessary. Also, be sure you can spell all the words.

Group 1. Suffixes -er, -or, -ar, -ist, -ant, -ent

The nouns of this group are *agent nouns:* they refer generally to a person, and in a few cases to an instrument or machine, that performs an action indicated by the verb. All the words in the noun list can occur in the pattern "They were looking for the _____." Try the nouns in this pattern and make sure the meaning of each sentence formed is clear to you.

VERBS	NOUNS	VERBS	NOUNS
act	actor	garden	gardener
beg	beggar	govern	governor
collect	collector	help	helper
compose	composer	invent	inventor
conquer	conqueror	lead	leader
dance	dancer	lie	liar
defend	defendant	light	lighter
	(*also* defender)	manage	manager
depend	dependent	manufacture	manufacturer
direct	director	mine	miner
drive	driver	own	owner
dust	duster	paint	painter
employ	employer	perform	performer
examine	examiner	play	player
farm	farmer	preach	preacher
fasten	fastener	print	printer
fight	fighter	read	reader

VERBS	NOUNS	VERBS	NOUNS
receive	receiver	sing	singer
remind	reminder	smoke	smoker
report	reporter	speak	speaker
reside	resident	suffer	sufferer
ride	rider	teach	teacher
rob	robber	tour	tourist
rule	ruler	trade	trader
run	runner	translate	translator
sail	sailor	type	typist
sell	seller	visit	visitor
serve	servant	vote	voter
	(*also* server)	wait	waiter
settle	settler	wrap	wrapper
ship	shipper	supply	supplier

Group 2. Suffix -al

The nouns of this group and Groups 3–7 can occur in the pattern "We heard about the _____." Try the nouns in this pattern and make sure the meaning of each sentence formed is clear to you.

VERBS	NOUNS	VERBS	NOUNS
approve	approval	propose	proposal
arrive	arrival	refuse	refusal
bury	burial	try	trial
dismiss	dismissal		

Group 3. Suffixes -ure, -ture, -ature

VERBS	NOUNS	VERBS	NOUNS
enclose	enclosure	mix	mixture
depart	departure	please	pleasure
fail	failure	press	pressure
fix	fixture	seize	seizure
furnish	furniture	sign	signature

Group 4. Suffixes -y, -ery, -ary

VERBS	NOUNS	VERBS	NOUNS
bound	boundary	injure	injury
bribe	bribery	inquire	inquiry
deliver	delivery	recover	recovery
discover	discovery	rob	robbery

Group 5. Suffix -age

Verbs	Nouns	Verbs	Nouns
carry	carriage	pass	passage
marry	marriage	spoil	spoilage
pack	package	wreck	wreckage

Group 6. Suffix -ing

Verbs	Nouns	Verbs	Nouns
begin	beginning	meet	meeting
belong	belonging(s)	open	opening
build	building	save	saving(s)
clothe	clothing	scold	scolding
cross	crossing	suffer	suffering
drown	drowning	swell	swelling
earn	earning(s)	train	training
greet	greeting	write	writing
happen	happening	understand	understanding

Group 7. Miscellaneous Pairs

Verbs	Nouns	Verbs	Nouns
behave	behavior	know	knowledge
compare	comparison	laugh	laughter
grow	growth	pray	prayer
hate	hatred	serve	service
heal	health		

EXERCISES

A. Underline the suffix in each of the following words:

settler	owner	dependent	helper
pressure	greeting	package	departure
opening	arrival	visitor	behavior
favorite	discoverer	boundary	laughter

B. Give two nouns related to each of the following verbs, **one** which refers to a person and one which does not.

Example: collect—**collector, collection**

govern	operate	perform	direct
rob	organize	translate	employ

sign	suffer	act	build
explore	begin	compose	train

C. Each verb below is given with a suffix. Put the verb and suffix together and spell the resulting word correctly.

Example: run -er — **runner**

inquire -y	carry -age
try -al	wrap -er
supply -er	serve -ice
please -ure	play -er
type -ist	marry -age

D. Fill each blank with an agent noun related to the verb in each sentence.

Example: A person who translates is a **translator.**

1. A person who suffers is a ....

2. A person who types is a ....

3. A person who smokes is a ....

4. A person who lies is a ....

5. A person who teaches is a ....

6. A person who sings is a ....

7. A person who farms is a ....

8. A person who preaches is a ....

9. A person who dances is a...............

10. A person who votes is a ....

11. A person who composes music is a ....

12. A person who collects money is a ....

13. A person who directs a play is a ....

14. A person who leads others is a ....

15. A person who prints books is a ....

16. A person who reports the news is a ....

17. A person who manages a business is a ....

18. A person who drives a car is a ....

19. A person who employs people is an ....

20. A person who invents things is an ....

E. Fill each blank in the answer with a noun related to the verb in the question.

Example: Did they **propose** a plan?

Yes, they did; but they never told me about the **proposal.**

1. Did they **deliver** the package?

Yes, they did; but they never told me about the ....

2. Did they **dismiss** the worker?

Yes, they did; but they never told me about the ....

3. Did they **refuse** the money?

Yes, they did; but they never told me about the ....

4. Did they **discover** the theft?

Yes, they did; but they never told me about the ....

5. Did they **approve** the plan?

Yes, they did; but they never told me about the ....

6. Did they **rob** the bank?

Yes, they did; but they never told me about the ....

7. Did they **meet** the guests?

Yes, they did; but they never told me about the ....

8. Did they **compare** the scores?

Yes, they did; but they never told me about the ....

9. Did they **try** the criminal?

Yes, they did; but they never told me about the ....

10. Did they **mix** the colors?

Yes, they did; but they never told me about the ....

6

Review: Formal Contrasts and Derivation

So far in our study of English words we have devoted our attention mainly to nouns and verbs. In the following chapters we shall continue to examine nouns and verbs, their occurrence in patterns, and the forms they have when they occur in different sets of patterns. We shall also be concerned in later chapters with adjectives and adverbs. But before we proceed, let us review briefly what we have studied in the first five chapters.

Our first consideration has been *form*—the occurrence of words in particular patterns and the shapes of the words when they occur in these patterns; our second consideration had been *meaning*—pairing and grouping words which are somehow related to each other because of a similarity of meaning (as well as form). **Beg** and **beggar,** for example, are obviously related, but not **pill** and **pillar.** **Agreement, movement,** and **shipment** have a word element in common, so we group them together; **entrance, marriage,** and **flight,** on the other hand, have no such word element in common, so we would not ordinarily group them together in the same way.

At the beginning we needed a method of separating word classes. We took several sentence patterns and found that for certain words in the patterns we could substitute other words. One substitution group we called nouns, and the other we called verbs. We saw that some words have the same form whether they occur as nouns or as verbs, but a large number of words in the two groups differ in form— by a suffix which the noun has, but not the verb. Some words did not fit any of the patterns we used; we said they do not occur as nouns or verbs. These words we left for later discussion, and we shall see that they belong to other word classes.

We define nouns as words which occur in a certain set of patterns, and verbs as words which occur in another set of patterns. These two sets of patterns are different; they have different shapes or forms.

So we say that there are *formal* differences between nouns and verbs
in that there are pattern differences in their occurrence—position in
the sentence, what comes before the noun or verb, what comes after
the noun or verb, etc. You will remember that nouns fit patterns like

> I saw a(n) _____.
> His _____ surprised everyone.
> He doesn't have any _____.
> The _____ is interesting.
> Some _____(e)s are over there.

And verbs fit patterns like

> We must _____.
> Please _____ them.
> Let's _____.
> Don't _____ it.
> They can _____.
> They didn't _____ him.

When we compare nouns and verbs themselves, we find that some
are identical in form; many others are similar in form. For example,
brush as a verb and **brush** as a noun are identical; the verb **complain**
and the noun **complaint** are similar, but not identical. Those which
are not identical, we say, have formal differences too. Here the differences are in the actual forms or shapes of the words. We shall
see, however, that differences of pattern and differences of word
form usually go together; that is, certain patterns call for certain
word forms, and certain word forms can occur only in certain
patterns. In the last two chapters we saw many pairs of nouns and
verbs which have formal differences in their endings: the nouns have
suffixes, but the verbs do not. Later we shall see formal differences in
words of different classes at the beginnings of the words; we shall
also see formal differences inside the words of different classes,
while the beginnings and endings remain the same.

We have used the words *derive, derivation*, and *derivational* as if
we were describing a real process of word formation in the English
language. Our discussion of nouns derived from verbs suggests that
the verbs existed first, and the nouns were "developed" from the
verbs simply by adding a suffix. We do not know for a fact that it all
happened this way. Actually, we are not concerned with the historical development of words. *Derivation*, as we use the term in this

book, is not a historical process at all. It is a descriptive term which we use for convenience. If we say that the noun **failure** is derived from the verb **fail**, we are not saying that first there was a verb **fail**, and then speakers of English later added the suffix -**ure** to form the noun **failure**. This may or may not have been the case. What we mean is that there is a verb **fail** and a noun **failure**; the latter word is longer, having an extra syllable spelled -**ure** (which we label a derivational suffix). And this contrast between the verb **fail** and the noun **failure** has parallels in other noun and verb forms: **depart— departure, please—pleasure, seize—seizure,** etc.

EXERCISES

A. Some of the words below occur both as verbs and nouns. The others occur as verbs only, but with the addition of a suffix they can also occur as nouns. Look at each word and tell whether it can occur as a noun or whether it requires a suffix in order to occur as a noun. If a suffix is required, tell which suffix may be used. (Do not use the suffix -**ing** in this exercise.)

brush	depart	wreck	enclose
astonish	recover	pray	connect
destroy	mix	behave	separate
resign	adopt	bury	guide
insure	fish	cook	deceive
doubt	prepare	refer	retire
hammer	bribe	compete	

B. Give two nouns related to each of the following verbs, one which refers to a person and one which does not.

Example: discover—**discoverer, discovery**

employ	produce	fly	heal
serve	think	educate	complain
give	write	pack	build
grow	sign	begin	explore
settle	propose		

C. Fill each blank with a noun related to the verb used in the first part of the sentence.

Example: They **inquired** about the house, but I never knew the reason for their **inquiry.**

1. They **failed** the examination, but I never knew the reason for their ....
2. They **attacked** the young policeman, but I never knew the reason for their ....
3. They **met** late last night, but I never knew the reason for their ....
4. They **compared** the football scores, but I never knew the reason for their ....
5. They **demanded** immediate payment, but I never knew the reason for their ....
6. They **laughed** when they saw him, but I never knew the reason for their ....
7. They **signaled** the driver, but I never knew the reason for their ....
8. They **complained** about the guest, but I never knew the reason for their ....
9. They **quarreled** for several minutes, but I never knew the reason for their ....
10. They **explored** all the islands, but I never knew the reason for their ....
11. They **requested** sixteen books, but I never knew the reason for their ....
12. They **interfered** whenever they could, but I never knew the reason for their ....
13. They **struggled** as long as possible, but I never knew the reason for their ....
14. They **decided** it was good, but I never knew the reason for their ....
15. They **argued** a long time, but I never knew the reason for their ....
16. They **preferred** the brick house, but I never knew the reason for their ....

CHAPTER 7

Verbs With Underlying Noun Forms;

Contrasts in Stem Forms

Verbs With Underlying Noun Forms

In Chapter 2 we saw that many nouns and verbs have the same form: **work, drink, walk, help,** etc. In Chapters 3, 4, and 5 we saw that many nouns and verbs differ in form, mainly in that the nouns have a derivational suffix: **punish—punishment, act—action, lead—leader,** etc.

Here we see three groups of nouns and verbs which differ in form, mainly in that the verbs have a derivational suffix. Some of the verbs—**hasten, apologize,** and **sympathize,** for example—can occur in the pattern "You don't need to _____." The other verbs can also occur in this pattern if additional words are added; that is, "You don't need to _____ . . ."—for example: You don't need to **frighten us.** Try each of the verbs in the pattern "You don't need to _____." If it does not fit, see if it will fit when you add some more words.

Group 1. Suffix -en

Nouns	Verbs	Nouns	Verbs
fright	frighten	strength	strengthen
haste	hasten	threat	threaten
length	lengthen		

Group 2. Suffixes -ze, -ize

Nouns	Verbs	Nouns	Verbs
apology	apologize	memory	memorize
colony	colonize	standard	standardize
critic	criticize	sympathy	sympathize

Group 3. Suffixes -fy, -ify, -efy

Nouns	Verbs	Nouns	Verbs
beauty	beautify	solid	solidify
class	classify	terror	terrify
liquid	liquefy		

Stems

Words like **work, drink, walk, help, punish, act, threat,** and **solid** are called *stems*. Stems may precede derivational suffixes, and stems may also include derivational suffixes. For example, the word **govern** is a verb stem which may precede the derivational suffix -ment; **government** is a noun stem which includes -ment.[6] Notice these:

NOUNS AND VERBS (stem with no suffix): **work, drink, walk, help**
VERBS (stem with no suffix): **punish, act, hear**
NOUNS (verb stem and suffix): **punishment, action, hearer**
NOUNS (stem with no suffix): **threat, solid**
VERBS (noun stem and suffix): **threaten, solidify**

In a number of instances the difference between nouns and verbs is marked by a difference in the stem form. Here we see five groups of verbs and nouns which show this kind of difference. The nouns in these groups can occur in the pattern "That _____ was not considered." Try the nouns in this pattern and make sure the meaning of each sentence formed is clear to you.

Group 4. Ending [z] contrasting with [s]

Verbs	Nouns	Verbs	Nouns
advise [z]	advice [s]	house [z]	house [s]
excuse [z]	excuse [s]	use [z]	use [s]

Group 5. Ending [d] contrasting with [s] (or [z])

Verbs	Nouns	Verbs	Nouns
applaud	applause [z]	offend	offense [s]
succeed	success [s]	pretend	pretense [s]
defend	defense [s]		

---

[6] Stems which contain no derivational suffixes or prefixes are also called *bases.* Bases usually carry the "meaning" of the word. Words like **govern, work, drink, walk, help, punish, act, threat,** and **solid** are both bases and stems. They are bases because they contain no other word element (suffix or prefix), and they are stems because we can add inflectional suffixes to them.

Group 6. Ending [v] contrasting with [f]

VERBS	NOUNS	VERBS	NOUNS
believe	belief	prove	proof
halve	half	relieve	relief

Group 7. Difference in Syllable Stress

VERBS	NOUNS	VERBS	NOUNS
insúlt	ínsult	recórd	récord
permít	pérmit	refúse	réfuse
presént	présent	subjéct	súbject
prodúce	próduce	suspéct	súspect
progréss	prógress		

Group 8. Miscellaneous Pairs

VERBS	NOUNS	VERBS	NOUNS
bathe	bath	sell	sale
bleed	blood	shoot	shot
breathe	breath	sing	song
choose	choice	sit	seat
feed	food	speak	speech
lose	loss	strike	stroke

Final and Non-Final Stem Forms

In our study of noun and verb forms so far, we have seen that stems and derivational suffixes go together nicely most of the time without any problems. We pointed out in Chapter 3, however, that sometimes the form of the stem when occurring with a suffix is different from the form of the stem without a suffix; for example: **educate—education, run—runner, memory—memorize, describe—description, explode—explosion, fly—flight,** etc. Many of these differences are simply spelling problems. (See spelling rules, footnotes 3, 4, and 5 in Chapter 4.) The others are differences in stem form and present more than just spelling problems.

It will make our description easier if we recognize two stem formations: one form without a derivational suffix which we shall call a *final* form, and the other form with one or more derivational suffixes which we shall call a *non-final* form. Notice the following examples:

Final Forms	Non-Final Forms	
describe	descrip-	(as in **description**)
explode	explos-	(as in **explosion**)
liquid	liqu-	(as in **liquefy**)

The forms in the first column—the final forms—can occur without a suffix. The forms in the second column—the non-final forms—occur only before a derivational suffix.

EXERCISES

A. If you take a word consisting of a stem plus a suffix and remove the suffix, the remaining stem is a non-final form. In some instances the spelling of the non-final form and the corresponding final form are identical; in other cases they are not.

Stem and Suffix	Non-Final Stem Form	Final Stem Form
government	govern-	govern
frighten	fright-	fright
burial	buri-	bury
flight	fligh-	fly

Each word in the list below consists of a noun stem plus a suffix or a verb stem plus a suffix. Remove the suffix, write the non-final form of the stem, and then write the final form.

Example: enclosure—**enclos-, enclose**

apologize	comparison	furniture	obedience
gift	thought	refusal	entrance
beautify	robbery	supplier	pronunciation
shipper	carriage	inquiry	solution
division	argument	pleasure	repetition

B. Give a related noun for each of the following verbs:

presént	advise	applaud
prove	defend	believe
sell	recórd	suspéct
choose	breathe	succeed
insúlt	lose	feed

C. Fill each blank with a verb form (past participle) related to the noun in parenthesis.

Example: (standard) The procedures were **standardized.**

1. (class)   The procedures were ....

2. (defense)   The procedures were ....

3. (critic)   The procedures were ....

4. (memory)   The procedures were ....

5. (strength)   The procedures were ....

6. (présent)   The procedures were ....

7. (length)   The procedures were ....

8. (choice)   The procedures were ....

9. (threat)   The procedures were ....

10. (applause)   The procedures were ....

D. Fill each blank with a verb form (past tense) related to the noun in parenthesis.

Example: (belief) The captain **believed** the guards.

1. (advice)   The captain .... the guards.

2. (defense)   The captain .... the guards.

3. (house)   The captain .... the guards.

4. (offense)   The captain .... the guards.

5. (use)   The captain .... the guards.

6. (ínsult)   The captain .... the guards.

7. (choice)   The captain .... the guards.

8. (excuse)   The captain .... the guards.

9. (relief)   The captain .... the guards.

10. (súspect)   The captain .... the guards.

CHAPTER 8

Prefixes and More Noun Suffixes

Prefixes

A word element preceding a stem is called a *prefix*. In a few instances, nouns differ from verbs in that the verb has a prefix.

In the first two groups of words below we see this kind of difference. The verbs can occur in the pattern "They were _____(e)d." Try the verbs in this pattern, and make sure the meaning of each sentence formed is clear to you.

Group 1. Prefix en-

NOUNS	VERBS		NOUNS	VERBS
camp	encamp		force	enforce
circle	encircle		joy	enjoy
courage	encourage		slave	enslave

Group 2. Miscellaneous Pairs

NOUNS	VERBS		NOUNS	VERBS
earth	unearth		prison	imprison
friend	befriend		witch	bewitch
knowledge	acknowledge			

In most cases, unlike the examples given above, prefixes do not mark a difference in word class. Generally, both the prefixed form and the unprefixed form of a word belong to the same class and pattern alike in sentences. However, the prefix usually does mark a "meaning" difference between pairs. Two such meaning differences are "negation" (**dis-, un-, in-, non-**) and "error" (**mis-**).

Here are five groups of nouns with and without prefixes. The unprefixed as well as the prefixed nouns can occur in the pattern "Their _____ made us unhappy." Try the prefixed nouns in this pattern, and make sure that the meaning of each sentence formed is clear to you.

Group 3. Noun Stems with Prefix dis-

advantage	disadvantage	obedience	disobedience
agreement	disagreement	pleasure	displeasure
appearance	disappearance	satisfaction	dissatisfaction
honor	dishonor	comfort	discomfort

Group 4. Noun Stems with Prefix un-

attractiveness	unattractiveness	evenness	unevenness
certainty	uncertainty	importance	unimportance
consciousness	unconsciousness	pleasantness	unpleasantness
concern	unconcern	popularity	unpopularity
employment	unemployment	selfishness	unselfishness

Group 5. Noun Stems with Prefix in-, im-, ir-

convenience	inconvenience	morality	immorality
equality	inequality	purity	impurity
justice	injustice	regularity	irregularity

Group 6. Noun Stems with Prefix non-

existence	nonexistence	occurrence	nonoccurrence
fulfillment	nonfulfillment	resistance	nonresistance
interference	noninterference	support	nonsupport

Group 7. Noun Stems with Prefix mis-

behavior	misbehavior	information	misinformation
conduct	misconduct	pronunciation	mispronunciation
fortune	misfortune	statement	misstatement

Here are three groups of verbs with and without prefixes. Both the unprefixed and the prefixed verbs can occur in the pattern "We _____(e)d them." Try the prefixed verbs in this pattern, and make sure the meaning of each sentence formed is clear to you.

Group 8. Verb Stems with Prefix dis-

arrange	disarrange	like	dislike
color	discolor	obey	disobey
connect	disconnect	own	disown
continue	discontinue	prove	disprove

Group 9. *Verb Stems with Prefix* un-

button	unbutton	pack	unpack
cover	uncover	pin	unpin
fasten	unfasten	roll	unroll
fold	unfold	saddle	unsaddle
load	unload	tie	untie
lock	unlock	wrap	unwrap

Group 10. *Verb Stems with Prefix* mis-

count	miscount	pronounce	mispronounce
judge	misjudge	place	misplace
lead	mislead	spell	misspell
number	misnumber	understand	misunderstand

We saw above that some verbs are derived from nouns by the addition of a prefix (Groups 1 and 2). We saw that other prefixes do not mark a difference in word classes (Groups 3–10); the noun or the verb belongs to the same word class whether it has a prefix or not.

More Noun Suffixes

Similarly, a few noun suffixes do not mark a difference in word class.

Here are four groups of nouns with and without suffixes. Whether suffixed or not the words are nouns. All of them can occur in the pattern "He'll never forget the _____." Try the suffixed nouns in this pattern, and make sure the meaning of each sentence formed is clear to you.

Group 11. *Suffix* -ess

actor	actress	poet	poetess
host	hostess	waiter	waitress

Group 12. *Suffixes* -st, -ist

art	artist
colony	colonist
science	scientist

Group 13. Suffix -ship

companion	companionship	owner	ownership
friend	friendship	workman	workmanship
member	membership		

Group 14. Miscellaneous Pairs

bag	baggage	mile	mileage
agent	agency	music	musician
crime	criminal	neighbor	neighborhood
engine	engineer	poet	poetry
king	kingdom	scene	scenery
law	lawyer	slave	slavery
library	librarian	thief	theft
message	messenger	treasure	treasury

EXERCISES

A. Underline the prefixes and suffixes in the following words:

unconcern	imprison	slavery
friendship	encircle	nonoccurrence
misplace	colonist	historian
baggage	kingdom	enjoy
displeasure	poetess	neighborhood

B. Fill each blank with the proper prefix:

1. It was definitely a matter of ....comfort.

2. It was definitely a matter of ....certainty.

3. It was definitely a matter of ....conduct.

4. It was definitely a matter of ....equality.

5. It was definitely a matter of ....resistance.

6. It was definitely a matter of ....information.

7. It was definitely a matter of ....regularity.

8. It was definitely a matter of ....satisfaction.

9. It was definitely a matter of ....employment.

10. It was definitely a matter of ....support.

11. It was definitely a matter of ....morality.

12. It was definitely a matter of ....interference.

13. It was definitely a matter of ....behavior.

14. It was definitely a matter of ....agreement.

15. It was definitely a matter of ....honor.

C. Fill each blank with the proper prefix:

1. He always ....connects the wires.

2. He always ....pronounces the names.

3. He always ....spells the words.

4. He always ....locks the doors.

5. He always ....likes the neighbors.

6. He always ....obeys the orders.

7. He always ....ties the rope.

8. He always ....buttons the coats.

9. He always ....understands the messages.

10. He always ....numbers the pages.

D. Fill each blank with a noun (plural form) related to the preceding noun in the sentence.

Example: Our interest was in **art** and **artists.**

1. Our interest was in **crime** and ....

2. Our interest was in **science** and ....

3. Our interest was in **law** and ....

4. Our interest was in **libraries** and ....

5. Our interest was in **messages** and ....

6. Our interest was in **music** and ....

7. Our interest was in **colonies** and ....

CHAPTER 9

How We Recognize Nouns

There are several ways we can recognize nouns in English sentences—several "signals" that guide us. Some of these we have already mentioned.

Inflectional Suffixes

In Chapter 3 we called attention to certain inflectional suffixes which you have probably studied elsewhere in more detail. The ones we use with nouns are the pluralizer (-s, -es) and the possessive markers (-'s and -s'). These suffixes help us recognize nouns in the following sentences:

1. If we had no **animals** like you, there would be no **prospectors** and few gold **mines.**
2. Jenet knew the **trails** and water **holes** better than Tappan.
3. Sylvia remembered that one of the **oak's** upper **branches** touched the trunk of the big pine.
4. She seemed to know what was beyond a **burro's** ability.
5. The blowing sand was almost as bad as the **day's** heat.
6. The **gulls'** eyes were tiny and black.

Derivational Suffixes

In Chapters 3, 4, and 5 we noted a number of contrasts between noun and verb forms, and we examined several derivational suffixes used in noun formations. The main ones were:

SUFFIXES	EXAMPLES
-ment	improvement, payment
-ion, -tion, -ation, -ition, -cation	discussion, description, invitation, repetition, application
-ance, -ence	appearance, preference
-t	complaint, gift
-er, -or	farmer, inventor

Suffixes	Examples
-al	arrival, burial
-ure, -ture	failure, mixture
-y, -ery	inquiry, robbery
-age	marriage, passage
-ing	beginning, opening

These suffixes help us recognize nouns in the following sentences:

7. Sylvia's gray eyes were dark with **excitement**.
8. Jenet would have taken the prize in any **competition** with other burros.
9. They had no **complaints** about the cow's milk.
10. Desert **wanderers** like Tappan preferred to camp at lonely spots.
11. The good woman suspected that Sylvia's late **arrival** was not on account of the cow.
12. Remembering the day's **pleasure** ahead of him, the guest hurried to dress himself.

We shall examine some additional noun suffixes in Chapter 14—those we use for deriving nouns from adjectives. The main ones are:

Suffixes	Examples
-ness	coldness, foolishness
-y, -ty, -ity	difficulty, loyalty, reality
-th	length, truth

These suffixes help us recognize nouns in the following sentences:

13. Few prospectors had the **toughness** and **ability** of Tappan.
14. Everybody knew the **difficulty** of finding the cow within a short time.
15. The baby burro may gain enough **strength** to go with us.

Determiners

Nouns occur with a group of words called *determiners:*

the	its	each	many	more
a	our	every	much	most
an	their	no	few	one
my	this	both	several	two
your	that	some	either	ten
his	these	any	neither	twenty-one
her	those	all		

Determiners precede nouns but do not always occur immediately in front of nouns; sometimes other words come between. In the following sentences the determiners help us recognize nouns:

16. He did not like the **water** at this **oasis** very well.
17. Some green **grass** and a few **trees** proved the **presence** of water.
18. He had never found a **lot** of gold in one **place**.
19. There's no **reward** for your **faithfulness**.
20. Several **groups** of outlaws lived in these **mountains**.

A noun with a possessive suffix (-'s, -s') marks a following word as a noun in the same way that determiners do:

21. Jenet's **ears** were standing straight up.
22. His bullet had gone through the man's **head**.

Position

Nouns fill certain positions in English sentences. One such position is before a verb as "subject" of the sentence; another position is after the verb as "object" of the verb. Position helps us recognize nouns in these sentences:

23. **Tappan** found **tracks** near his camp.
24. Desert **plants** provided **food** for Jenet.

Position does not mark nouns as clearly as suffixes and determiners. Most of the time we can recognize nouns without reference to position.

In a sentence like "Your **possessions** are safe" the word in heavy type is marked as a noun in all the ways we have mentioned: first, by the occurrence of an inflectional suffix (-s); second, by the occurrence of a derivational suffix (-ion); third, by a determiner (**your**); and fourth, by the noun position before the verb **are** and the "agreement" of a plural noun with a plural verb form.

EXERCISES

A. Underline the determiners in the following sentences:

1. At many idle moments he sat looking at the great desert valleys, or watching some desert insect or animal, or admiring the colors of some desert flowers.
2. Tappan wandered across the desert from one edge to another, and his burros traveled with him.
3. Jenet's behavior was about the same on all occasions.

4. Tappan had broken this habit at its beginning.

5. He spent several days digging gold and had six small bags of it.

6. Many times she had put her hand on its rough trunk and looked up at those dark branches waving in the wind.

7. Almost every night during the summer Sylvia had to come and look a long time before she found the cow.

8. She knows every foot of ground in the woods as well as any wild creature living there.

9. Sylvia gave no signs of interest in talking about birds; she was thinking about the wonderful things she could buy with ten dollars.

10. Some day, Jenet, we'll die here in the desert. Our bones will lie on the sand. And nobody will know or care.

B. In the sentences below some nouns are shown in heavy type. Underline the inflectional suffixes once and the derivational suffixes twice.

1. Besides the **feeling** of **loyalty** to the **commander** of the **boat**, there was **friendship** and **companion-ship**.

2. The **birds** sat comfortably in **groups**; the **rough-ness** of the **sea** did not disturb them at all.

3. The **moon** produced a **reflection** on the water.

4. There were no hurried **words**, no **shouts**, no wild **excitement**.

5. The **sound** of the **pine's** green **branches** was still in her **ears**.

6. Each **time** a **man** took his **eyes** from the **waves**, he turned his **attention** toward the **shore**.

7. When an old **newspaper** fell into their **hands**, there were some lively **discussions**.

8. They stood looking at him with such strange **expres-sions** on their **faces** that his **knees** began to shake.

9. He was a **descendant** of the **historian** by that **name**, who wrote one of the earliest **accounts** of the **province**.

    10. The **group** returned to the more important **concerns** of the **election**.

C. The words in heavy type in the sentences below are nouns. Each is marked as a noun in one or more ways—by an inflectional suffix, a derivational suffix, a determiner, or position. Tell which marker or markers are present in each case.

    1. **Necessity** is the **mother** of **invention**.
    2. You can't teach new **tricks** to an old **dog**.
    3. **Truth** never hides in dark **corners**.
    4. Any **fool** can ask **questions**, but only a smart **man** can answer them.
    5. **Haste** makes **waste**.
    6. One **man's** meat is another **man's poison**.
    7. A liar needs a good **memory**.
    8. A **friend's** envy is worse than an **enemy's** hatred.
    9. Every **child** loves his **nurse** and forgets her when he grows up.
    10. All **work** and no **play** makes **Jack** a dull **boy**.

CHAPTER **10**

How We Recognize Verbs

We have seen that certain signals help us recognize nouns—inflectional suffixes, derivational suffixes, etc. Similar signals help us recognize verbs, some of which we have already mentioned.

Inflectional Suffixes

In Chapter 3 we reviewed certain inflectional suffixes used with verbs which you have probably studied elsewhere in detail: 3rd person present tense marker (**-s, -es**); past tense marker (**-d, -ed**); [7] present participle marker (**-ing**); and past participle marker (**-d, -ed**).[7] In the following sentences these suffixes help us recognize verbs:

1. He **thinks** we're **fishing.**
2. Surely the signal **means** something.
3. **Thinking** and **planning,** he **continued** his work, **trying** his best to act natural.
4. Tappan **felt** that he was **being followed** by a ball of fire.
5. Finally he **realized** what had **happened.**
6. The low pressure **caused** by the heat was now **yielding** to the higher pressure from outside.

Derivational Suffixes and Prefixes

In Chapters 6 and 7 we noted some contrasts between verb and noun forms. We examined a few derivational suffixes and prefixes used in verb formations. The main ones were the following:

Affixes	Examples
-en	hasten, strengthen
-ze, -ize	apologize, standardize

---

[7] Many "irregularities" of past tense and past participle formations also serve as verb markers. Contrasts between the various forms of so-called irregular verbs are, for the most part, patterned.

270

AFFIXES	EXAMPLES
-fy, -ify, -efy	beautify, solidify, liquefy
en-	encircle, enjoy

These *affixes* (suffixes and prefixes) help us recognize verbs in the following sentences:

7. She remembered a red-faced boy in the city who used to **frighten** her.
8. Since no one was awake to **sympathize,** he leaned to one side and swore softly into the sea.
9. There never was a child who **enjoyed** the out-of-doors so much.
10. The sight of land **encouraged** them.

We shall see in Chapter 16 that we use some of these same affixes to derive verbs from adjectives; for example:

AFFIXES	EXAMPLES
-en	deepen, ripen
-ize	civilize, modernize
en-	enable, enlarge

These affixes help us recognize verbs in the following sentences:

11. **Loosening** the ropes of Jenet's pack, he freed her from the load.
12. A moment's thought was enough for Tappan to **realize** the seriousness of his situation.
13. His condition did not **enable** him to stand for more than a moment.

Auxiliaries

Verbs occur with a group of words called *auxiliaries.* Auxiliaries and verbs combine to make verb phrases:

Group 1:	can/could	must	
	may/might	dare	and simple
	shall/should	need	form of verb
	will/would	(had) better/best	
	do/does/did		

Group 2:	am/is/are/was/were	and present
	get/gets/got	participle form
	keep/keeps/kept	of verb

Group 3: am/is/are/was/were   and past par-
       get/gets/got   ticiple form
       have/has/had   of verb

Group 4: have/has/had
       ought
       used   to   and simple
       am/is/are/was/were   form of verb
       get/gets/got

       am/is/are/was/were $\begin{cases} \text{about} \\ \text{going} \end{cases}$

Less frequent, but not at all uncommon, are verb phrases consisting of two auxiliaries and a verb form. And occasionally we find verb phrases with three or even four auxiliaries and a verb form.

Auxiliaries mark verbs very much like determiners mark nouns. The occurrence of an auxiliary is a signal that a verb is coming. In the following sentences the auxiliaries help us recognize verbs:

14. I must **act** natural; but I can't **stay** here any longer.
15. Even if he did **reach** the other side of the valley, he would **find** himself in the region of the Funeral Mountains.
16. She was afraid that morning might **come** too soon.
17. His rifle was **leaning** against this pile of things.
18. There are two or three rare ones I've been **hunting** for five years.
19. The sun had **gone** behind the mountain, but it had **left** the rocks so hot that Tappan could not **touch** them.
20. If I hadn't **watched** her, she would have **gone** without food herself in order to feed them.
21. The great pine tree could be **seen** from miles away.
22. He was about to **go** into the upper end of Death Valley.
23. They were going to **let** him dig the gold and then steal it.
24. If he buried the gold, he would have to **return** for it later.

Position

Verbs fill certain positions in English sentences. The position at the beginning of a sentence can be filled by a verb stem or preceded by **please, let's, do,** or **don't.** This produces a type of sentence used in requests; for example:

25. **Look** at those mountains ahead; they seem to call us.
26. Don't **be** afraid, little girl.
27. Let's **give** the boys a chance to rest.

Verbs and verb phrases can occupy a position between two nouns, with or without determiners:

28. Jenet **saved** his life.
29. The short limbs **caught** her clothes.
30. The air **must find** its way upward.
31. Two more hours of such heat **would finish** Tappan.

Most of the time we can recognize verbs without reference to position. The same is true for prefixes and derivational suffixes. We can, as a rule, identify verbs most readily by inflectional suffixes and auxiliaries.

In a sentence like "The children have **memorized** a poem" the word in heavy type is marked as a verb in all the ways we have mentioned: first, by the occurrence of an inflectional suffix (**-d**); second, by the occurrence of a derivational suffix (**-ze**); third, by an auxiliary (**have**); and fourth, by position (verb phrase between two nouns).

EXERCISES

A. Underline the auxiliaries in the following sentences:

1. Jenet was lying down, and her pack was resting on the ground beside her.
2. He could fight evil men, but he could not fight this heat.
3. Even if they tried to follow him, they would never catch him.
4. His entire body was wet, as if he had fallen into the spring.
5. Much to his surprise he did discover gold—lots of gold.
6. I've dug almost all the gold.
7. Our bones will lie on the sand, and no one will know or care.
8. He knew that he might easily overlook valuable ore.
9. The child realized that she must hurry.
10. I have to leave early tomorrow morning.
11. Where did you find her this time, Sylvy?
12. Oh, no, they are stuffed and preserved, dozens and dozens of them.
13. It was a human whistle—the kind she used to hear in the city.

14. If she's afraid of people, she should go to the farm.

15. Maybe you can give me some milk.

B. The words in heavy type in the sentences below are verbs. Each is marked as a verb in one or more ways—by an inflectional suffix, a derivational suffix, an auxiliary, or position. Tell which marker or markers are present in each case.

1. Something **begins** as a custom and **becomes** the law of the land.

2. A leopard can't **change** his spots.

3. Walls **have** ears and mountains **have** eyes.

4. **Take** the weather as it **comes**; nothing can be **done** about it.

5. Too many cooks will **ruin** the soup.

6. Let's **stay** in good company; we might **become** one of its members.

7. One rotten apple has **spoiled** a barrel-full.

8. An old dog doesn't **bark** without a reason.

9. Don't **quit** your job because of a bad boss; your next one may **be** worse.

10. I'll **do** my best; no man can **do** more.

CHAPTER 11

Review: Meaning and Form

We have classified some words as nouns and some words as verbs according to the patterns they fit, not according to their meaning. In Chapter 3 we called attention to the traditional idea of noun and verb classification, namely that nouns are the "names of persons, places, and things," and verbs "express the occurrence of an action or the existence of a state or condition." In thousands of instances this seems to be true, but in thousands of other instances it does not seem to be true. Certainly **Thomas, California,** and **door** name a person, a place, and a thing respectively; also **run** and **is** can express the occurrence of an action and the existence of a state or condition respectively. But isn't just as much action expressed by **punishment** (noun) as **punish** (verb)? Is **punishment** (noun) actually the name of a person, place, or thing? Similarly, is more action expressed by **applaud** (verb) than **applause** (noun)? And is **applause** really the name of a person, place, or thing? If the verb **smell** expresses the existence of a state or condition in the sentence "The flowers smell nice," isn't the same state or condition expressed by the noun **smell** in "The flowers have a nice smell"? Is **smell** in either sentence the name of a person, place, or thing?

These questions point out some of the difficulties we would face if we used meaning instead of form as a basis for setting up our word classes. Of course we cannot disregard meaning entirely; all words have meaning of some kind, and we have to know these meanings in order to use the words properly.

The meanings of words present many special problems. Serious students of language usually agree that any word is very difficult to define adequately. Our best aid in dealing with problems of meaning is the dictionary. It describes objects and processes; it gives *synonyms* (words with similar meanings) and *antonyms* (words with opposite meanings); and it sometimes gives a few sentences to illustrate the use of the word defined. A foreign language dictionary, instead of providing synonyms in the same language, of course, gives corresponding words and phrases in a foreign language and, ordinarily, some examples to show how the word defined can be used in sentences.

Even the best dictionary definitions, however, are not entirely satisfactory. Knowing the meaning of a word includes knowing all the situations in which a native speaker of the language might use the word. Take a word like **hand**, for example. In many situations **hand** refers to "the part of the human arm below the wrist, including the palm, fingers, and thumb, used for grasping and gripping." But speakers of English use the word **hand** in many other situations without this reference. Notice these sentences:

The judge **handed** down a decision on the case.
   (hand down = announce, deliver)
We have several products on **hand**.
   (on hand = available, ready)
On the one **hand**, he thought he should go; on the other **hand**, he thought he should stay.
   (on the one hand = from one point of view; on the other hand = from another point of view)
Don't let those children get out of **hand**.
   (out of hand = out of control)
She would like to try her **hand** at teaching.
   (try her hand = test her skill or interest)
The king ruled with a heavy **hand**.
   (with a heavy hand = with sternness or severity)
This is all first-**hand** information.
   (first-hand = from the original source)
They live from **hand** to mouth most of the time.
   (from hand to mouth = spending or using immediately what is obtained)
In the card game last night I had several good **hands**.
   (hand = cards held by a player at any one time)
The matter is out of my **hands** now.
   (out of my hands = not my responsibility)
The **hands** of the clock are broken.
   (hand = pointer)

Our team won the game **hands** down.
  (hands down = easily, without effort)
They definitely had the upper **hand** in the race.
  (upper hand = advantage)
He plays tennis every day to keep his **hand** in.
  (keep his hand in = keep in practice)

All words, of course, have form and meaning. One way to proceed in the study of word occurrences and word formations is to examine meanings first and examine forms second. Because of the difficulties of describing and classifying meaning, our procedure is the reverse: first we examine similarities and contrasts of form; and second we examine similarities and contrasts of meaning. Form is our basic guide—always. In our description a given word is not a noun or a verb because it has a certain meaning. It is a noun if it will fit patterns which nouns fit, or it is a verb if it will fit patterns which verbs fit. The word may fit both sets of patterns, in which case it is both a noun and a verb.

For purposes of recognizing words in the two word classes we have studied so far—nouns and verbs—we have called attention to various markers (or signals). Some mark nouns, and some mark verbs. Actually we don't even have to know the meaning of a word in order to know that it is a noun or a verb.

Take a sentence like

Foodle those bloobers there.

We don't know what **foodle** and **bloobers** mean, but we recognize **foodle** as a verb and **bloobers** as a noun. We know that **foodle** is something we can do to **bloobers**, and that **bloobers** (whatever they are) can be **foodled**. We know too that this is a command or request: somebody is telling another person (or persons) to **foodle** some **bloobers**.

Or take a sentence like

We have to hide our wackers.

We don't know what a **wacker** is, but we recognize it as a noun. And we know that a **wacker** is something small enough to hide and that there are at least two of them.

Or take a sentence like

We wackered the books last night.

In this case **wacker** is marked as a verb, and we know that **wacker** is something we can do to books.

Although form is our basic guide, meaning sometimes plays an important part in our classification of words. We cannot draw conclusions about related words on the basis of form alone. We must depend on meaning to support these conclusions. Notice these two sentences:

> We tried to remember the **address** of his house.
>
> We have to **address** the envelope.

Most native speakers of English would probably agree that the noun **address** in the first sentence is related to the verb **address** in the second sentence. There is a common element of meaning in the two words as they appear in these examples: in the first case, location in terms of a street and house number; and in the second case, putting the street and house number on an envelope.

Now notice these two:

> I broke my **watch** last night.
>
> I want to **watch** the game.

Most native speakers of English would probably agree that the noun **watch** in the first sentence has nothing to do with the verb **watch** in the second sentence. The meanings in these cases certainly suggest that the two words are unrelated, even though the forms are the same. Because the spelling is the same a few people might feel that the words are somehow related, but there is no common element of meaning.

Now notice these two:

> I did not like the **pear**.
>
> I did not like the **pair**.

Here we have two words which sound alike, but are spelled differently. Probably no native speaker of English would say that the noun **pear** in the first sentence is related to the noun **pair** in the second sentence. We call these words *homonyms;* that is, words which sound alike but have different meanings.

We see, then, that we cannot disregard meaning. Similarities of meaning must support our conclusions concerning related words which are based on form. If they do not support our conclusions, then the conclusions are incorrect.

EXERCISES

A. Possible dictionary definitions for four words are shown below. See if you can make five sentences in which each of the words has no reference to the dictionary definition. For example, here is a dictionary definition for the word **back**: "the part of the body opposite the front." Now here are some sentences in which **back** does not refer to the definition:

1. The books have broken **backs**.
2. After class he went **back** to his room.
3. That chair has no **back**.
4. She went out the **back** door when she left.
5. We sat in the **back** of the theater.

Use your dictionary, if you wish, while doing this exercise.

    a. **Run:** "to go by moving the legs rapidly, faster than walking."
    b. **Time:** "the period between two events or during which something exists, happens, or acts."
    c. **Stand:** "to be or remain in an upright position, supported on the feet."
    d. **Come:** "to move from a place thought of as 'there' to or into a place thought of as 'here'."

B. In the sentences below several nonsense words are given in heavy type. We can recognize them as nouns or verbs by certain markers or signals. Look at each of these words and tell whether it is a noun or a verb.

1. **Steegity** is the **zupper** of **octition**.
2. **Rumpth** never **fubbles** in dark **follyledges**.
3. Too many **warfers** will **coopen** the **sabbage**.
4. Don't **filibize** your **sluckies** before they **undify**.
5. One **dood's marfle** is another **dood's nargle**.
6. You can't **stoove** new **bligs** to an old **howzit**.
7. When the **tich glooved** away, the **mombs** began to **vickle**.
8. **Hindstance** always makes **ceiverment**.
9. **Nokettleness** does not **englob** frequently.
10. He had been **jollygigging** for six **vobes**.

C. Give a related verb for each of the following nouns:

Example: repetition—repeat

hindrance	treat	disturbance
product	confusion	population
suggestion	combination	liar
retirement	contents	burial
weight	colony	signature
beauty	description	recovery
conqueror	leader	package
opening	knowledge	hatred

D. Fill the space between parentheses with a noun related to the verb shown in heavy type. If two nouns are possible, give both.

Example: (memory)   Will you **memorize** the poem?

1. (   ) Will you **classify** the words?

2. (   ) Will you **believe** the teacher?

3. (   ) Will you **arrive** on time?

4. (   ) Will you **prepare** the lesson?

5. (   ) Will you **choose** the books?

6. (   ) Will you **translate** the sentence?

7. (   ) Will you **fail** the examination?

8. (   ) Will you **deliver** the message?

9. (   ) Will you **compare** these figures?

10. (   ) Will you **interrupt** the conversation?

CHAPTER **12**

Adjectives and Nouns: Differences in Patterning

We made our first identification of nouns and verbs by testing words in two sets of sentence patterns. Those which fit one set of patterns we called nouns and those which fit the other set of patterns we called verbs. We shall see now that *adjectives* fit a third set of patterns. In this and the following two chapters we shall see some of the formal differences between adjectives and nouns.

Adjectives

Adjectives occur in patterns like

He seemed _____.

They were very _____.

Words like **angry, tired,** and **careful** occur as adjectives. The following are normal English sentences:

He seemed **angry.**   They were very **angry.**

He seemed **tired.**   They were very **careful.**

Words like **horses, usually,** and **go** will not fit these patterns. These are not English sentences:

* He seemed **horses.**   * They were very **usually.**

* He seemed **go.**   * They were very **go.**

Some positions in English sentences are shared by adjectives and nouns. Take a pattern like "He was _____," for example. We have normal English sentences like

He was **happy.**   He was **kind.**

He was **interesting.**   He was **angry.**

We also have normal English sentences like

He was **governor.**   He was **captain.**

He was **Robert.**   He was **Smith.**

The position "a(n) _____ man" is a position for adjectives; but nouns occur in this position too.

281

ADJECTIVES	NOUNS
a **hungry** man	a **city** man
an **old** man	an **insurance** man
a **foolish** man	a **desert** man

However, we can separate adjectives and nouns occurring in this position. Adjectives will fit both blanks in one of these sentences, but nouns will not.

A _____ person is a person who is _____.

A _____ thing is a thing that is _____.

In the phrase "a tall man," then, **tall** is an adjective, because a tall man is a man who is tall. But in "a college man," **college** is not an adjective, because a college man is not a man who is college. **College** in this phrase is a noun.

Words Which Are Both Adjectives and Nouns

A few words occur both as adjectives and as nouns. Some of the common ones are the following:

American	fat	particular
average	hollow	plain
cold	human	public
dear	ideal	secret
elastic	light	solid
equal	moral	sore
English	native	square
explosive	official	special
evil	orange	welcome

The following, for example, are normal English sentences:

ADJECTIVES: They were very **American**.   He seemed **average**.

NOUNS: I saw an **American**.   The **average** was eighty.

Inflectional and Derivational Suffixes

Again we distinguish between inflectional and derivational suffixes. Some adjectives can occur with certain inflectional suffixes which you have probably studied already:

DICTIONARY FORM:	cold	large	lucky
COMPARATIVE:	colder	larger	luckier
SUPERLATIVE:	coldest	largest	luckiest

Most other adjectives, you will remember, can occur with **more** and **most**:

DICTIONARY FORM: interesting   beautiful
COMPARATIVE: **more** interesting   **more** beautiful
SUPERLATIVE: **most** interesting   **most** beautiful

Derivational suffixes mark a class difference between many adjectives and nouns. In some instances the adjective has the suffix; in others the noun has it. A large number of pairs showing these contrasts are given in Chapters 13 and 14.

EXERCISES

A. In each of the groups of words below, there are four adjectives and one noun or four nouns and one adjective. See if you can pick out the word which does not belong with the others. Remember that adjectives will fit a pattern like "They were very _____" or "He seemed _____." Nouns will fit a pattern like "That/those _____ surprised us."

1. dust, strange, lonely, dangerous, silent.
2. snow, difficult, weather, winter, storm.
3. forest, mountains, sand, fragrant, moss.
4. tall, pleasant, peaceful, trees, thick.
5. beautiful, smoke, happy, warm, healthy.
6. high, meat, stranger, enemy, wanderer.
7. pines, name, careful, people, advice.
8. old, creature, heavy, selfish, dark.
9. silence, burro, deep, shelter, branches.
10. shady, grass, indifferent, dry, fierce.
11. weight, still, loud, necessary, soft.
12. method, supplies, sacks, bright, rifle.
13. box, big, strong, lazy, long.
14. big, harmless, fist, different, awkward.
15. pain, caution, generous, snowshoe, snowbank.

B. In the numbered sentences below, the words in heavy type pattern as adjectives. See if you can make a sentence in which each of these words will pattern as a noun.

Example: Are your hands **cold?**
         I like heat better than **cold.**

1. My arm felt **sore** when I woke up this morning.
2. Sometimes dogs seem almost **human.**
3. Mr. Thompson is a **dear** friend.
4. Those papers look very **official.**
5. Witches control **evil** spirits.
6. The sides of that triangle are **equal.**
7. Miss Osgood is certainly a **particular** person.
8. The tree trunk looks completely **hollow.**
9. His new bicycle is **orange** and black.
10. There was a **secret** meeting at 10 o'clock last night.
11. Tappan wore **plain** clothes most of the time.
12. The morning sun was a **welcome** sight.

C. Look again at the list of words which occur both as adjectives and as nouns. Select one word from the list and make a sentence in which it patterns as an adjective. Then see if you can think of ten other adjectives which you can substitute for the one you selected. Take **plain,** for example. You can make a sentence like "It was a **plain** envelope." And for **plain,** you can substitute various other adjectives:

> It was a plain envelope.
> pink
> dirty
> long
> white
> small
> rough
> short
> big
> beautiful
> soft

D. Now select another word from the list and make a sentence in which it patterns as a noun. Then see if you can think of ten other nouns which you can substitute for the one you selected. Take **square,** for example; you can make a sentence like "He took a pencil and drew a **square.**" And for **square,** you can substitute various other nouns:

He took a pencil and drew a square.
        triangle.
        picture.
        flower.
        building.
        house.
        dog.
        car.
        horse.
        leaf.
        wagon.

CHAPTER 13

Adjectives With Underlying Noun Forms

Here are some lists of adjectives with underlying noun forms. Look over these lists carefully, and be sure you know the meanings of all the words given. If necessary, consult your dictionary. All the words in the adjective lists can occur in the pattern "They were _____." Try the adjectives in this pattern and make sure the meaning of each sentence formed is clear to you. Also, be sure you can spell all the words listed. You will notice that spelling changes sometimes accompany derivation.

Group 1. Suffix -y

NOUNS	ADJECTIVES	NOUNS	ADJECTIVES	NOUNS	ADJECTIVES
anger	angry	haste	hasty	shade	shady
bag	baggy	health	healthy	silk	silky
blood	bloody	hill	hilly	silver	silvery
bush	bushy	hunger	hungry	sleep	sleepy
curl	curly	ice	icy	smoke	smoky
dirt	dirty	juice	juicy	snow	snowy
dust	dusty	leaf	leafy	soap	soapy
ease	easy	luck	lucky	stone	stony
fault	faulty	milk	milky	storm	stormy
glass	glassy	mud	muddy	sun	sunny
grass	grassy	powder	powdery	thorn	thorny
grease	greasy	risk	risky	wave	wavy
greed	greedy	rust	rusty	wealth	wealthy
guilt	guilty	sand	sandy	wind	windy
hair	hairy				

Group 2. Suffix -ly

NOUNS	ADJECTIVES	NOUNS	ADJECTIVES	NOUNS	ADJECTIVES
cost	costly	love	lovely	order	orderly
coward	cowardly	man	manly	time	timely
friend	friendly	mother	motherly		

286

Group 3. Suffix -ful

Nouns	Adjectives	Nouns	Adjectives	Nouns	Adjectives
beauty	beautiful	help	helpful	sorrow	sorrowful
care	careful	hope	hopeful	success	successful
cheer	cheerful	joy	joyful	thought	thoughtful
deceit	deceitful	law	lawful	truth	truthful
delight	delightful	pain	painful	use	useful
doubt	doubtful	peace	peaceful	waste	wasteful
event	eventful	plenty	plentiful	watch	watchful
faith	faithful	power	powerful	wonder	wonderful
fear	fearful	respect	respectful	youth	youthful

Group 4. Suffix -less

Nouns	Adjectives	Nouns	Adjectives	Nouns	Adjectives
age	ageless	home	homeless	sense	senseless
care	careless	hope	hopeless	shape	shapeless
end	endless	law	lawless	spot	spotless
fault	faultless	leaf	leafless	taste	tasteless
fear	fearless	life	lifeless	use	useless
harm	harmless	noise	noiseless	value	valueless
heart	heartless	power	powerless	worth	worthless

Group 5. Suffixes -ous, -ious

Nouns	Adjectives	Nouns	Adjectives
courage	courageous	mountain	mountainous
danger	dangerous	mystery	mysterious
envy	envious	number	numerous
fame	famous	poison	poisonous
joy	joyous	space	spacious

Group 6. Suffixes -al, -tal, -ial, -tial

Nouns	Adjectives	Nouns	Adjectives
accident	accidental	experiment	experimental
coast	coastal	form	formal
colony	colonial	horizon	horizontal
confidence	confidential	influence	influential
conversation	conversational	music	musical
critic	critical	nature	natural
education	educational	origin	original

NOUNS	ADJECTIVES	NOUNS	ADJECTIVES
ornament	ornamental	season	seasonal
person	personal	universe	universal
practice	practical		

Group 7. Suffixes -ic, -etic, -atic

NOUNS	ADJECTIVES	NOUNS	ADJECTIVES
artist	artistic	poet	poetic
base	basic	sympathy	sympathetic
patriot	patriotic	system	systematic

Group 8. Suffix -ish

NOUNS	ADJECTIVES	NOUNS	ADJECTIVES
book	bookish	fool	foolish
child	childish	self	selfish
fever	feverish	sheep	sheepish

Group 9. Suffix -like

NOUNS	ADJECTIVES	NOUNS	ADJECTIVES
business	businesslike	life	lifelike
child	childlike	war	warlike
lady	ladylike	workman	workmanlike

Group 10. Suffixes -ed, -en

NOUNS	ADJECTIVES	NOUNS	ADJECTIVES
disease	diseased	skill	skilled
gold	golden	wood	wooden
horn	horned	wool	woolen
salary	salaried		

Group 11. Endings -ion, -iety contrasting with -ious

NOUNS	ADJECTIVES	NOUNS	ADJECTIVES
ambition	ambitious	religion	religious
anxiety	anxious	suspicion	suspicious
caution	cautious	variety	various

Group 12. Miscellaneous Pairs

NOUNS	ADJECTIVES
circle	circular
fortune	fortunate
satisfaction	satisfactory

EXERCISES

A. Underline the suffixes in each of the following words:

bushy	skilled	childlike
beautiful	warlike	wooden
leafless	foolish	lifeless
mountainous	golden	feverish
poetic	systematic	thoughtful
original	silvery	orderly
friendly	shapeless	formal

B. Give an adjective related to each of the nouns below. If two adjectives are possible, give both.

Example: noise—**noisy, noiseless**

hope	storm	circle
horizon	fear	book
envy	business	fortune
time	disease	cost

C. Each noun below is given with a suffix. Put the noun and suffix together and spell the resulting word correctly.

mud -y	peace -ful
plenty -ful	wave -y
use -less	mystery -ous
nature -al	influence -tial
sympathy -etic	sheep -ish
number -ous	salary -ed
joy -ous	space -ious

D. Fill each blank with an adjective related to the noun which appears before the comma.

Example: He talked a great deal about **hope,** and I think he was **hopeful** himself.

1. He talked a great deal about **courage,** and I think he was .... himself.

2. He talked a great deal about **hunger,** and I think he was .... himself.

3. He talked a great deal about **fever,** and I think he was .... himself.

4. He talked a great deal about **wealth,** and I think he was
.... himself.

5. He talked a great deal about **ambition,** and I think he was
.... himself.

6. He talked a great deal about **sympathy,** and I think he was
.... himself.

7. He talked a great deal about **success,** and I think he was
.... himself.

8. He talked a great deal about **caution,** and I think he was
.... himself.

9. He talked a great deal about **music,** and I think he was
.... himself.

10. He talked a great deal about **sleep,** and I think he was
.... himself.

11. He talked a great deal about **fame,** and I think he was
.... himself.

12. He talked a great deal about **doubt,** and I think he was
.... himself.

13. He talked a great deal about **envy,** and I think he was
.... himself.

14. He talked a great deal about **power,** and I think he was
.... himself.

15. He talked a great deal about **suspicion,** and I think he was
.... himself.

CHAPTER 14

Nouns With Underlying Adjective Forms;
Contrasts in Stem Forms

Here we see several groups of nouns with underlying adjective forms. Examine these groups carefully for spelling and meaning. All the words in the noun lists can occur in the pattern "He hasn't told me about the _____ yet." Try the nouns in this pattern and make sure the meaning of each sentence formed is clear to you.

Group 1. Suffix -ness

ADJECTIVES	NOUNS	ADJECTIVES	NOUNS
awkward	awkwardness	ill	illness
bitter	bitterness	kind	kindness
black	blackness	lonely	loneliness
clean	cleanness	mad	madness
clear	clearness	mild	mildness
close	closeness	neat	neatness
cold	coldness	pale	paleness
conscious	consciousness	polite	politeness
dark	darkness	prompt	promptness
dry	dryness	reasonable	reasonableness
dull	dullness	rough	roughness
faint	faintness	rude	rudeness
firm	firmness	sick	sickness
foolish	foolishness	slow	slowness
forgetful	forgetfulness	smooth	smoothness
fresh	freshness	soft	softness
gentle	gentleness	stiff	stiffness
good	goodness	strange	strangeness
great	greatness	thick	thickness
happy	happiness	thin	thinness
idle	idleness	truthful	truthfulness

291

Adjectives	Nouns	Adjectives	Nouns
useful	usefulness	weak	weakness
wasteful	wastefulness	wicked	wickedness
watchful	watchfulness	yellow	yellowness

Group 2. Suffixes -y, -ty, -ity

Adjectives	Nouns	Adjectives	Nouns
able	ability	original	originality
active	activity	peculiar	peculiarity
certain	certainty	poor	poverty
cruel	cruelty	popular	popularity
curious	curiosity	public	publicity
difficult	difficulty	punctual	punctuality
electric	electricity	pure	purity
equal	equality	rapid	rapidity
formal	formality	real	reality
generous	generosity	regular	regularity
honest	honesty	responsible	responsibility
jealous	jealousy	royal	royalty
loyal	loyalty	safe	safety
modest	modesty	scarce	scarcity
moral	morality	simple	simplicity
noble	nobility	sincere	sincerity
opportune	opportunity	stupid	stupidity

Group 3. Suffix -th

Adjectives	Nouns	Adjectives	Nouns
broad	breadth	true	truth
deep	depth	warm	warmth
long	length	wide	width
strong	strength	young	youth

Group 4. Ending t contrasting with ce

Adjectives	Nouns	Adjectives	Nouns
absent	absence	patient	patience
distant	distance	present	presence
important	importance	silent	silence
obedient	obedience	violent	violence

Group 5. Ending t contrasting with cy

ADJECTIVES	NOUNS	ADJECTIVES	NOUNS
efficient	efficiency	secret	secrecy
frequent	frequency	urgent	urgency
permanent	permanency		

Group 6. Miscellaneous Pairs

ADJECTIVES	NOUNS	ADJECTIVES	NOUNS
brave	bravery	literary	literature
foreign	foreigner	proud	pride
free	freedom	strange	stranger
hard	hardship	wise	wisdom
high	height	young	youngster
just	justice		

EXERCISES

A. Underline the suffixes in each of the following words:

promptness	length	cruelty
truth	honesty	justice
wisdom	purity	softness
hardship	usefulness	breadth

B. Give a noun related to each of the adjectives below.

Example: kind—**kindness**

stupid	good	original
wicked	electric	young
brave	popular	difficult
high	free	polite
warm	rude	able

C. Each adjective below is given with a suffix. Put the adjective and suffix together and spell the resulting word correctly.

lonely -ness	noble -ity
curious -ity	deep -th
strong -th	safe -ty
foreign -er	dry -ness
thin -ness	scarce -ity

D. Fill each blank with a noun related to the adjective at the beginning of the sentence.

Example: **Active** men are noted for their **activity.**

1. **Truthful** men are noted for their ....

2. **Generous** men are noted for their ....

3. **Patient** men are noted for their ....

4. **Efficient** men are noted for their ....

5. **Brave** men are noted for their ....

6. **Wise** men are noted for their ....

7. **Strong** men are noted for their ....

8. **Punctual** men are noted for their ....

9. **Awkward** men are noted for their ....

10. **Loyal** men are noted for their ....

E. Fill each blank with a noun related to the adjective which appears in the first part of the sentence.

Example: She looked at the **wide** road and was really impressed by its **width.**

1. She looked at the **rough** sea and was really impressed by its ....

2. She looked at the **violent** storm and was really impressed by its ....

3. She looked at the **high** mountain and was really impressed by its ....

4. She looked at the **long** car and was really impressed by its ....

5. She looked at the **silent** forest and was really impressed by its ....

6. She looked at the **pale** moon and was really impressed by its ....

7. She looked at the **clear** water and was really impressed by
   its ....

8. She looked at the **difficult** problem and was really impressed by
   its ....

9. She looked at the **important** paper and was really impressed by
   its ....

10. She looked at the **dull** knife and was really impressed by
    its ....

CHAPTER 15

Adjectives and Verbs: Differences in Patterning

Adjectives

In this and the following chapter we shall see some of the formal differences between adjectives and verbs.

We have seen that adjectives occur in patterns like

He seemed _____.

They were very _____.

Words like **happy, tired,** and **beautiful** occur as adjectives, but not **horse, usually,** and **go.**

We have also seen that verbs fit patterns like

Let's _____.

Don't _____ it.

Words like **go, carry,** and **stop** occur as verbs, but not **village, happy,** and **usually.**

Certain positions in English sentences are shared by adjectives and verbs, some of which are also shared by nouns. Both adjectives and nouns, for example, fit the pattern "He was _____," which we saw in Chapter 12.

He was **happy.**   He was **captain.**

He was **kind.**   He was **Robert.**

Verbs will fit this pattern too.

He was **running.**   He was **killed.**

He was **smoking.**   He was **followed.**

The position "a(n) _____ man" is a position for adjectives and nouns; but verbs occur in this position too.

ADJECTIVES	NOUNS	VERBS
a **hungry** man	a **city** man	a **laughing** man
an **old** man	an **insurance** man	an **employed** man

Furthermore, verbs as well as adjectives will fit both blanks in these sentences:

A _____ person is a person who is _____.
A _____ thing is a thing that is _____.

A laughing man, for example, is a man who is laughing, and a moving car is a car that is moving.

We can, however, separate adjectives from both nouns and verbs in this position. A word like **very, rather,** or **somewhat** will fit in front of the adjectives.

> a **very** hungry man
> a **rather** old man
> a **somewhat** foolish man

But these words—**very, rather,** and **somewhat**—will not fit in front of the nouns and verbs. The following are not English phrases:

* a **very** city man   * a **very** laughing man
* a **rather** insurance man   * a **rather** employed man
* a **somewhat** desert man   * a **somewhat** fighting man

Similarly, these are normal English sentences:

> He was **very** happy.
> He was **rather** kind.

But these are not English sentences:

> * He was **very** captain.
> * He was **somewhat** Robert.

Nor are these:

* He was **very** running.   * He was **very** killed.
* He was **rather** smoking.   * He was **somewhat** followed.

Words Which Are Both Adjectives and Verbs

A few words occur both as adjectives and as verbs.[8] Some of the common ones are the following:

average	clear	dirty
blind	complete	dry
brown	cool	dull
calm	correct	empty
clean	direct	equal

---

[8] Several words occur as adjectives, as nouns, and as verbs. Four of them are **average, equal, hollow,** and **welcome.** Note the following:

Nouns:	The **average** was interesting.	The **welcome** was interesting.
Adjectives:	He seemed **average.**	They were very **welcome.**
Verbs:	Let's **average** the scores.	Let's **welcome** them.

faint	near	tame
fit	open	thin
free	quiet	tidy
hollow	slow	upset
idle	smooth	welcome
level	steady	wet

The following, for example, are normal English sentences:

ADJECTIVES: He seems **cool.** They were very **dry.**
VERBS: Let's **cool** it.   Don't **dry** it.

Derivational suffixes and prefixes mark a difference between many adjectives and verbs. In some instances the adjective has the affix; in others the verb has it. A number of contrasting pairs are given in Chapter 16.

EXERCISES

A. In each of the groups of words below, there are four adjectives and one verb or four verbs and one adjective. See if you can pick out the word which does not belong with the others. Remember that adjectives will fit a pattern like "They were very _____" or "He seemed _____." Verbs will fit a pattern like "Let's _____" or "Don't _____ it."

1. sew, long, necessary, flat, slow.
2. tie, look, rest, cover, rich.
3. good, take, tall, careful, dark.
4. wear, old, pale, heavy, straight.
5. fill, fold, asleep, return, work.
6. tap, change, awkward, answer, remain.
7. large, examine, nervous, angry, stiff.
8. hit, rub, bring, uneasy, scatter.
9. mild, sweep, afraid, wise, faithful.
10. listen, accept, unhappy, turn, continue.
11. impatient, keep, neat, important, foolish.
12. powerful, clean, youthful, paint, true.
13. smoke, walk, spread, carry, guilty.
14. friendly, move, foolish, young, big.
15. fortunate, discuss, sad, bright, eager.

B. In the numbered sentences below, the words in heavy type pattern as adjectives. See if you can make a sentence in which each of these words will pattern as a verb.

Example: His hands were **dry.**

   Dry your hands with that towel.

1. The grass remained **wet** all night.
2. After 4 o'clock the room was completely **empty.**
3. This sentence looks **correct;** ask the teacher if there are any mistakes in it.
4. The child has **dirty** hands; tell him to wash them.
5. There are no hills along the river; the land there seems to be **smooth.**
6. When you have some **free** time, call me on the telephone.
7. The train sounds **near** already. What time does it reach the station?
8. You can't cut very well with those **dull** scissors.
9. Give me a **clean** handkerchief, please.
10. We expect **calm** weather this weekend.

C. Look again at the list of words which occur both as adjectives and nouns. Select one word from the list and make a sentence in which it patterns as an adjective. Then see if you can think of ten other adjectives which you can substitute for the one you selected. Take **tame,** for example. You can make a sentence like "Those animals are **tame.**" And for **tame,** you can substitute various other adjectives:

>   Those animals are tame.
>   sick.
>   powerful.
>   wild.
>   strong.
>   afraid.
>   young.
>   noisy.
>   quiet.
>   lively.
>   hungry.

D. Now select another word from the list and make a sentence in which it patterns as a verb. Then see if you can think of ten other verbs which you can substitute for the one you selected. Take **faint,** for example. You can make a sentence like "She **fainted** when she saw Mr. Higginbotham." And for **fainted,** you can substitute various other verbs:

She fainted when she saw Mr. Higginbotham.
     stopped
     cried
     shouted
     laughed
     moved
     screamed
     fell
     ran
     listened
     returned

CHAPTER **16**

Adjectives With Underlying Verb Forms and Verbs With Underlying Adjective Forms

Adjectives With Underlying Verb Forms

Here are some lists of adjectives with underlying verb forms. Examine these lists carefully, and be sure you know the meanings of all the words given. All the words can occur in the pattern "They were _____." Try the adjectives in this pattern and make sure the meaning of each sentence formed is clear to you. Also, be sure you can spell all the words listed. You will notice that spelling changes sometimes accompany derivation.

Group 1. Suffixes -ent, -ant

VERBS	ADJECTIVES	VERBS	ADJECTIVES
confide	confident	obey	obedient
depend	dependent	observe	observant
differ	different	please	pleasant
excel	excellent	urge	urgent

Group 2. Suffixes -able, -ible

VERBS	ADJECTIVES	VERBS	ADJECTIVES
agree	agreeable	love	lovable
avoid	avoidable	measure	measurable
comfort	comfortable	notice	noticeable
defend	defensible	pardon	pardonable
depend	dependable	prefer	preferable
enjoy	enjoyable	read	readable
explain	explainable	reason	reasonable
fashion	fashionable	sense	sensible
favor	favorable	value	valuable
laugh	laughable	work	workable

301

Group 3. Suffixes -ive, -tive, -ative, -itive

VERBS	ADJECTIVES	VERBS	ADJECTIVES
act	active	explode	explosive
attend	attentive	extend	extensive
attract	attractive	imagine	imaginative
create	creative	possess	possessive
destroy	destructive	select	selective
effect	effective	sense	sensitive
expend	expensive		

Group 4. Suffixes -ed, -en

VERBS	ADJECTIVES	VERBS	ADJECTIVES
advance	advanced	note	noted
complicate	complicated	overjoy	overjoyed
crowd	crowded	prejudice	prejudiced
curve	curved	spot	spotted
damage	damaged	stripe	striped
detail	detailed	swell	swollen
determine	determined	tire	tired
disappoint	disappointed	trouble	troubled
experience	experienced	trust	trusted
fade	faded		

Group 5. Suffix -ing

VERBS	ADJECTIVES	VERBS	ADJECTIVES
amuse	amusing	entertain	entertaining
annoy	annoying	fit	fitting
astonish	astonishing	interest	interesting
charm	charming	invite	inviting
comfort	comforting	puzzle	puzzling
cut	cutting	refresh	refreshing
dare	daring	sport	sporting
deserve	deserving	surprise	surprising
disappoint	disappointing	will	willing
disgust	disgusting		

Group 6. Miscellaneous Pairs

VERBS	ADJECTIVES	VERBS	ADJECTIVES
continue	continuous	séparàte	séparate
forget	forgetful	sleep	asleep
imagine	imaginery	slip	slippery
live	alive	tire	tiresome
quarrel	quarrelsome	trouble	troublesome
perféct	pérfect	wake	awake
satisfy	satisfactory		

Verbs With Underlying Adjective Forms

Here are three groups of verbs with underlying adjective forms. Examine these groups carefully for spelling and meaning. All of the verbs given can occur in the pattern "They were _____(e)d." One or two, however, do not fit the pattern as well as the others. Try the verbs in this pattern and make sure the meaning of each sentence formed is clear to you.

Group 1. Suffix -ize

ADJECTIVES	VERBS	ADJECTIVES	VERBS
civil	civilize	modern	modernize
equal	equalize	real	realize

Group 2. Suffix -en

ADJECTIVES	VERBS	ADJECTIVES	VERBS
bright	brighten	sharp	sharpen
damp	dampen	short	shorten
dark	darken	soft	soften
deaf	deafen	stiff	stiffen
deep	deepen	straight	straighten
fat	fatten	sweet	sweeten
light	lighten	thick	thicken
loose	loosen	tight	tighten
mad	madden	weak	weaken

Group 3. Prefix en-

ADJECTIVES	VERBS
able	enable
large	enlarge
rich	enrich

EXERCISES

A. Underline the affixes (suffixes and prefixes) in each of the following words:

loosen	different	charming
observant	preferable	astonishing
enjoyable	tighten	sensible
attractive	troublesome	modernize
deepen	slippery	awake
enrich	alive	trusted

B. Give an adjective related to each of the verbs below.

Example: work—**workable**

depend	sleep	urge
possess	forget	pardon
tire	obey	act
entertain	create	interest

C. Each verb below is given with a suffix. Put the verb and suffix together and spell the resulting word correctly.

please	-ant	excel	-ent
value	-able	sense	-itive
extend	-ive	continue	-ous
fade	-ed	annoy	-ing
dare	-ing	swell	-en

D. Fill each of the blanks with an adjective related to the verb which appears in the first part of the sentence.

Example: If a child **obeys** his parents, we say he is **obedient.**

1. If a person **amuses** us, we say he is ....

2. If we can **depend** on a person, we say he is ....

3. If a man **observes** everything that happens, we say he is ....

4. If something **explodes** easily, we say it is ....

5. If a person is **sleeping** right now, we say he is ....

6. If something **continues** without stopping, we say it is ....

7. If we can **measure** a certain object, we say it is ....

8. If something **interests** us a great deal, we say it is ....

9. If someone or something **disappoints** us, we say we are

   ....

10. If one object **differs** from the others of a group, we say it is

    ....

11. If a woman's beauty **attracts** the attention of many men, we

    say she is ....

12. If a person **quarrels** a good deal of the time, we say he is

    ....

E. Fill each of the blanks with a verb form (past participle) related to the adjective which appears in the first part of the sentence.

Example: The knives are **sharper** now; they have just been **sharpened.**

1. The ropes are **tighter** now; they have just been ....

2. The rooms are more **modern** now; they have just been ....

3. The curtains are **straighter** now; they have just been ....

4. The houses are **larger** now; they have just been ....

5. The dresses are **shorter** now; they have just been ....

6. The clothes are **damper** now; they have just been ....

CHAPTER **17**

Adjectives With Prefixes; Prefixes in Derivation

Adjectives With Prefixes

In the last group of contrasting pairs given in the preceding chapter we noted the prefix **en-** which marks a difference between adjectives and verbs. As you will remember in our previous discussion of prefixes (Chapter 8), we pointed out that most of the time prefixes do not mark a class difference. Both the prefixed form and the unprefixed form of a word usually belong to the same class. However, the prefix does mark a meaning difference between pairs.

Here are four groups of adjectives with and without prefixes. The prefixes used give the words a "negative" meaning. The unprefixed as well as the prefixed adjectives can occur in the pattern "They appeared to be _____." Try the prefixed adjectives in this pattern, and make sure that the meaning of each sentence formed is clear to you.

Group 1. Adjective Stems with Prefix dis-

agreeable	disagreeable	obedient	disobedient
contented	discontented	orderly	disorderly
continuous	discontinuous	pleased	displeased
honest	dishonest	respectful	disrespectful
honorable	dishonorable	satisfied	dissatisfied
loyal	disloyal	similar	dissimilar

Group 2. Adjective Stems with Prefix un-

afraid	unafraid	civilized	uncivilized
ambitious	unambitious	clear	unclear
artistic	unartistic	comfortable	uncomfortable
ashamed	unashamed	common	uncommon
attractive	unattractive	educated	uneducated
changeable	unchangeable	equal	unequal

eventful	uneventful	official	unofficial
fair	unfair	patriotic	unpatriotic
faithful	unfaithful	pleasant	unpleasant
fortunate	unfortunate	popular	unpopular
friendly	unfriendly	real	unreal
grateful	ungrateful	reasonable	unreasonable
happy	unhappy	satisfactory	unsatisfactory
healthy	unhealthy	scientific	unscientific
imaginative	unimaginative	selfish	unselfish
important	unimportant	skilled	unskilled
interesting	uninteresting	steady	unsteady
just	unjust	successful	unsuccessful
kind	unkind	true	untrue
lawful	unlawful	usual	unusual
natural	unnatural	willing	unwilling
necessary	unnecessary	wise	unwise

Group 3. Adjective Stems with Prefixes in-, im-, ir-

active	inactive	perfect	imperfect
complete	incomplete	possible	impossible
convenient	inconvenient	practical	impractical
dependent	independent	probable	improbable
direct	indirect	proper	improper
expensive	inexpensive	pure	impure
formal	informal	regular	irregular
human	inhuman	responsible	irresponsible
moral	immoral	sincere	insincere
patient	impatient		

Group 4. Adjective Stems with Prefix non-

alcoholic	nonalcoholic	explosive	nonexplosive
destructive	nondestructive	political	nonpolitical
educational	noneducational	racial	nonracial
existent	nonexistent	resistant	nonresistant

Are Prefixes Inflectional or Derivational?

We have seen in earlier chapters that derivational suffixes usually mark a difference in word classes. In many chapters of this book, in fact, we have listed related words of different classes which are distinguished by these suffixes. In Chapter 8, however, we noted a few noun suffixes which we also called derivational, but which do not separate word classes; for example, **-ess, -ist, -ship** as in **waitress, artist, friendship**. But they do serve, like other derivational suffixes, in the building of stems to which we can add inflectional suffixes.

Inflectional suffixes, you will remember, never mark a difference in word class. They occur in sets or *paradigms*. Some noun paradigms, for example, have as many as four members: **boy, boys, boy's, boys'**. Most noun paradigms, however, are limited to two or three members; and a few nouns have no paradigmatic forms at all. Verbs usually have five paradigmatic forms: **walk, walks, walked, walking, walked; rise, rises, rose, rising, risen**. Inflected adjectives and adverbs ordinarily have three paradigmatic forms: **slow, slower, slowest**.

In a few instances we have noticed that prefixes separate word classes in the same way that derivational suffixes ordinarily do. In Chapters 8 and 16 we saw that prefixes sometimes mark a difference between nouns and verbs and between adjectives and verbs: **circle—encircle; large—enlarge**. We shall see in Chapter 21 that prefixes sometimes mark a difference between adjectives and adverbs and between nouns and adverbs: **long—along; shore—ashore**. Elsewhere, prefixes do not distinguish the words of one class from those of another class. But they do serve in the derivation of stems in the same way as the noun suffixes of Chapter 8—stems to which we can add inflectional suffixes. Therefore, we consider all prefixes in English **derivational**. The difference between word elements which are inflectional or derivational, then, is not whether they mark a class difference, but whether they are used in stem-building.

EXERCISES

A. Underline the prefixes and suffixes in the following words:

unfaithful	imperfect	nonracial
discontinuous	unselfish	uneventful
nonexistent	noneducational	informal
inactive	disagreeable	disrespectful
unnatural	unfortunate	impure

B. Fill each blank with the proper prefix.

1. His house is ....comfortable.

2. His wife is ....happy.

3. His brother is ....satisfied.

4. His son is ....patient.

5. His servant is ....honest.

6. His club is ....political.

7. His occupation is ....pleasant.

8. His daughter is ....dependent.

9. His neighbor is ....kind.

10. His sister is ....efficient.

C. Fill each blank with the proper prefix.

1. All of his employees were ....agreeable.

2. All of his questions were ....clear.

3. All of his children were ....popular.

4. All of his drinks were ....alcoholic.

5. All of his clothes were ....expensive.

6. All of his customers were ....pleasant.

7. All of his statements were ....true.

8. All of his suggestions were ....practical.

9. All of his friends were ....orderly.

10. All of his promises were ....sincere.

CHAPTER **18**

How We Recognize Adjectives

We have seen that certain signals help us recognize nouns and verbs—inflectional and derivational suffixes, determiners, auxiliaries, etc. Similar signals help us recognize adjectives, some of which we have already mentioned.

Inflectional Suffixes

In Chapter 12 we reviewed certain inflectional suffixes used with adjectives which you have probably studied elsewhere in detail: the comparative marker (-er) and the superlative marker (-est). These suffixes occur with some adjectives, and they also occur with some adverbs. In the following sentences these suffixes (together with other signals) help us recognize adjectives:

1. Stephen's work was much **harder** than the title suggests.
2. "Maybe it's **easier** to write that kind of poetry," suggested Roberts.
3. Louisa's face was **paler** and **smoother** than Joe's, and people thought she looked **older**.
4. The **biggest** consumer in town is Mrs. Arnold Peters.
5. Sitting at her window during long afternoons, she spent the **happiest** hours of her life.
6. The farmer was smoking the **worst** [9] tobacco the peddler had ever smelled.
7. The stranger insisted that this was the **best** supper he had eaten in a month.

Derivational Suffixes

In Chapter 13 we noted a number of contrasts between noun and adjective forms, and we examined several derivational suffixes used in adjective formations. The main ones were:

---

[9] The irregular forms serve as markers just as the regular forms.

Suffixes	Examples
-y	hasty, wealthy
-ly	friendly, timely
-ful	beautiful, painful
-less	careless, worthless
-ous, -ious	dangerous, spacious
-al, -tal, -ial, -tial	accidental, influential
-ic, -etic, -atic	basic, sympathetic
-ish	childish, selfish
-like	businesslike, lifelike
-ed, -en	horned, woolen

In Chapter 16 we noted contrasts between verbs and adjective forms, and we examined some additional suffixes used in adjective formations. The main ones were:

Suffixes	Examples
-ent, -ant	different, pleasant
-able, -ible	comfortable, sensible
-ive, -tive, -ative, -itive	active, imaginative
-ed, -en	crowded, swollen
-ing	daring, surprising

These suffixes help us recognize adjectives in the following sentences:

8. He frequently cut **funny** stories and articles from the local newspapers.
9. You know I can't afford a **costly** gift.
10. For ten years they tried to make our chicken farm **successful**.
11. Finally they decided it was **hopeless**.
12. With **nervous** hands she lighted a lamp.
13. Father became a little **feverish** in his anxiety to please.
14. I hope next year I can make things more **pleasant**.
15. It was mother's idea that the restaurant would be **profitable**.
16. An **attractive** young woman pressed through the crowd to see the man with the gray beard.
17. On a chicken farm **surprising** things sometimes happen.

Intensifiers

Adjectives (and adverbs too) occur with a group of words called *intensifiers*. Some of the common ones are:

very	pretty	so	less
quite	mighty	too	least
somewhat	a little	more	enough
rather	a bit	most	

Intensifiers do not mark adjectives and adverbs as clearly as determiners mark nouns and auxiliaries mark verbs. **Very, pretty, mighty, a little, more, most, less,** and **least,** for example, also occur with nouns. But since intensifiers frequently occur in patterns with adjectives and adverbs, they serve (together with other signals) to mark these word classes. In the following sentences, intensifiers help us recognize adjectives:

18. Stephen's father had died when he was very **young.**
19. You'll probably think it's pretty **bad.**
20. Father became a little **angry** with Joe Kane.
21. This is one of the facts which makes life so **discouraging.**
22. The Gales were too **poor** to go to the movies.
23. This made Stephen less **efficient** than ever as a bill collector.

Position

Adjectives fill certain positions in English sentences. One such position is between a determiner and a noun; for example, "a(n) _____ friend:" a **tall** friend, an **old** friend. In Chapter 12 we saw that nouns can fill this position: a **girl** friend, an **animal** friend; and in Chapter 15 we saw that verbs can also fill this position: a **sleeping** friend, an **employed** friend. Another position is after a linking verb (**be, become, see, look, feel, appear, sound, taste, smell, grow, remain**); for example: "He was _____:"

He was **helpful.**
He was **sick.**

Nouns and verbs can fill this position too:

He was **captain.**   He was **laughing.**
He was **Edward.**   He was **killed.**

We can separate adjectives from nouns and verbs in these positions by placing an intensifier like **very, somewhat,** or **rather** in front of the word in question. An intensifier will fit before an adjective, but not before a noun or verb. **Tall** and **old,** then, are adjectives because a **very tall** friend and a **very old** friend are normal English. **Girl, animal, sleeping,** and **injured,** on the other hand, are not adjectives because * a very **girl** friend, * a very **animal** friend, * a very **sleeping** friend, and * a very **employed** friend are not English at all. Similarly, **helpful** and **sick** are adjectives:

He was very **helpful.**
He was very **sick.**

But **captain, Edward, laughing,** and **killed** are not adjectives; these are not English sentences:

* He was very **captain.**   * He was very **laughing.**
* He was very **Edward.**   * He was very **killed.**

Nouns and verbs occur in the two positions mentioned, but apparently with less frequency than adjectives. So these positions do serve (together with other signals) to mark this class of words. In the following sentences position helps us recognize adjectives:

24. Stephen had just returned from an **unsuccessful** collection tour.
25. The **bald** path on top of his head was like a **broad** road.
26. Something happened to the two people; they became **ambitious.**
27. Stella thought it was **wonderful.**
28. Tappan's mind grew **old** quickly.

EXERCISES

A. Underline the intensifiers in the following sentences:

1. "You see," said Miss Higginbotham, "that this story about me is quite untrue."
2. The stranger looked rather weary; Dominicus guessed the man had walked all night.
3. He realized that such an action was very unlikely.
4. Stella thought it was pretty good.
5. Then he went to bed, quite satisfied with his position in life.
6. Small chickens, just starting the journey of life, look so bright, but they are really very stupid.
7. In the future he was going to adopt a more cheerful outlook on life.
8. He pointed to the most remarkable of his treasures.
9. Joe decided that the man in front of him was somewhat insane but harmless.

10. My uncle has been kind enough to give me a place to live in his house.

B. In the sentences below, the adjectives are shown in heavy type. Underline the inflectional suffixes once and the derivational suffixes twice.

1. He decided that he had been an **unsuccessful** man in the past because he had not been **cheerful**.
2. Father believed that the **younger** people wanted a place to go, and that he and mother could provide an **attractive** place for them.
3. He gave Joe Kane a **friendly** tap on the shoulder.
4. After that moan came others, growing **louder** and **longer** until there was a **continuous** sound.
5. One August, the **hottest** and **driest** of his desert experience, Tappan was working in the Panamint Mountains.
6. It was not a **healthy** burro, although its mother was the **strongest** and **toughest** of all the burros he had owned.
7. Desert plants provided **suitable** food for Jenet.
8. This also made her **different** from other burros.
9. Sylvia remained **motionless,** not moving a foot or even a finger.
10. There, when she made the **dangerous** pass from one tree to another, her **great** adventure would really begin.

C. The words in heavy type in the sentences below are adjectives. Each is marked as an adjective in one or more ways—by an inflectional suffix, a derivational suffix, an intensifier, or position. Tell which marker or markers are present in each case.

1. The **foolish** man chooses his wife by her looks.
2. Women and cats are always **ungrateful.**
3. One is never too **old** to learn.
4. A **good** teacher sets a **good** example.
5. Silence is **golden.**
6. Two heads are **better** than one.
7. The **largest** fish come from the **largest** sea.
8. Boys that fight aren't very **bright.**
9. Some people are born **lucky.**
10. A word to the wise is **sufficient.**

CHAPTER **19**

Review: Latin, Greek, and English

In earlier chapters, we have discussed three kinds of word elements which we called *prefixes, suffixes,* and *stems.* Stems are very numerous. It would not be worth our while to try to make a complete list of stems; we can find thousands of them in the dictionary. *Affixes* (prefixes and suffixes), on the other hand, are much less numerous; it is possible to make a complete list of them without difficulty, provided, of course, we can decide exactly what an English affix is.

Some books list various word elements as prefixes and suffixes which we have not mentioned; for example,

-ism	re-	-id
Americanism	reread	humid
heroism	regain	liquid
patriotism	receive	solid
realism	remain	splendid

Since the readings and word-study materials of this book have been prepared largely within a limited vocabulary list of high-frequency words, some word elements which we would call affixes do not appear. Words with the suffix -ism, for instance, are low-frequency words and have not been used in these materials.

Thousands of English words and word elements are of Latin and Greek origin. A high percentage of these, especially the ones of Latin origin, have changed considerably in meaning through the centuries. The forms clearly suggest a relationship between large numbers of English and Latin words, but the meanings often seem so unlike, we might consider them unrelated if we knew nothing about their Latin origins. Part of the Latin vocabulary in English came into the language directly from Latin; a great deal of it, however, came into the language through French.

The word element re- which we noted above is definitely an English prefix. We have words like reread, regain, reintroduce, and

315

rewind, and new words in English are still being created with this word element joined to verb stems. There is a consistent form **re-** and a consistent element of meaning—"again, back." **Re-** is clearly a Latin prefix also, with a similar or perhaps the same meaning, but if this meaning is still present in the English words **react, receive, relax, relieve, remain,** and **respect,** it is certainly difficult to recognize.

The other word element, **-id,** which we noted above, is a perfectly good Latin suffix, marking a difference between verbs and adjectives: **humere, humidus; liquere, liquidus,** etc. But **-id** serves no function of this kind in English, and we find no consistent element of meaning in the English words **humid, liquid, solid,** and **splendid.** So we hesitate to consider it an English suffix at all.

There are today two points of view concerning many of these related ancient and modern words and word elements. Let's take the English word **compete,** for example. In Latin we have a prefix **com-,** "with," and a root or stem form **pet-,** "seek." From one point of view, **com-** is both a Latin prefix and an English prefix. From the other point of view, **com-** is a Latin prefix but not an English prefix; and the word **compete** is not divisible into two parts in this way. The disagreement rests largely on prefixes rather than suffixes. Suffixes (that is, derivational suffixes), you will remember, ordinarily mark class differences, whereas prefixes ordinarily mark meaning differences.

We are listing below a number of Latin and Greek prefixes— the ones often listed in handbooks devoted to English word study— along with their original meanings and some examples from English. Look these over carefully, and use your dictionary to check the meanings of the words which are unfamiliar to you. You will probably form some ideas of your own concerning the two points of view we have mentioned.

Latin Prefixes

We have already noted **dis-** "negative" (disagree, displeasure), **in-** (injustice, inactive), and **re-** (reread, regain).

PREFIXES	MEANING	EXAMPLES
ab-	away from	abrupt, abnormal
ad-, ar-, as-, at-, *etc.*	to, toward	admit, arrive, associate, attend

PREFIXES	MEANING	EXAMPLES
ambi-	both	ambidextrous, ambiguous
ante-	before	antedate, anteroom
bene-	well	benefit, benevolent
bi-	two	bicycle, biannual
circum-	around	circumnavigate, circumference
com-, col-, con-, co-, *etc.*	together with	complete, collect, concord, cooperate
contra-	against	contradict, contrast
de-	down from	depend, depression
dis-	apart from	dismiss, distribute
ex-, ef-, e-	out of	exhale, effect, event
extra-	beyond, outside of	extraordinary, extracurricular
in-, il-, im-, *etc.*	into	incline, illustrate, impose
inter-	between	interfere, interruption
intra-	within	intramuscular, intrastate
intro-	within	introduce, introvert
mal-	bad	malcontent, malnutrition
multi-	many	multiply, multimillionaire
ob-, oc-, of-, op-	toward, against	observe, occur, offend, oppose
per-	throughout, completely	percussion, persistence
post-	after, behind	postpone, postwar, postnasal
pre-	before	predict, prepare
pro-	forward	proceed, project, progress
se-	aside	separate, secret
semi-	half	semicircle, semiprecious
sub-, suf-, sup-	under	submerge, suffer, support
super-	above, over	superscript, supervise supernatural
supra-	above in position	supranasal, supraliminal
trans-	across, beyond	transfer, transmit, transcontinental

PREFIXES	MEANING	EXAMPLES
tri-	three	triangle, triplicate
uni-	one	uniform, universal
vice-	in place of	vice-president, viceroy

Greek Prefixes

PREFIXES	MEANING	EXAMPLES
a-	not	asylum, anesthetic
ana-	up, backward	analysis, anatomy
anti-	against	antiseptic, antisocial
apo-	away from, off	apology, apoplexy
cata-	down, against	catalogue, catastrophe
ec-, ex-	out of	eccentric, exodus
en-	in	energy, entomology
mono-	one, alone	monotonous, monopoly
para-	beside, beyond	paralysis, parasite
peri-	around	periphery, periscope
poly-	many	polyglot, polysyllabic
pro-	before	prologue, prophet
syn-, sym-, syl-	with, together	syntax, sympathy, syllable

The two points of view concerning whether the prefixes listed above are really English prefixes need not trouble us here. A more detailed account of English word building than is possible in this book would undoubtedly give a fuller discussion of these prefixes. Most of them are like **re-**; that is, they appear in words of ancient origin which have undergone considerable change in meaning, and there is usually no underlying free form. Take **receive**, for example. If we remove the prefix (**re-**), we have **-ceive**, which is a bound form like **re-**. On the other hand, most of them are still active prefixes; that is, we still form new words with them, especially technical terms. But when this happens, the prefix is ordinarily attached to a free form and it ordinarily has a consistent meaning; for example, **readvertise, recapture, redecorate, reorganize,** and **revisit,** with re- meaning "again."

The vocabulary selected for our word study in this book is very limited. Most of the words given above to exemplify Latin and Greek prefixes do not appear on our limited list. For a fuller discussion of all the facts concerning these prefixes we would need to go much farther beyond our selected vocabulary—into a large number of low-frequency words.

Native Prefixes

Before leaving this matter, we should note a few native English prefixes which are often listed along with Latin and Greek prefixes. Most of these also appear as separate words; and it would be more accurate to regard the examples in the list below as compounds instead of prefixes plus stems. We have already listed un- (uncertainty, unattractive), be- (befriend, bewitch), mis- (misfortune, miscount), and a- (alive, asleep).

PREFIXES	MEANING	EXAMPLES
by-	near, different from the usual	bypass, by-product
for-	off, away	forbid, forget
fore-	in front of	forepaw, forecast
off-	from	offshore, offspring
out-	outside of, going beyond	outdoors, outcast, outlive, outwalk
over-	above, beyond	overcoat, overcautious
under-	below	underline, underpass

EXERCISES

A. Using your dictionary, see if you can find one word which begins with each of the prefixes listed below. Look for words which have an underlying free form; for example, **reappear:** prefix **re-** and underlying form **appear.**

ante- (L.)	extra- (L.)	poly- (G.)	sub- (L.)
anti- (G.)	inter- (L.)	post- (L.)	syn- (G.)
bi- (L.)	mono- (G.)	pre- (L.)	tri- (L.)
circum- (L.)	multi- (L.)	pro- (L.)	uni- (L.)
de- (L.)	para- (G.)	semi- (L.)	

B. Give a related noun for each of the following adjectives:

Example: spacious—**space**

important	childish	circular
secret	horned	high
proud	anxious	deep

violent	hasty	wooden
warlike	frequent	mysterious
suspicious	silent	systematic
envious	free	horizontal

C. Give a related verb for each of the following adjectives:

pleasant	obedient	forgetful
valuable	tiresome	alive
able	large	soft
swollen	imaginative	destructive
urgent	comfortable	quarrelsome
equal	modern	stiff

D. Fill each blank with an adjective related to the noun in the first part of the sentence.

Example: In discussing **beauty** he mentioned many **beautiful** paintings.

1. In discussing **danger** he mentioned many .... games.

2. In discussing **suspicion** he mentioned many .... people.

3. In discussing **pain** he mentioned many .... experiences.

4. In discussing **poison** he mentioned many .... plants.

5. In discussing **education** he mentioned many .... institutions.

6. In discussing **art** he mentioned many .... creations.

7. In discussing **events** he mentioned many .... years.

8. In discussing **costs** he mentioned many .... experiments.

9. In discussing **colonies** he mentioned many .... regions.

10. In discussing **mysteries** he mentioned many .... events.

E. Fill each blank with a noun related to the adjective at the beginning of the sentence.

Example: **Obedient** children are noted for their **obedience**.

1. **Mild** cigars are noted for their ....

2. **Cold** winters are noted for their ....

3. **Jealous** husbands are noted for their ....

4. **Strong** ropes are noted for their ....

5. **Popular** girls are noted for their ....

6. **Forgetful** professors are noted for their ....

7. **Urgent** messages are noted for their ....

8. **Idle** men are noted for their ....

9. **Warm** blankets are noted for their ....

10. **Important** events are noted for their ....

CHAPTER **20**

Adverbs and Adjectives: Differences in Patterning

We have identified nouns, verbs, and adjectives as groups of words which fit three sets of sentence patterns respectively. Now we shall see that adverbs fit a fourth set of patterns. In this and the following chapter we shall examine some of the formal differences between adverbs and adjectives. Also in the following chapter we shall examine some contrasts between adverbs and nouns.

Adverbs

Adverbs occur in patterns like

They walked _____.

He did it very _____.

Words like **often, cheerfully, out,** and **well** occur as adverbs. The following are normal English sentences:

They walked **often.**	He did it very **often.**
They walked **cheerfully.**	He did it very **cheerfully.**
They walked **out.**	He did it very **well.**

Words like **bench, go,** and **empty** do not fit these patterns. These are not English sentences:

* They walked **bench.**	* He did it very **bench.**
* They walked **go.**	* He did it very **go.**
* They walked **empty.**	* He did it very **empty.**

It may seem to you that certain positions in English sentences are shared by adverbs and adjectives. However, this is usually only a matter of verb sub-classes. In two previous lessons we mentioned a group of verbs called *linking verbs*, the main ones being

be	feel	taste	grow
become	look	sound	remain
seem	appear	smell	

Other verbs are called *non-linking verbs.* Ordinarily, linking verbs pattern with adjectives and non-linking verbs pattern with adverbs.

But the verbs in these two sub-classes are not rigidly fixed. Notice this contrast:

> The child **looked happy.**
> The child **looked happily.**

The first sentence tells us that the child seemed to be happy, regardless of what he was doing; the second sentence tells us that the child was happy while he was looking (possibly at or for something). In the first sentence **looked** is a linking verb, and in the second sentence **looked** is a non-linking verb. Here are some other contrasts, but without the "minimal" difference between adjective and adverb forms:

LINKING VERBS	NON-LINKING VERBS
He **appeared** tired.	He **appeared** suddenly.
She **grew** old.	She **grew** quickly.
The bell **sounded** loud.	The bell **sounded** clearly.
The man **turned** red.	The man **turned** around.
She **fell** sick.	She **fell** down.
The water **ran** deep.	The water **ran** quietly.

The pairs of verbs, of course, have a meaning difference.

Words Which Are Both Adverbs and Adjectives

A few words occur both as adverbs and adjectives. Some of the common ones are:

alone	first	low
backward	hard	near
behind	high	next
early	late	right
far	lively	well
fast	last	wrong
fine	long	

The following, for example, are normal English sentences:

ADJECTIVES:	He seemed **early.**	They were very **fast.**
ADVERBS:	They left **early.**	He did it very **fast.**

Inflectional and Derivational Suffixes

Like adjectives, some adverbs can occur with certain inflectional suffixes which you have probably studied already:

DICTIONARY FORM:	fast	hard	near
COMPARATIVE:	faster	harder	nearer
SUPERLATIVE:	fastest	hardest	nearest

Most other adverbs, you will remember, can occur with **more** and **most:**

DICTIONARY FORM:	rapidly	promptly
COMPARATIVE:	**more** rapidly	**more** promptly
SUPERLATIVE:	**most** rapidly	**most** promptly

In some descriptions of English word classes adjectives and adverbs are grouped together as one word class. The two groups have a good deal in common, it is true. The comparative and superlative suffixes occur with certain adjectives and certain adverbs, and both groups of words pattern with intensifiers. If we put all adjectives and adverbs in one class, then we would have to consider the -ly ending an inflectional suffix like -er and -est. Those words ending in -ly would fall in a sub-class of the large adjective-adverb class, and the words we have been calling adjectives would fall in another sub-class. Most of the time we would find that these two sub-classes pattern differently in English sentences.

Because of this difference in patterning and because of the -ly ending which serves as a marker for hundreds of adverbs, we have chosen to consider adjectives and adverbs as separate word classes. So the ending -ly in our grouping is a derivational suffix signaling a difference between adverbs and adjectives in most cases and a difference between adverbs and nouns in others. A large number of pairs showing these contrasts are given in Chapter 21.

EXERCISES

A. In each of the groups of words below, there are four adverbs and one adjective or four adjectives and one adverb. See if you can pick out the word which does not belong with the others. Remember that adverbs will fit a pattern like "They walked _____" or "He did it very _____." Adjectives will fit a pattern like "They were very _____" or "He seemed _____."

1. often, unhappy, steep, dark, sick.
2. forth, normally, quickly, lonely, fearlessly.
3. big, motionless, around, peaceful, insane.
4. away, unfortunate, alive, wise, neat.
5. homeward, original, frequently, seriously, sometimes.

6. loud, by, narrow, lazy, cruel.
7. cautiously, carefully, home, abnormal, ahead.
8. pleasantly, along, stupidly, reasonable, quietly.
9. peaceful, envious, happy, foolish, easily.
10. awkward, hungry, watchful, small, suddenly.
11. nervously, upstairs, ridiculous, occasionally, differently.
12. lucky, hastily, aside, slowly, across.

B. In the numbered sentences below, the words in heavy type pattern as adverbs. See if you can make a sentence in which each of these words will pattern as an adjective.

Example: Nobody went with her; she went **alone**.
           He seems to be **alone** most of the time.

1. They came to work **early** this morning.
2. Don't drive too **far**.
3. He turned the corner so **fast**, I didn't see him.
4. This bus is running **late** tonight.
5. She speaks English very **well**.
6. I think you wrote that sentence **wrong**.
7. If you do it at all, please do it **right**.
8. Rip Van Winkle carried the load **high** into the mountains.
9. Have you been working **hard** all day?
10. He's standing too **near**; ask him to move back.

C. Look again at the list of words which occur both as adverbs and adjectives. Select one word from the list and make a sentence in which it patterns as an adverb. Then see if you can think of ten other adverbs which you can substitute for the one you selected. Take **first**, for example. You can make a sentence like "She came to see us **first**." And for **first** you can substitute various other adverbs:

        She came to see us first.
                     often.
                     recently.
                     again.
                     frequently.
                     promptly.
                     suddenly.
                     early.
                     there.
                     finally.
                     today.

D. Now select another word from the list and make a sentence in which it patterns as an adjective. Then see if you can think of ten other adjectives which you can substitute for the one you selected. Take **backward,** for example. You can make a sentence like "He was a **backward** child." And for **backward,** you can substitute various other adjectives:

> He was a backward child.
>> quiet
>> noisy
>> happy
>> hungry
>> nervous
>> sick
>> lazy
>> good
>> different
>> tired

CHAPTER 21

Adverbs With Underlying Adjectives and Noun Forms

Adverbs With Underlying Adjective Forms

Here are two lists of adverbs with underlying adjective forms. Look over these lists carefully, and be sure you know the meanings of all the words given. If necessary, consult your dictionary.

Group 1. Suffixes -y, -ly

The adverbs in this group can occur in the pattern "They spoke _____." Try them in this pattern and make sure the meaning of each sentence formed is clear to you. Also, be sure you can spell all the words listed. You will notice that spelling changes sometimes accompany derivation.

ADJECTIVES	ADVERBS	ADJECTIVES	ADVERBS
accidental	accidentally	efficient	efficiently
awkward	awkwardly	excellent	excellently
beautiful	beautifully	excessive	excessively
bold	boldly	extensive	extensively
brave	bravely	fair	fairly
calm	calmly	false	falsely
cautious	cautiously	favorable	favorably
cheerful	cheerfully	foolish	foolishly
clear	clearly	fierce	fiercely
cold	coldly	firm	firmly
continuous	continuously	formal	formally
cool	coolly	free	freely
correct	correctly	frequent	frequently
cruel	cruelly	gay	gaily
direct	directly	general	generally
eager	eagerly	gentle	gently
easy	easily	glad	gladly
effective	effectively	gradual	gradually

ADJECTIVES	ADVERBS	ADJECTIVES	ADVERBS
happy	happily	quick	quickly
hasty	hastily	quiet	quietly
honest	honestly	rapid	rapidly
hot	hotly	recent	recently
humble	humbly	regular	regularly
idle	idly	rude	rudely
immediate	immediately	sad	sadly
independent	independently	sensible	sensibly
intentional	intentionally	separate	separately
joyful	joyfully	severe	severely
kind	kindly	sharp	sharply
loud	loudly	simple	simply
merry	merrily	sincere	sincerely
mild	mildly	slow	slowly
miserable	miserably	soft	softly
moderate	moderately	solemn	solemnly
natural	naturally	sorrowful	sorrowfully
nice	nicely	splendid	splendidly
occasional	occasionally	steady	steadily
ordinary	ordinarily	stiff	stiffly
patient	patiently	strange	strangely
peculiar	peculiarly	stupid	stupidly
perfect	perfectly	sudden	suddenly
plain	plainly	suspicious	suspiciously
polite	politely	terrible	terribly
prompt	promptly	wild	wildly
proper	properly	willing	willingly
proud	proudly	wise	wisely
public	publicly	wonderful	wonderfully

Group 2. Prefix a-

The adverbs in this small group can occur in the pattern "They can sing _____ if they want to." Try them in this pattern and make sure the meaning of each sentence formed is clear to you.

ADJECTIVES	ADVERBS	ADJECTIVES	ADVERBS
broad	abroad	loud	aloud
long	along	round	around

Adverbs With Underlying Noun Forms

Here we see three groups of adverbs with underlying noun forms. Examine these groups carefully for spelling and meaning. All the adverbs can occur in the pattern "They went _____." Try them in this pattern and make sure the meaning of each sentence formed is clear to you.

Group 1. Suffix -ly

NOUNS	ADVERBS	NOUNS	ADVERBS
day	daily [10]	month	monthly
former	formerly	night	nightly
hour	hourly	week	weekly
instant	instantly	year	yearly
leisure	leisurely		

Group 2. Suffix -ward(s)

NOUNS	ADVERBS	NOUNS	ADVERBS
back	backward(s)	north	northward
east	eastward	south	southward
front	frontward(s)	west	westward
home	homeward		

Group 3. Prefix a-

NOUNS	ADVERBS	NOUNS	ADVERBS
board	aboard	part	apart
cross	across	shore	ashore
ground	aground	side	aside
head	ahead	way	away

Adverbs With Prefixes

We noted in Chapter 17 that the prefixes **dis-**, **un-**, and **in-** (**im-**, **ir-**) occur with adjectives. These same prefixes can occur with certain adverbs ending in -ly:

---

[10] Daily, hourly, leisurely, monthly, nightly, weekly, and yearly also pattern as adjectives in some positions; daily, weekly, and monthly, when referring to publications, also pattern as nouns.

agreeably	disagreeably	honestly	dishonestly
happily	unhappily	naturally	unnaturally
intentionally	unintentionally	wisely	unwisely
correctly	incorrectly	perfectly	imperfectly
formally	informally	regularly	irregularly

EXERCISES

A. Underline the prefixes and suffixes in the following words:

incorrectly	homeward	apart
abroad	aside	westward
idly	continuously	unnaturally
cheerfully	daily	sensibly

B. Give an adverb form for each of the following adjectives and nouns:

Example: easy—easily

free	recent	front
round	head	merry
way	long	year
north	wild	loud

C. The adjectives listed below were not given in Group 1 at the beginning of this chapter. See if you can give an adverb related to each of these adjectives and use it correctly in a sentence.

Example: frequent—**frequently**   He came to see us **frequently.**

busy	extraordinary	permanent
certain	fortunate	reasonable
common	generous	thorough
curious	lawful	tight
entire	loose	urgent
especial	original	usual

D. Fill each blank with an adverb related to the adjective which appears in the first part of the sentence.

Example: Even though he was an **awkward** fellow, he didn't do everything **awkwardly.**

   1. Even though he was a **cautious** fellow, he didn't do everything ....

   2. Even though he was a **cheerful** fellow, he didn't do everything ....

3. Even though he was an **efficient** fellow, he didn't do everything ....

4. Even though he was a **foolish** fellow, he didn't do everything ....

5. Even though he was a **gentle** fellow, he didn't do everything ....

6. Even though he was an **honest** fellow, he didn't do everything ....

7. Even though he was a **prompt** fellow, he didn't do everything ....

8. Even though he was a **quiet** fellow, he didn't do everything ....

9. Even though he was a **sensible** fellow, he didn't do everything ....

10. Even though he was a **wise** fellow, he didn't do everything ....

E. Fill each blank with an adverb related to the adjective or noun in heavy type.

Example: A **brave** soldier usually fights **bravely.**

1. A person on his way **home** is headed ....

2. An **eager** worker is one who works ....

3. A magazine appearing every **month** is published ....

4. A person going toward the **east** is moving ....

5. A person who takes a bath every **day** bathes ....

6. A **clear** thinker is a person who thinks ....

7. A person who does something in an **instant** does it ....

8. A person with a **soft** voice usually speaks ....

9. A boat carrying people from a ship to the **shore** is taking them ....

10. A person removing the various **parts** of an object is taking it ....

CHAPTER 22

How We Recognize Adverbs

We have seen certain signals that help us recognize nouns, verbs, and adjectives—inflectional and derivational suffixes, determiners, auxiliaries, etc. Similar (and some of the same) signals help us recognize adverbs; we have mentioned most of these signals already.

Inflectional Suffixes

In Chapter 18 we saw that the comparative suffix (-er) and the superlative suffix (-est) occur with certain adjectives. These suffixes also occur with some adverbs. In the following sentences these suffixes (together with other signals) help us recognize adverbs:

1. They said the headless horseman could travel **faster** than any human being.
2. He took a big drink of water and began to walk **slower.**
3. Mother worked **hardest** of all.
4. The freight train arrived **earliest.**
5. He enjoyed fun and laughter **best.**
6. The dog howled **worse** when Katrina began to sing.

Derivational Prefixes and Suffixes

In Chapter 21 we noted a number of contrasts between adjective and adverb forms and between noun and adverb forms. We also examined a few affixes which separate these word classes. These were:

AFFIXES	EXAMPLES
-y, -ly	idly, bravely
a-	along, aloud
-ly	hourly, instantly
-ward(s)	frontward(s), northward
a-	ahead, away

These affixes help us recognize adverbs in the following sentences:

7. **Lately** this had been Ichabod's habit.
8. **Fortunately** he did not have to worry about interfering parents.
9. The shots from my own gun broke the stillness **around.**
10. Stephen read them **aloud** for Stella's approval.
11. The ghost rides **nightly** to the scene of battle.
12. It was about midnight when Ichabod started **homeward.**
13. After ten years on a chicken farm we threw everything **aside.**
14. The American urge to get **ahead** took possession of them.

Intensifiers

In Chapter 18 we noted a group of words called intensifiers which pattern with adjectives and also adverbs. These were:

very	pretty	so	less
quite	mighty	too	least
somewhat	a little	more	enough
rather	a bit	most	

In the following sentences intensifiers (along with other signals) help us recognize adverbs:

15. He didn't have to wait very **long.**
16. And so in these ways Ichabod managed to live pretty **well.**
17. He extended one hand rather **nervously** over the counter.
18. It would double the amount if you arranged the lines somewhat **differently.**
19. Without noticing the scene of great wealth he had thought about so **often,** he went to find his horse.

Position

Adverbs fill certain positions in English sentences. Some of these positions are after verbs, before verbs, after an auxiliary in a verb phrase, and at the end of a sentence following a noun. Of course words belonging to other classes fill most of these positions too. One noticeable difference, however, is that words of other classes are usually marked in some way as nouns, verbs, or adjectives, whereas the adverbs are often without formal markers. Position helps us recognize adverbs in the following sentences:

20. I wandered **there** one day about noontime.
21. They **always** shook their heads and decided that Brom Bones was the cause of them.
22. This valley has **long** been known as Sleepy Hollow.
23. Stephen could **only** increase the number of lines from nineteen to thirty.
24. Dominicus stared at the man **stupidly.**
25. First it was necessary to rebuild the place **inside.**

EXERCISES

A. The words in heavy type in the sentences below are adverbs. Each is marked as an adverb in one or more ways—by an inflectional suffix, a derivational suffix or prefix, an intensifier, or position. Tell which marker or markers are present in each case.

1. **Sooner** or **later** the dog catches the rabbit.
2. An apple a day keeps the doctor **away.**
3. The wife and the car **always** need something.
4. There is no man who **never** made a mistake.
5. The way one feels **often** depends on the weather.
6. The old man at home and the young man **abroad** can lie as much as they wish.
7. The man who lives in the mountains thinks he has something, but he **really** has nothing.
8. Where one door shuts **quickly** another opens **quickly.**
9. He has one foot in the grave **already.**
10. Opportunity **rarely** knocks more than once.

B. In the sentences below certain words appear in heavy type. Tell whether each word is an adverb or an adjective.

1. Everyone who lives **there** for a time is subject to this **strange** power.
2. Ichabod's schoolhouse stood in a rather **lonely** but **pleasant** location, just at the foot of a **wooded** hill, with a stream running **nearby.**
3. He helped the farmers **occasionally** in the **lighter** work of their farms.
4. His powers of discovering and remembering **unusual** facts about witchcraft were **extraordinary,** and they were **probably** increased by living in this neighborhood.

5. He delighted them **equally** with his stories of witchcraft and the **terrible** sights and sounds in the air.

6. The schoolmaster enjoyed sitting **safely** in a **comfortable** corner of the room lighted by a shining wood fire.

7. **Often** he trembled at the sight of some bush covered with snow; its appearance was so **ghostlike.**

8. A corner cupboard, **purposely** left open, showed **immense** treasures of old silver and well-preserved china.

9. Although his attention was something like the **gentle** touch of a bear, the neighbors believed that Katrina did not **altogether** dislike him.

10. Ichabod was not one to give up **easily;** he was **yielding** but **tough.**

11. He was not **foolish** enough to battle **openly** with his rival, for **real** danger threatened anyone who opposed Brom Bones.

12. A **terrible** rivalry **gradually** arose between Brom and the teacher of Sleepy Hollow.

13. Ichabod knew the **greater** strength of his rival very **well** and dared not go into battle against him.

14. When the people at a gathering saw this well-known head ornament floating **around** among a group of **hard** riders, they **always** expected excitement.

15. Fat, **awkward** pigs made **low, contented** noises as they ate their **plentiful** supply of food and rested **peacefully** in the shade.

CHAPTER 23

Other Word Groups

Our attention in the preceding chapters has been devoted almost entirely to the four great word classes in English—nouns, verbs, adjectives, and adverbs. As we have noted before, about 90 per cent of all English words fall into these classes. In our discussions, however, we have mentioned other word groups—some as sub-classes of the four main classes, and some as markers of the four main classes.

Proper Nouns and Pronouns

In Chapter 1 we mentioned *proper nouns* and *pronouns*, both of which we considered sub-classes of nouns. Proper nouns are mostly the names of people and places, and they do not ordinarily pattern with determiners: **Thomas, Edward, Johnny, Mac, Mr. Jones, Mrs. Nelson, Dr. King; Asia, England, California, New York, Mount Everest, Lake Louise.** A few proper nouns, however, do occur with the determiner **the: the United States, the Dominican Republic, the Netherlands, the Atlantic Ocean, the Queen of Bermuda, the Catskill Mountains.**

Pronouns do not pattern with determiners at all. Here is a list of words which occur frequently as pronouns:

I	me	mine	myself
you	yours	yourself	yourselves
he	him	his	himself
she	her	hers	herself
it	its	itself	
we	us	ours	ourselves
they	them	theirs	themselves

all	either	much	some	this	one
any	few	neither	such	those	two
both	many	none	that		ten
each	most	several	these		

336

anybody	everybody	nobody	somebody
anyone	everyone	no one	someone
anything	everything	nothing	something

We could set up other sub-classes of nouns according to their meanings. However, we have seen some of the difficulties of classifying words on the basis of meaning, and we do not advise this kind of classification. We could also set up sub-classes of nouns according to their relations to other words; for example, those which occur as the *subject* of a sentence and those which occur as the *object* of a verb. But relations fall outside of our study of words in this book.

Linking and Non-Linking Verbs

In several chapters we mentioned a sub-class of verbs which we called *linking verbs*. These ordinarily pattern with adjectives, whereas *non-linking verbs* ordinarily pattern with adverbs. We noted, however, that these two sub-classes are not rigidly fixed. Here is a list of verbs which occur usually as linking verbs:

appear	feel	remain	sound
be	grow	seem	taste
become	look	smell	

There is a traditional grouping of verbs into two sub-classes called *transitive* and *intransitive verbs;* the former consists of verbs which take an object, and the latter consists of verbs which do not. This classification also has to do with relations and goes beyond our study of words here.

Structure Words

The other word groups we have discussed are those which signal the four main classes. These are sometimes called *structure words* or *function words*.

The first group we listed was *determiners;* these signal nouns:

the	its	each	many	more
a	our	every	much	most
an	their	no	few	one
my	this	both	several	two
your	that	some	either	ten
his	these	any	neither	twenty-one
her	those	all		

Several words which appear on the pronoun list, p. 336, also appear on the determiner list above: **his, her, its, this, that, these, those, each, both, some, any, all, many, much, few, several, either, one, two, ten.** We have seen that some words occur as both nouns and verbs, verbs and adjectives, adjectives and adverbs, etc.; we also find that some words occur as both determiners and pronouns. When they pattern with nouns they are determiners; when they do not they are pronouns.

The second group we listed was *auxiliaries;* these signal verbs:

am, is, are, was, were	may, might
(had) better, best	must
can, could	need
dare	ought
do, does, did	shall, should
get, gets, got	used
have, has, had	will, would

You have probably noticed that some of these also occur as verbs: **am, is, are, was, were; dare; do, does, did; get, gets, got; have, has, had; need; used.**

The third group we listed was *intensifiers;* these signal adjectives and adverbs. Here is a list of words which frequently occur as intensifiers:

very	pretty	so	less
quite	mighty	too	least
somewhat	a little	more	enough
rather	a bit	most	

Many of these, you will remember, also occur with nouns: **very, pretty, mighty, a little, more, most, less,** and **least.**

There are several additional groups of structure words which we have not mentioned in this book. We shall list these below and discuss some of them briefly.

The largest group is *prepositions,* which pattern with a following noun:

aboard	against	at	beside	concerning
about	along	before	besides	despite
above	alongside	behind	between	down
across	among	below	beyond	during
after	around	beneath	by	for

from	near	over	till	upon
in	of	per	toward	with
inside	off	since	under	within
into	on	through	until	
like	onto	throughout	up	

Besides these, there are several combinations which function like the single-word prepositions:

according to	by means of	in spite of
ahead of	down under	on account of
apart from	due to	on top of
back of	in front of	out of
because of	in place of	up to

Notice that many of these prepositions also occur as adverbs.

PREPOSITIONS	ADVERBS
They walked **along** the road.	They walked **along**.
They went **by** the house.	They went **by**.
They climbed **up** the mountain.	They climbed **up**.

We give the name *subordinators* to a group of words which subordinate part of a sentence to another part or to the rest of the sentence. The main ones are:

after	if	though	whereas	who
although	provided	until	wherever	whoever
as	since	what	whether	whom
as if	so that	when	which	whomever
because	than	whenever	whichever	whose
before	that	where	while	why
how				

Here are some examples:

Let's find the man **who** just came in.
The money **that** we needed was already spent.
He ate the meat **because** he was hungry.
When they reached the shore, the boat was gone.

Notice that a few subordinators also occur as prepositions and adverbs: **after, before,** and **since.**

Conjunctions join together two sentences or parts of a sentence, and they also join the last two parts of a series. The main ones are:

and	for	or	yet
but	nor	so	

Here are some examples:

> The pay he received would hardly have been enough to supply him with food, **for** he was a big eater.
>
> He was satisfied with his wealth, **but** he was not proud of it.
>
> Baltus Van Tassel was a successful **and** generous farmer.
>
> A straw hat, a fine ribbon, **or** a white dress showed some influence from the city.

We notice that when conjunctions join sentences, as in the first two examples above, they always stand between the two sentences.

Sentence connectors also join two sentences, but their position is not fixed like the conjunctions. The main sentence connectors are:

accordingly	furthermore	moreover
also	hence	nevertheless
at least	however	then
besides	indeed	therefore
consequently	in addition	thus
for example	in fact	

A sentence connector may stand between the two sentences it joins, it may stand at the end of the second sentence, or it may stand in the middle of the second sentence; for example:

> He knew the greater strength of his rival; **therefore,** Ichabod did not battle with him openly.
>
> He knew the greater strength of his rival; Ichabod did not battle with him openly, **therefore.**
>
> He knew the greater strength of his rival; Ichabod, **therefore,** did not battle with him openly.

Question words, as the name suggests, mark sentences as questions. The main ones are:

how	where	whom
what	which	whose
when	who	why

These question words, you will notice, also appear on the subordinator list, p. 339.

There are also several miscellaneous words which we have not mentioned elsewhere, some of which occur frequently in English sentences. The word **there**, which occurs in sentences like "**There are** no boats on the lake," is a widely-used structure word. **Please** and **let's** are structure words which signal request sentences, and **not** which we use to make sentences negative. Other words with special patterning are *hesitation forms* like **well** and **uh**; *attention-claimers* like **hey, oh**, and **say**; *responses* like **yes, no, okay, right, why, sure**, and **uh-huh**; and certain *formulas* like **hello, hi, good-by**, and **so long**.

EXERCISES

A. In the numbered sentences below, the words in heavy type occur as pronouns. See if you can make a sentence in which each of these words will occur as a determiner.

Example: Shall I bring the red book or the green book? Bring **both**.
He had scratches on **both** arms.

1. Don't take all the ornaments; we don't have **many**.
2. Three boys helped him with the work, and he gave **each** a dollar.
3. We looked for squirrels all day, but we couldn't find **any**.
4. How much does **this** cost?
5. Katrina still lives near Tarry Town; we see **her** occasionally.
6. We can lend you two horses; we have **several**.
7. They offered me a ham sandwich and a beef sandwich, but I didn't want **either**.
8. Everybody had good mirrors except Ichabod; **his** was broken.
9. They don't need any paper now; they bought **some** a few minutes ago.
10. What do you call **that**?

B. In the numbered sentences below, the words in heavy type occur as verbs. See if you can make a sentence in which each of these words will occur as an auxiliary.

Example: Ichabod **had** two sticks in the schoolroom.
He **had** finished the book by nightfall.

1. The schoolmaster's name **was** Ichabod Crane.
2. He **got** an invitation to the Van Tassels' party.
3. Our companions **need** some horses.
4. Nobody knew what Gunpowder **did**.
5. **Were** you at home last night?

6. He thought that witches **used** the schoolhouse for a meeting-place.
7. We **have** plenty of schoolbooks now.
8. They can't tell us where the farm **is**.
9. **Are** the children thirsty?
10. Let's find out what kind of work he **does**.

C. In the numbered sentences below, the words in heavy type occur as prepositions. See if you can make a sentence in which each of these words will occur as an adverb.

Example: They walked **along** the road.
We're going to the movies. Would you like to come **along**?

1. I went **aboard** the ship yesterday afternoon.
2. **Besides** these books we have several others.
3. The dog ran **through** the village last night.
4. He jumped **over** the fence as he ran.
5. **Within** two weeks you will have your handkerchiefs.
6. Let's go **around** the house and sit down on the bench.
7. Ichabod rode **across** the river very quickly.
8. The branches of the tree were far **above** our heads.
9. Sylvia looked down at the white heron **below** her.
10. They always want to rest a while **before** dinner.

CHAPTER 24

Review and Conclusion

Patterns in Derivation

Just as there is patterning in the occurrence of words in English sentences—patterning which we have used to set up our four word classes—there is also a certain amount of patterning in English word derivation. We have noticed in the derivation of nouns from verbs, for example, the existence of sets: we derive a group of nouns from a group of verbs by means of one suffix; we derive another group of nouns from another group of verbs by means of a second suffix; etc. In the final group we list several miscellaneous pairs; as a rule we do not have enough examples of these to show a clear derivational pattern.

Learning to derive words correctly comes only with practice. It is impossible, for practical purposes, to make rules concerning which verbs take -ment, which take -ion, which take -ence, which take -al, etc. to form nouns. We simply have to learn these matters through practice. The derivation of agent nouns from verbs by means of the suffix -er and the derivation of adverbs from adjectives by means of the suffix -ly are fairly regular processes, but there are various exceptions.

When we compare the words of two classes, the derivational patterns are fairly obvious: generally a set of stems belonging to one word class occurs with a particular affix to form a new set of stems which belong to another class; for example, the verbs agree, govern, pay, etc. occur with the suffix -ment, and the resulting words— agreement, government, payment, etc.—are nouns. Ordinarily only one affix is required to change the class. Your problem here is learning which stems can occur with which affixes. If you had no other problem than this, learning to derive words in English would be rather easy. But, as we have seen, you face many additional problems: there are the miscellaneous pairs, some without clear derivational patterns; there are many words with the same form which belong to different classes; there are many stem forms which contrast, even without the occurrence of an affix; there are many spelling changes which accompany derivation; and there are also various other problems which we have not mentioned because of our limited space.

Besides the fairly regular processes of deriving agent nouns from verbs and adverbs from adjectives, there is little else we can say about regular formations. There is, however, one other matter which might be helpful for you to remember, but it is by no means a regular process. Some nouns ending in **-ion** have a corresponding adjective ending **-ive.** Many of these forms are derived from verbs.

Verbs	Nouns	Adjectives
describe	description	descriptive
explode	explosion	explosive
persuade	persuasion	persuasive
repeat	repetition	repetitive
select	selection	selective
suggest	suggestion	suggestive

And a number of nouns ending in **-ance** or **-ence** have a corresponding adjective ending **-ant** or **-ent** respectively. Many of these forms are derived from verbs also.

Verbs	Nouns	Adjectives
confide	confidence	confident
differ	difference	different
excel	excellence	excellent
obey	obedience	obedient
observe	observance	observant

We often see groups of three related words which belong to different classes, as the ones listed above. It is not unusual to find four such related words—all belonging to different classes—especially since it is possible to derive an adverb from almost any adjective by adding **-ly.**

Nouns	Verbs	Adjectives	Adverbs
beauty	beautify	beautiful	beautifully
danger	endanger	dangerous	dangerously
helper	help	helpful	helpfully
length	lengthen	long	along
sadness	sadden	sad	sadly
safety	save	safe	safely

You have probably noticed that two and sometimes three derivational suffixes occur together. In the word **dangerously**, for example, we have the noun stem **danger**, the adjective suffix -ous, and the adverb suffix -ly. And in the word **truthfulness** we have an adjective stem **tru-** (true), a noun suffix -th, an adjective suffix -ful, and another noun suffix -ness; we can also add the prefix **un-** and get **untruthfulness**.

It is worth noting also that two or more words of a single class are frequently derived from the same stem by using different affixes.

NOUNS	VERBS	ADJECTIVES	ADVERBS
act	act	active	actively
actor	activate		
actress			
action			
activity			
activeness			
continuation	continue	continual	continually
continuity		continuous	continuously
continuousness		continuative	continuatively
continuance		continuable	
continuum			
continuer			

Conclusion

A high percentage of English words, as we have noted, fall into one or more of the four great word classes discussed in this book—nouns, verbs, adjectives, and adverbs. These classes are unlimited; new experiences bring new words, and these classes continue to grow. At the same time certain words in these classes are used less and less and finally disappear from the active vocabulary of the language.

Vocabulary does not make the language. The language is a system of sounds and the patterned arrangement of these sounds. The sounds and patterns change slowly, whereas vocabulary comes and goes. When I was a high-school student, I noticed that my grandparents used many words which I did not use; on the other hand, I used many words which they did not use. Some of the words used regularly by my grandparents have disappeared from active use; and some of the words they never used are in current use today.

Although vocabulary does not make the language, you cannot go far in reading, writing, speaking, or understanding the language without a large number of words at your command. If you have worked through this book systematically and carefully under the guidance of a teacher or some other English-speaking person, then you now know a good deal about English words. You have increased your vocabulary to about 4,000 words.

This book, however, is little more than an introduction to vocabulary study. You should become thoroughly familiar with the information about words which your dictionary contains, and you should consult your dictionary the moment you have a question about a particular word.

There is no reason why you should not continue to increase your English vocabulary as time goes on. It will grow as you continue to read and write and converse in the language. Ask an English teacher or professor for suggestions to help you build your vocabulary, and follow the suggestions you get. Above all, practice using the language—reading, writing, speaking, and listening to English—as much as your opportunities allow. Language ability, like any other skill, comes only through practice.

EXERCISES

A. Give an adjective, verb, and noun form related to each of the following adverbs:

Example: hastily—**hasty, hasten, haste**

joyfully	continuously	suspiciously
favorably	actively	softly
freely	deeply	intentionally
astonishingly	dangerously	quickly

B. Give an adjective and noun form related to each of the following adverbs:

accidentally	efficiently	generously
bravely	faithfully	lawfully
certainly	foolishly	miserably
curiously	fortunately	naturally
safely	patiently	peculiarly
truly	suddenly	strongly

C. Fill the blanks in the second and third sentences with verbs and nouns respectively which are related to the adjective in the first sentence.

Example: My children are very **obedient**.

They always **obey** me.

Such **obedience** surprises everybody.

1. Our children are very **destructive**.

They .... everything they find.

Such .... surprises everybody.

2. Our children are very **different**.

They always .... in their opinions.

Such a .... surprises everybody.

3. Our children are very **forgetful**.

They always .... what we tell them.

Such .... surprises everybody.

4. Our children are very **imaginative**.

They .... all sorts of things.

Such .... surprises everybody.

5. Our children are very **amusing**.

They always .... their friends.

Such .... surprises everybody.

6. Our children are very **dependent**.

They .... on us for everything.

Such .... surprises everybody.

7. Our children are very **helpful**.

They .... us in every way they can.

Such .... surprises everybody.

8. Our children are very **creative**.

They .... all kinds of wonderful things.

Such .... surprises everybody.

9. Our children are very **suspicious.**

They even .... their best friends.

Such .... surprises everybody.

10. Our children are very **annoying.**

They .... all the people they meet.

Such .... surprises everybody.

Index